Oral Literature
of the
Maasai

NAOMI KIPURI

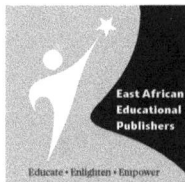

East African
Educational
Publishers

Educate • Enlighten • Empower

East African Educational Publishers
Nairobi • Kampala • Dar es Salaam • Kigali • Lusaka • Lilongwe

Published by
East African Educational Publishers Ltd.
Elgeyo Marakwet Close, off Elgeyo Marakwet Road,
Kilimani, Nairobi
P.O. Box 45314, Nairobi - 00100, KENYA
Tel: +254 20 2324760
Mobile: +254 722 205661 / 722 207216 / 733 677716 / 734 652012
Email: eaep@eastafricanpublishers.com
Website: www.eastafricanpublishers.com

East African Educational Publishers also has offices or is represented in the following
countries: Uganda, Tanzania, Rwanda, Malawi, Zambia, Botswana and South Sudan.

First published 1983
Reprinted 1993
This impression 2020

ISBN 978-9966-46-173-5

Contents

Dedicated to Memusi, with expectations that he grows to learn to appreciate and love this heritage that I so cherish, and which has moulded many a life in this little corner of the globe.

Acknowledgements

Without assistance from a long list of friends and relatives, it would not have been possible to write a book of this kind. It is not possible to name everyone here, but since they know themselves, I wish to record my deep gratitude for their contributions. I am particularly indebted to my mother, Maayio enole Kipury, for spending many hours narrating patiently most of the stories in this book. She also sang to me many women's songs, and gave explanations whenever my inexperienced mind failed me. I am also extremely grateful for the help offered by David ole Tuukuo and Mumeita ole Kipees, who contributed some of the stories and proverbs. Without the cultural knowledge of Moses ole Marima and Matuyia ole Kurao, which they so willingly shared with me, my appreciation of some riddles and poems would have been limited. Lastly, many thanks go to Ann Ndung'u for her tireless effort in typing the manuscript.

Foreword

In this collection of Maasai oral literature, Naomi Kipuri has provided an enchanting avenue into the wisdom, mores, values, art and literary creativity of Maa-speaking peoples of East Africa. Known for their commitment to a pastoralist lifestyle, the Maasai number around 2 million spread across both Kenya and Tanzania. They feature prominently in mass-circulated iconography of Africa – in safari brochures, coffee table books, mobile phone ads, and on postcards shouldering video cameras in a cheap contrast of supposed 'tradition' with presumed 'modernity'. In these images, Maasai are subjects of narratives constructed by others. They are presented as proud cattle-keepers who reject the demands and exigencies of today's world. However noble and romantic that may at first appear, the disturbing subtext is that they are out of synch with contemporary life, a cultural throwback to a bygone era. Yet nothing could be further from the truth.

This volume offers a strong rejoinder to those dangerous discourses. It contains a wide array of stories, songs, poetry, creation myths, heroic legends, trickster tales, allegories, riddles, proverbs and more composed by Maasai for Maasai. But they are rendered here for broader audiences by Kipuri, who painstakingly collected them, transcribed and beautifully translated them so that readers could appreciate them both in their original Maa and in English. She organizes them into chapters according to genre, each of which is preceded by a thorough and illuminating introduction. These oral art forms educate and elucidate. They describe the rewards that come to the just, and the punishments suffered by the greedy or lazy, the selfish or unkind. They offer explanations for the origins of Maasai moieties and clans, and of cultural practices such as marriage.

They tell how features in the landscape where Maasai live came into being and describe the personalities of others who share that landscape, such as the clever hare, the wise mongoose and the greedy hyena.

And through variations in colour, tone, emphasis and character that Kipuri draws out and explicates, these stories reveal the richness of Maasai cosmology, philosophy and ethos, even as they expose problematic aspects such as patriarchy and cultural prejudice against hunter-gatherer Okiek.[1]

The release of this new edition is especially timely given escalating pressures on Maasai and other pastoralist communities to abandon their way of life and assimilate to the mainstream. Both the Tanzanian and Kenyan governments have instituted policies that impede and undermine pastoralism despite the fact that pastoralists (with the Maasai being the majority) provide both nations with 80-90% of their meat and dairy needs.[2] This is, of course, very short-sighted but the alignment of (1) development fads that promote modern ranches over traditional pastoralism, with (2) longstanding cultural prejudices against pastoralists, and (3) an influx of agro-industrial investments in Africa since the global food crisis of 2008 is creating a highly precarious situation for the Maasai. Recent government initiatives, for instance, circumscribe the mobility on which pastoralism depends by outlawing movement across district borders in the name of preventing spread of livestock disease, and by privatizing or re-allocating communal pastures, water sources and migratory corridors that Maasai have accessed for generations.[3] Politicians are also trying to legislate limits on the size of herds, and in some cases ordering draconian "destocking campaigns", based on controversial (and scientifically unfounded) ideas about the "carrying capacity" of the land.

---

[1] Referred to in these stories by their more common, but derogatory name, of Dorobo.

[2] Helen de Jode and Ced Hesse, *Strengthening Voices: How Pastoralist Communities and Local Government Are Shaping Strategies for Adaptive Environmental Management and Poverty Reduction in Tanzania's Drylands* (Tanzania: IIED, KDSC and TNRF, 2011), p. 9. Also, Elisabeth Farmer and James Mbwika, *End Market Analysis of Kenyan Livestock and Meat: A Desk Study*, micro REPORT #184 (Washington, DC: USAID, 2012), p.1.

[3] Recent high profile cases include the dispossession of over 150,000 hectares of Maasai territory in Loliondo division, Ngorongoro district, Tanzania to a private corporation based in the United Arab Emirates that organizes hunting safaris for royalty, and a 12,000 hectares parcel to a Boston-based tour operator.

Without ease of movement to shift herds seasonally for access to pasture and water, and without the ability to maintain herds at traditional levels, the Maasai will be unable to sustain their way of life.

It is important to note that both Kenya and Tanzania are signatory states to the 2007 United Nations Declaration on the Rights of Indigenous Peoples (UNDRIP). They are thus bound to the principles enshrined within it, which include rejecting discrimination against indigenous populations and ensuring their rights to self-determination, to their land, and to practise their cultural traditions. Globally, Maasai are recognized as indigenous people yet their own governments resolutely deny the existence of any indigenous populations.[4] And yet, the Maasai are continually misrepresented in public pronouncements, both official and unofficial, as raiders and thieves, who disregard the land rights of others by trespassing where they will, and whose herds destroy the environment, wreak havoc on farmers' crops, and imperil water sources and wetlands.

Upon investigation, what one finds instead is that it is Maasai territories that are being invaded. Farmers, both large and small-scale, whose territories are now over-populated and over-cultivated are encroaching on Maasai territories with impunity, attracted also because they surmise the virgin soil there must be rich in nutrients even if rainfall is meager. And investors and elites, who view Maasai territory as underutilized and rich in agricultural or mining or conservationist potential, are joining forces to grab ever more Maasai lands. Unfortunately, this continues a long history of forced re-settlement of Maasai from their territories, which dates back to the arrival of colonial settlers in the Kenyan highlands in the late 19th century up through the creation and expansion of multiple national parks in the 1960s onwards that continue to bear Maa names (Maasai Mara, Serengeti, Tarangire, Ngorongoro, Manyara) in memory of those whose land it once was.[5]

---

[4]International understandings of "indigenous" entail having a sense of cultural distinctiveness (self-identification), desire to retain a traditional mode of lifestyle, identification by others as being culturally distinctive, and a condition of political marginalization.

[5]Lotte Hughes, *Moving the Maasai: A Colonial Misadventure* (New York: Palgrave Macmillan, 2006), also Diana Vinding and Sille Stidsen, eds., *The Indigenous World 2005* (Copenhagen: IWGIA, 2005), p.467.

One irony is that Maasai have developed their lifestyle in response to the semi-arid environment of their territories and have managed not only to adapt and survive under harsh conditions but to contribute around 40% of the agricultural GDP in their respective countries.[6] Traditional pastoralism is as study after study has shown. Yet curiously this passes unrecognized and governments risk endangering their meat and dairy supplies by threatening pastoralism. Try imagining a dinner party in Kenya or Tanzania without *nyama choma* or *chai masala!* A second irony is that Maasai territories keep being appropriated for new national parks precisely because they are such excellent guardians of the land and its flora and fauna. In 1961 Tanzania had only one national park, the famous Serengeti, but today it boasts sixteen, several of which are the direct result of Maasai evictions (add Mkomazi and Ruaha national parks to the list above). Thus contrary to depictions of Maasai as causing environmental destruction or degradation, Maasai have proven to be such superior custodians of the land that they are now losing to countless conservation initiatives.

Maasai communities nonetheless continue to pursue their way of life, which is documented and praised through their oral literature and songs. In the area of Kiteto district where I have worked for a number of years in Maasai communities, one song frequently sang by warriors details their love for the land and its features:

> *Serai! Serai!*
> *My Serai grassland, your warriors are as fierce as fire!*
> *Mutambaalo valley with the narrow stream*
> *Serai, where the lion dances with its flowing mane*
> *Mutambaalo! Kipaya!*
> *My Serai grassland, your warriors are as fierce as fire!*
> *Lion, you cannot deceive me there.*
> *Serai! Serai! Serai!*

The compilation of literary forms that Kipuri produced in this volume can thus serve not only as a repository of Maasai artistic creativity and worldview but as evidence of their territories and claims to land. Newly discovered songs recorded in the 1850s, for instance by the famous

---

[6] de Jode and Hesse, *op cited.*, Farmer and Mbwika, p.3.

ethnomusicologist Hugh Tracey who traveled from South Africa to record music of the Maasai, may yield vital information on where they were located before experiencing eviction and political marginalization.[7] Oral literature defines a people and certifies their existence. It affirms their distinctiveness and preserves their cultural knowledge. Folklorists and anthropologists have long recognized this. However, its political value before international entities like the United Nations and its legal value before courts of law have yet to be tested. The first step, however, entails documenting and preserving it. For successfully accomplishing this in exquisite fashion, we must thank Naomi Kipuri and all the Maasai she consulted who shared their stories, riddles, proverbs and songs with her.

Kelly Askew

Professor of Anthropology and Afro-American/African Studies

The University of Michigan

August 2016

---

[7]Communication with Diane Thram, director of the International Library of African Music (ILAM), Rhodes University, South Africa.

Preface

When I was growing up, telling and listening to stories, posing riddles, singing songs, telling jokes and playing all sorts of games, constituted a natural part of the evening's entertainment. This pattern has since been upset to the extent that as I was collecting some of the narratives in this book, few narrators could tell one story from the beginning to the end. Several narratives were told in a confused manner. Others were merged into one, and many more had been wholly forgotten, except for the songs accompanying them.

This book is an attempt to record, and hence preserve, part of the rich heritage of Maasai oral literature before it is completely forgotten. By so doing, it is hoped that its literary significance and values will be learnt and appreciated.

Although the original texts are in Maa, a free English translation has been provided for each text so that English speakers can understand them, and young African readers will be able to record their own oral literature by collecting similar examples in their own languages, thus building up a stock of what has been ignored for centuries.

This book is divided into five chapters. Chapter One deals with the dominant features and style of Maasai literature. In Chapter Two we have stories arranged into categories according to their functions: myths, legends, ogre tales, trickster and other animal tales, and man stories. The third chapter contains riddles. Chapter Four contains proverbs, and in the last chapter we have songs and poetry, including prayers and blessings. A brief introduction explaining oral literature forms is given at the beginning of each chapter. There are also footnotes to explain the meaning of some references.

A few questions and discussion topics are also given at the end of each chapter to aid the student in his or her study of oral literature.

Looking at some of the bibliographies on the Maasai, one gets the impression that the "field" has been exhausted. The Maasai are probably some of the most famous, or infamous, people in Africa, coming close only to the Zulu of Southern Africa. Yet there is relatively little comprehensive work that has been produced on the Maasai. Needless to say, their history has not even been recorded fully except in short incidental and scattered pieces of literature. It is hoped that this book will benefit many Maa speakers, especially the young and growing children whose chances of learning it from the indigenous sources are fast diminishing. It is also expected to be of interest to students of oral literature.

Sources of Material

Most of the material recorded in this book was collected mainly from Kajiado District, Kenya, between 1973 and 1975. The material itself may have been passed down from time immemorial, except for some praise songs that were composed for a particular purpose during a specific time in history.

Although there are slight variations in the versions of narratives or in the tone and rhythm of the accompanying songs, depending on the geographic area where they were recorded, the differences in the forms and types of recorded oral literature are basically minor. The material in this book can hence be regarded as a representation of Maasai oral literature.

Although many oral artists contributed a greater portion of the material in this book, a substantial number of narratives, riddles, proverbs and songs were written from the author's own childhood reminiscences. In such cases, the author has played the role of an oral artist.

Orthography

No special orthography has been used in this book. Maa is a highly tonal language, but tone has not been indicated in these texts. Those interested in Maa scientific orthography are referred to Tucker and Mpaayei, *A Maasai Grammar with Vocabulary*. Mention must, however, be made of the slight variations in the orthography used, in as much as it differs from that used by other scholars. I have preferred to use the triagraphy ng' adapted from Kiswahlli and other African languages to represent the velar nasal sound which, phonetically, is represented by the sound [n] and which has been used by Tucker and Mpaayei. I hope that the apostrophe effects the necessary distinction.

The palatal fricative sound [tf] which is rendered either as 'ch' or 'c', orthographically, creates a lot of confusion. I have therefore preferred to use 'ch' throughout, whenever the sound occurs. I have also indicated a trilled sound by doubling the letter 'r' (**rr**), except when the sound falls at the end of the word, in which case it is always trilled. Finally, I have had difficulty indicating diphthongs owing to their extreme complexity. For those who are keen to learn the correct pronounciation, it is suggested that they consult with Maa speakers.

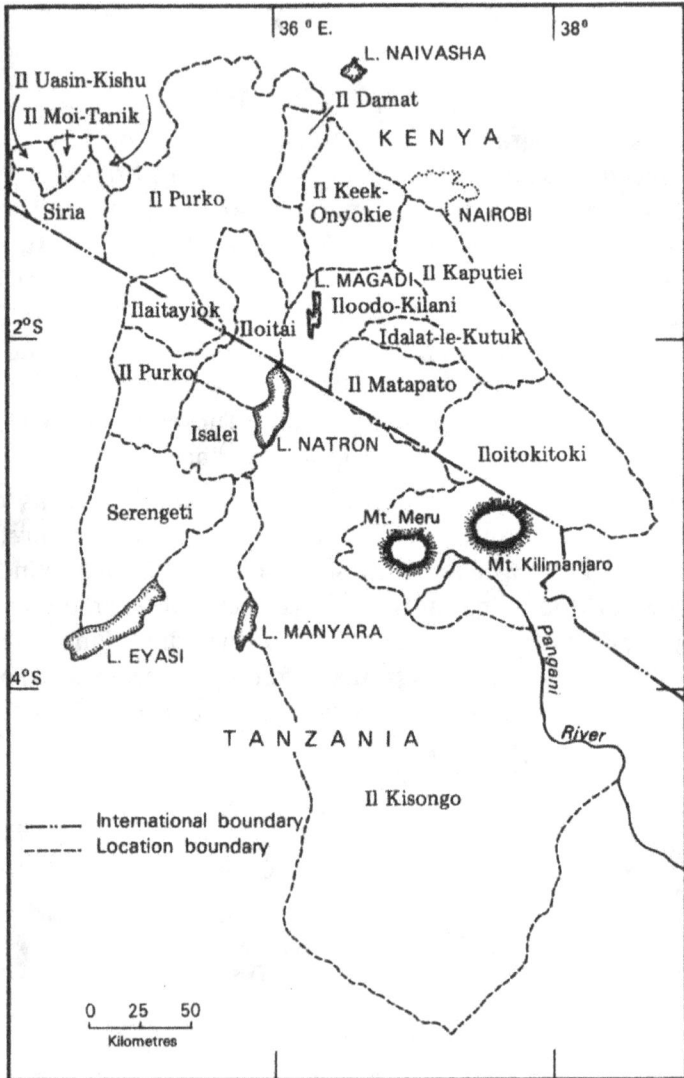

The distribution of Maa-speaking pastoralists since ca. 1930

CHAPTER ONE

Introduction

The Maasai people of Kenya and Tanzania speak the language Maa which is an Eastern Nilotic language. Nilotes are Eastern-Sudanic speeking people (a sub-family of Nilo-Saharan). Nilotes include Western Nilotes (Nuer, Dinker, Acholi, Luo), Southern Nilotes (Kalenjin, Barbaig and Datoga of Tanzania and Pokot). Eastern Nilotes include the Bari of North-Western Uganda and Southern Sudan who are distinguished from the rest. Then there are the two related sub-families: Teso-Turkana or what historians call the "Ateker" group which also include the Karamojong, Toposa, Nyangatom, Jie, etc. This group divided from the Lotuko-Maa, the Lotuko remaining in Southern, the Maa moving Southwards from some region from Southern Sudan or Eastern Uganda. From their move, Maa speakers then came into contact with Eastern Cushitic-speakers – Rendile, Borana, Somali, etc near Lake Turkana from whom they adopted male and female circumcision and other cultural traits.

Although they present a linguistic and cultural unity, there are still noticeable dialectic and cultural differences among the various Maa speakers. The **Samburu** or **Ilooibor-Kineji**, the people of the white goats, the **Iltiamus** who practise fishing around Lake Baringo, keep a few livestock and do subsistence farming, and the hunter-gathering group, **Iltorrobo**, (Dorobo), form the third group of Maa speakers, although they speak another language that sounds like a dialect of Kalenjin. But since these people speak Maa, albeit with a heavy accent, and have acquired livestock, like the pastoral Maasai, they are gradually being assimilated, as a group, into the Maasai community. The **Ilkunono**, who subsist on iron smithing, in addition to keeping an insignificant number of livestock, also live alongside the Maasai, and although they are said to speak a language separate from Maa, it is a language spoken only by the senior members of the community, and risks becoming extinct. There are also other peripheral Maa groups such as the **Baraguyu, Ilarusa** and **Ilkurman**; the last two are semi-pastoral and subsist mainly on agriculture.

Then there are what one might term as the Maasai 'proper', who, except for slight dialectical variations, speak one language and have initially striven as much as possible to maintain a purely pastoral existence. They fall into sixteen politically independent **iloshon**, location or territorial units. These include Ilpurko, Ilmatapato, Ilkeek-onyokie, Ildalat-Ie-kutuk (Ilkankere), Ildamat, Iloodo-kilani, Ilkisongo, Iloitokitoki, Iloitai, Isikirari, Ilaitayiok, Isiria, Serenget, Ilmoitanik, Ilwuasin-kishu and Ilkaputiei. The forms of oral literature presented in this book are known and shared by these **iloshon**, with only slight variations. Climate change, loss of land and increased impoverishment has forced them to diversify into other livelihood systems and economic activities.

Background Information

According to popular oral tradition, the Maasai originated somewhere in the north, at a place called **Endikir-e-Kerio** (the scarp of Kerio). Although many scholars have referred to this place as the southeastern region of present-day Lake Turkana, some oral sources suggest that it may have been somewhere further north, probably in the northern part of Africa. Whatever the case may be, their migration southward ensued after a dry spell.

It is reported that a bridge was constructed, and after half the people and livestock had left the dusty depression, the bridge collapsed, throwing back the other half of the population. These people later managed to climb out of the valley, reaching the highland region as the present day Somali, Borana and Rendille peoples.

Since the middle of the nineteenth century, the present Maa-speaking peoples have occupied the region from near Mt Marsabit in northern Kenya to Kiteto in central Tanzania, a distance of about 700 miles from north to south, and about 200 miles from east to west. Within this vast region, the Maasai have come into contact with a great number of peoples of different cultural and linguistic backgrounds. There are the Cushitic-speaking pastoralists, such as the Somali, Borana, Rendille and Orma; the Nilotic-speaking semi-pastoralists such as the Turkana, Luo, Kalenjin, Latuka, Bari, Dinka, etc; and the Bantu-speaking agriculturalists, such as the Akamba, Abaluhya, Kikuyu, Kisii, Chagga, Pare, Hehe, Swahili and others.

2

The oral traditions of these peoples are riddled with stories about their encounters with the Maasai. Although some of these encounters tended to have been exaggerated, as in the case of the Swahili traders who hoped to retain a monopoly of trade with the inland region, the contact indeed produced some lasting effects on each of these groups, as well as on the Maa-speaking people. The narratives, songs and poetry in this collection contain evidence of this cultural interaction.

Climate, Vegetation and Environment

Topographically, Maasailand is part of the East African Plateau complex, which ranges from 3,000 to 6,000 ft in altitude. But the Great Rift Valley, running from north to south, divides the land into two regions, which vary greatly in topography as well as in vegetation. On the higher altitudes lying mainly on the western side of the Rift Valley, including the Mau and **Nabarn-intare** (Aberdare) ranges, we find the evergreen forest and associated vegetation cover; on the eastern side however, we find mainly grassland with sparse bushes, salt lakes on the floor of the rift valley and desert scrub (**olpurkel**). The average rainfall in the whole region ranges between 22 to 30 milimetres annually but rarely exceeds 14 milimetres in some parts. The rain generally falls in two seasons: the long rains from March to June, and the short rains from November to December. It is often torrential when it falls, and seasonal in character. This rainfall pattern is changing with climate change.

As rainfall is unreliable, the main sources of surface water for the Maasai during the dry season is in seepages. These take the form of soft stones or dry river bed wells (**Ilumbwa** or **Isinya**), springs, natural dams and pools, as well as permanent swamps.

The vegetation of Maasailand varies greatly in both composition and the degree of cover following the rainfall pattern. Apart from its obvious ecological significance, the vegetation cover plays an extremely important role in the social life of the Maasai community. From a very early age, children are expected to distinguish between the various plants and grasses and their uses. Grass is, for instance, used in the building of houses, for grasping in the hand as a sign of peace, as well as for blessings during rituals.

3

Trees and shrubs provide traditional medicines and herbs, some of which have special ritual value. According to a popular myth, it was the folk of the forest, the hyena, who taught the Maasai the medicinal uses of various plants. It is significant to note that the Maa word for tree is the same as that for medicine (**olchani; pl. ilkeek**), and that every ailment has a traditional treatment, if not a cure, obtained from leaves, roots, bark or the fruit of plants. The importance of trees and plants is also noted during rituals, when some of them are symbolically associated with certain notions of cosmology. The Oreteti tree *(Ficus naiaiensis)*, 'bark cloth fig', is one of these. Its size, shape, sturdiness and long life, epitomize the ideal in life, hence it is sang about and invoked in prayers and blessings.

Wildlife is abundant in Maasailand and important in the life of the people. Traditionally, the Maasai were not hunters, and they abhorred the consumption of wild animals. The lion hunt (**olamayio**) was the only form of hunting that was permitted, mainly to eliminate predators when they posed dangers to livestock, and as a sporting activity. Wild animals do, however, play an important role in the economic and social life of the Maasai either directly or indirectly, as is seen from their lore.

A large number of the objects of material culture, which the Maasai use, are obtained from the Dorobo, Ilkurman or Sonjo hunters in exchange for small stock. The proverb goes: *'mitum errap etii enkuo ntare',* 'you cannot obtain the arm-band while the ram is with the flock'. This underlines the seriousness of this exchange. Some of the products obtained include buffalo-hide shields; rhinoceros horns, for making tobacco and snuff containers; wildebeest and giraffe tails, used by elders as fly whisks; lion manes and ostrich feathers, made into warriors' head-dresses and spear covers in time of peace; colobus monkey skins, used for making leg bands and robes; hyrax skin, for making robes for distinguished elders; Kudu horns, used as war or ceremonial trumpets; and eland skin, used for making sandals and leather straps for carrying firewood and water containers.

Apart from their material significance, the Maasai love and tolerate wild animals. In oral literature, children sing songs and chants for them. And in the case of the *Teasing Song for the Dorobo Hunters*, we see the drawing of parallels between domestic and wild animals. A look at Maasai proverbs, riddles, poetry and songs shows the significance of wild animals in the social life of the people. The main reason why the Maasai despise the Dorobo hunters is because of what is seen as an abnormal desire to kill domestic as well as wild animals and destroy what, in the Maasai mind, should be left to exist for its own aesthetic value. Blacksmiths who make all sorts of weapons for the Maasai, and whose services are appreciated, are also ostracized because the Maasai believe their means of livelihood, the manufacture of lethal weapons, makes them unclean. The Dorobo, as well as other agricultural groups, are hence employed to perform "menial" jobs such as circumcision, digging wells and, in recent times, to graze livestock.

Diet and Economy

Being pastoralists, the Maasai raise cattle, sheep and goats, and donkeys are kept as beasts of burden. Their sole subsistence and wealth is derived from livestock. Milk, meat and blood form the staple diet, although maize-meal and other carbohydrates and vegetables now become essential parts of the diet although livestock products remain the ideal food. Milk is consumed on a daily basis, and during the dry season, when milk yields are low, it is mixed with fresh cow blood obtained by puncturing the jugular vein with a blunt arrow-head.

The blood is mixed with either fresh milk to produce what is called **nailang'a**, or is curdled to make **osaroi.** These two preparations are also given to convalescing patients at all times. Although sheep and goats are frequently slaughtered for food, cattle are reserved for rituals and ceremonial feasts, which are quite numerous in the life of the people. These include births, deaths, and all the rites of passage, and, depending on the occasion, the sex and colour of the cattle is ritually significant.

Livestock provide the Maasai with almost everything, ranging from domestic utensils to clothing, though the latter has been replaced by cotton sheets and blankets purchased from shops. But the social and economic role that livestock plays in Maasai life is of paramount significance. Livestock is procured and exchanged in kinship relations as well as for bridewealth. The latter, ranging between three and six animals is minimal compared to what other East African pastoralists have to pay. Exchange of gifts of livestock between friends and kinsmen is the basis of social relationships. When two people exchange heifers (enkashe, pl. nkasho), they address each other as pa-ashe. Cattle are also used in the payment of civil as well as capital fines such as for homicide. Despite the great importance attached to cattle, the Maasai, unlike other pastoralist groups such as the Nuer and Dinka, do not take on ox-names, nor do they imitate animals in any way. Despite the positive light in which livestock is viewed, it is not rare to hear a stupid person being referred to as a cow or sheep!

Settlement Pattern

The Maasai homestead consists of a large circular enclosure surrounded by a thorn bush fence. The size of the camp and the number of gates it has, depends on the number of families living in the camp, for, as the saying goes: 'one gate cannot contain two elders' *meishaa ilmoruk aare Kishomi.* When a woman is married, she builds her house on the right-hand side of her family's cattle entrance. The second wife builds hers on the left-hand side, the third on the right, and so on. Each of these camps, or homesteads, can hold from one to ten or so independent families, who are not necessarily related.

Maasai houses are rectangular in shape, with a slightly domed roof, and are built with wooden poles and saplings, intertwined with grass, and plastered with cow-dung. The entrance to the house is constructed in such a way that it faces the centre of the enclosure (**Olosinko**). The inside of the house consists of a small bed for the lady of the house; a big bed, for the husband, children and visitors; a hearth, with three cooking stones, separating the two beds; and a small pen for calves near the door. In recent years, all calf pens are now constructed outside reportedly for health reasons. There is also a small dish rack above the fireplace, and small holes are made in the walls by either bed and on the roof above the fireplace to act as ventilations and to let in light. In the centre of the homestead are small enclosures for the big calves, sheep and goats. This settlement pattern is often referred to in riddles and enigmas.

Political and Social Organization

The traditional Maasai system of governance is decentralized, with every age-set of every section (**olosho**) having its own elected political as well as ritual leaders. While the political leaders preside over meetings and secular functions, ritual leaders officiate at religious rituals. All these leaders are elected during the warriorhood stage, and retain their positions throughout their lives.

The diviner, **oloiboni**, acts as a prophet, shaman or seer, and officiates at rituals for all sections owing allegiance to him. He is the one who names the successive age-sets, with help from the elders; he opens and closes successive age-sets, and sees to the problems of women who have no children. Although he is not usually accorded any secular prerogative, a diviner can command a lot of power depending on his personality. This was the case with Mbatiany, who managed to command many Maasai sections.

The post of a diviner is confined to only one family in the **Nkidong'i** location and is inherited. Even today, the role of the oloiboni is still very important, being so deeply entrenched in the social life of the people to the extent that physical ailments that cannot be treated by a traditional physician are taken to the diviner. In recent years, the diviner institution has much wained through being demonized by Christianity. In oral literature, we see people and animals visiting him, and being given instructions, some of which seem nonsensical, such as Hare being told to jump over a fire four times to be cured. Depending on his position and character, a diviner can change from a seer into a sorcerer.

All Maa-speaking peoples share the descent system. At the base of this descent system are two **moieties** into which everyone falls irrespective of clan, section, location, or homestead. These are **Odomong'i** and **Orok-kiteng'**. They are further subdivided into clans, of which there were five originally; but another two were added later. These are again sub-divided into sub-clans. Exogamy is observed theoretically. While marriage within a clan was originally proscribed, this rule is slowly breaking down within the larger clans to the extent that it is now only restricted to the sub-clan level.

In the social organization of the Maasai, the age-set system, into which all males are recruited according to their approximate age and in fixed initiation groups, is of paramount importance. Despite a few rules that are observed in common, such as which section opens what ritual, each age-set normally organizes and regulates its age-set activities independent of the others. The age-set organization has remained very much the same through the years, except in the length of time for which young men remain warriors, which has been shortening over the years. Because of the school system, many boys have not been able to participate in the age set system. In order to correct this situation, some sections have designed mechanisms to induct the youth into the age-set system and impart some lessons during school holidays. While others are managing this transition, others are facing some expected challenges. For the proper understanding of some oral literature genres, it is essential to give a further explanation of the age-set pattern and its significance in the society.

The childhood stage is the one in which children perform small chores in the home, like running errands, looking after kids, calves and babies. They are also taught traditional lore informally, such as stories, riddles and rhymes by their parents and grandparents. As they grow older, the boys take to grazing cattle, sheep and goats, and their fathers and grandfathers teach them what there is to learn of traditional manly skills, as well as the various plants and animals and their uses. The girls, in turn, learn from the womenfolk. This arrangement is strictly 'adhered to because as the saying goes, *"elder olayioni o menye neder entito o ng'otonye,"* 'the boy chats with his father, the girl with her mother'.

The next stage signals adulthood, when initiation rites are observed. Initiation involves circumcision for men and clitoridectomy for women. After initiation, the boys become young men, **ilbarnot**, after recovery, warriors (**ilmurran**), elders (**ilmoruak**), and finally they retire as elders (**Iltasati**). There are important aspects to each of these stages.

Circumcision is an operation that candidates are expected to go through without flinching. The Maasai refer to flinching as **aipirri, akwet** (to run away), and need not be viewed in a literal sense. The simple act of blinking the eye-lashes is enough to have a person declared a coward, in which case fellow initiation friends will not eat or drink anything in his house, and will deprive him of the right to wear the favoured birds on his crown (See *The initiates' Song*). In short, it is a disgrace to the family for a boy to flinch.

Other important aspects of this stage are its attire and habits. The initiate wears long black greasy robes, keeps his hair long and greasy, like that of a woman in maternity. The impression he gives is summarized by the riddle, **Arro onyil** ("who looks like a greasy buffalo?"); the initiate, (**oloibartani**). He is also neither allowed to carry nor handle any type of weapons, and the meat he eats is cut into small pieces to facilitate easy eating without the use of a knife. He can, however, use a bow and blunt arrows to kill birds for his crown. The whole idea is to simulate a state of innocence and peacefulness in contrast to the later life of a warrior. During the convalescing stage, all that an initiate does is roam about the countryside encouraging, in the form of teasing, the younger boys to go through the operation without flinching. Some of the songs they sing are indeed scathing. This stage and the next lasts only a few months, then the young man becomes a warrior.

The warrior keeps his hair long, braided into pigtails, applies red ochre to his body, and carries a long bladed spear and shield. Contrary to popular belief, the warriors do not just roam about hunting lions, though this is indeed a sport that they alone can participate in.

The exercise is also a way of getting rid of lions when they become a nuisance to livestock. Warriors ordinarily live in their own special camps called **emanyatta**, pl. **imanyat** (ordinary villages are called **inkang'itie**, sing. **enkang'**), where they reside with their sponsors and instructors (**olpiron**, elders), who belong to the alternate age-set above them, and who impart the knowledge that society expects the warriors to have as adults. Through close association with, and imitation of, the elders, the warriors learn and acquire skills such as the use of proverbs and the art of oratory. Through associating with their peers, they learn the meaning of cooperation, unity and sharing. They are also exempted from tough domestic chores, except during the dry seasons, in order to allow them time to familiarise themselves with all parts of Maasailand, for, as the saying goes, *Enkong'u naipang'a eng'en* 'clever is the eye that has travelled'. During the dry seasons the warriors are expected to perform chores, such as watering the cattle, moving livestock to highland forested grazing areas, running long distances, errands and prospecting for water and pasture.

For their part, elders teach, direct and supervise the younger generation, as well as fencing the camps, watering the stock, and administering the general husbandry of the herd, such as castrating male steers and treating the sick. They also hold frequent meetings to discuss the management of livestock and other issues.

Women are not grouped into corporate age-sets like men are. They, however, tend to be identified, in status, with the male age-set with which they had danced as young unmarried girls and later as wives of particular age-sets. In Maasai society the women do most of the work in the home. The numerous chores for which they are responsible include gathering material for, and building houses, fetching water and firewood, milking and distributing food, cleaning milk utensils, sweeping the cattle, calf, sheep and goat enclosures, as well as the bearing and care of children.

Although the duty of grazing and watering the stock is normally a man's job, it is not infrequent for women to be called upon to give assistance when the need arises. Some women's songs and prayers in this collection are actually laments over the pathetic situation of their lot, for achievements in battle, or to urge them to take action.

Despite their apparent preoccupation with domestic chores, young women still find time to sing elaborate and poetic praises for men!

Dietary taboos and prescriptions accompany the age-set institution. During the warriorhood stage, the consumption of anything but livestock products is not only forbidden, but also sneered at. Beer and meat that has been seen by a woman, is considered taboo, and a warrior must never eat or drink anything without being in the company of an age-mate. Women have no such prescriptions. Most of these taboos are no longer adhered to.

CHAPTER TWO

The Dominant Features and Style of Maasai Oral Literature

In examining any art form, including oral literature, there are certain features of style that stand out. Among these are content, conventions and style. In all communities, each oral literature form has its own peculiar features and characteristics. Sometimes there are rules and conventions that have evolved over the years that have since been associated with each form or genre of oral literature. You have examined some of these features in general terms in *Oral Literature: A School Certificate Course.* In this chapter we will examine these features in reference to Maasai oral literature. It will be noticed that there are similarities to as well as differences from other Kenyan communities, as well as with most written literature.

Unlike some West African communities, where indigenous education has been formalized and is a monopoly of a few individuals, the Maasai traditional system of education, which includes imparting knowledge through various forms of oral literature, is characterized by its informality. Narrators as well as participants, and even the audience are all drawn in voluntarily. From being good listeners we develop into good narrators, and so the artistry is perpetuated.

The Social Setting of Stories

For a full appreciation of any lore, the social setting of the narration is of paramount importance. Setting includes the time and place where the narrative is told, and the participants.

Among the Maasai, the usual trend is for children as well as adults to assemble informally at the house of an elderly woman, whom many people call grandmother. In this house, one grandmother may commence relating a story, in the course of the evening the audience, which includes other adults, male or female, and children, take turns in narrating stories, until the young audience falls asleep.

11

Storytelling, posing of riddles and jokes are pass times that take place in the evening after super, when all the evening chores have been completed. These chores include milking and locking up calves in their respective enclosures, the latter being a job that is done mostly by children.

Children are forbidden to tell stories during daytime when they are looking after stock. They are warned that if they do so, their cattle, sheep and goats will wander off and get lost. Although this warning is sounded as a taboo, it is obvious that once a story-telling session is commenced, people get so involved that it may go on for hours on end with the herders and shepherds neglecting their duties. But there are always ways of getting around every taboo, and this one is no exception. Children have, therefore, adopted a method of knotting grass and bushes as a way of crossing their fingers to ward off misfortune and ameliorate the taboo. This is to enable them to recover any of the livestock that wanders off far into the bushes. Sometimes this charm works, but very often it does not. This is because story telling and listening can indeed be infectious.

The Storyteller as an Artist

As already noted, anyone can tell a story; no one is charged with the right or responsibility of a professional oral artist.

Some individuals, however, still excel as good narrators and acquire recognition as oral artists, especially achieved through performance. A good narrator usually identifies him/herself with characters in the tales quite strongly. These characters, as you will see later, can either be human beings, animals with fixed characteristics, or ogres, which are portrayed with human qualities and weaknesses.

A good narrator will imitate the appropriate sounds, gestures, movements and mannerisms of the characters. Hare, for example, often feigns weakness, and behaves like a young child whose ability to speak is not yet quite fully developed. In imitation, the narrator will lisp and make all sorts of phonemic errors that only a child can make. But Hare is not just an ordinary little child, but an exceedingly clever one too, and so a good artist portrays her accordingly. In contrast, when imitating Hyena, the narrator always speaks in a rough, heavy voice. A story can be good or bad depending on how it is told, and an accomplished artist employs many devices to make the audience enjoy the story. A well told tale is the one that evokes strong emotions in the audience, be they feelings of anger, apathy or humour.

The Audience

Just as the performance of the narrator is an important aspect of story telling, the audience plays an essential role, too. It is difficult to talk about one without the other. Some audiences are active while others are passive. This behaviour of the audience is not so much determined by the social group, but by the type of narrative, the manner of presentation, as well as the rapport developed between the artist and the audience.

Thus within one group, it is not uncommon to find an audience that joins the narrator in the singing of a song if it is part of a story, or to complete a favourite monologue, or even laugh or cheer at a humourous piece or openly express sorrow when the plot warrants it.

Yet the same audience may remain calm and seemingly unaffected by some other narratives. It may, however, be apparent that one group may have a natural tendency to appear more dramatic than another. The role of the audience is also noticeable in singing, where arms are thrust toward the singer in support of his or her contribution. Support from the audience is also apparent in lyrical verses, *eoko* and *enkijuka,* where the audience is free to make comments in the refrains. Often, the conclusion of an especially good rendition, be it a narrative, song, or any other art form, the audience indicates its appreciation of the art by offering their comments.

At the same time, the audience may indicate displeasure with the narrator or disagreement with the story quite indiscreetly. The highest appreciation of the artist's performance, however, is measured by the influence he/she has on the behaviour of the audience. To achieve this end, all possible artistic means are employed: these include movement of body and limbs, changes in tempo and pitch of voice, songs and gestures. The Maasai, however, did not clap hands to express appreciation. Hand-clapping was reserved for wonder and shock, but not continuously, just once.

Some Formulas in Oral Literature

As you will notice below, a story in Maa is introduced with the words **netii apa**, an equivalent of the English "once upon a time". This formula is constant in almost all narratives, except in those myths whose veracity is supposed to be highlighted. In the latter case, veracity is successfully achieved by underplaying the story-like semblance. Unlike in Dholuo, where the narrator and audience jointly say **thutinda** at the end of a story, there is no standard way of ending stories in Maa.

A Maasai narrator has a choice between several formulas. A common one goes: "and that is the end of my story". There is also: "and my story ends like that", or "my story ends in that length".

Riddles, of which there are two types in Maa, have fixed formulas that prepare the audience's response. The simple riddles are introduced by the propounder with the word, **oyiote**, "are you ready?" to which the audience respond by saying, **ee-wuo**, "it has come". Then the riddle is propounded. Complex riddles are opened with the question: "are you clever?" If the audience responds in the affirmative, which they always do irrespective of whether or not they are able to provide an answer, the riddle is then propounded.

Some forms of poetry have formulas, too. While **eoko** is introduced with a chorus or refrain, to get the rest of the singers in step with the rhythm, when introducing pieces such as **enkijuka**, the artist always begins by asking whether or not the others know him. The answer to this question is always negative, in order to give the singer or speaker a chance to praise himself and his accomplishments in wars and raids or any other feat worth telling.

The Style of Oral Literature

Events in oral narratives follow a certain sequence, just as they do in a written tale. The plot is a narrative of motivated action that may involve some conflict that is finally resolved. A story may have one or multiple plots. Some stories are narrated in a simple style, where events follow each other in a sequence.

This chronological mode of development is common in fiction but it is often altered for special effects. Some Maasai narratives are simple, while others are complex, hence the necessity of employing special techniques of style in the narration. Apart from simply getting the message across, a good narrator also takes the entertainment aspect of a narrative into consideration.

To achieve this, techniques such as flashbacks, suspense, repetition and others are used. A flashback is a shifting of focus to past occurrences to relate them to present events in the story. A similar effect is sometimes achieved when the narrator introduces a story within a story. Notice, for instance, how in story 9 the dog takes over the narration in such length and detail that we tend to forget the actual narrator.

Each of these techniques serves a particular purpose. Suspense holds the attention of the audience and keeps them alert throughout the narration. It also keeps them thinking and guessing and, therefore, exercising their minds. Repetition touches on another common technique of oral literature: song. Thus a song within a narrative may be repeated, not so much for its lexical or structural meaning, aspects which may often be irrelevant for the appreciation of the narrative, but for the beauty of the words and sounds. And depending on the audience's reactions, the raconteur may repeat a song as many times as he/she wants, sometimes creating occasions for it purposely. When a story is written down, however, it becomes cumbersome to repeat the song every so often, especially in the absence of a good narrator to add the entertainment aspect to the tale. Repetition also relieves any tension that may have built up in the course of the story.

As a device, repetition in other literary forms, such as songs, poetry, prayers and blessings, serves different purposes. It is often used to emphasize a point and to keep the audience aware of what it is doing. In prayer songs and blessings, you will notice the repeated calls to God to hear the people's prayer. You will also notice that this repetition is varied say from: **Na-Ai**, O God, to **Ee-Enkai**, Yes God. This is to break the monotony.

Symbolism, Imagery and Other Figures of Speech

Poets and distinguished orators, as well as good narrators and music composers, make liberal use of figures of speech. A symbol is an object that embodies an abstract idea. The Oreteti tree among the Maasai embodies long life because of its strong sturdy nature. When used in blessings, as is often the case, the tree symbol is understood without any need for interpretation. When a woman in a prayer song asks God for "long greasy hair", it is known, almost automatically, that she is asking for a child. This is because a woman in maternity keeps her hair long and greasy.

Imagery is the creation of mental figures of images, and is closely allied to similes. For example, the saying: "children are the bright moon", is a metaphor; while: "children are like the bright moon" is a simile. While a metaphor equates certain images with life situations, a simile compares them. Personification is where an inanimate object is conceived as embodying human qualities. This is commonly used in poetry. An idiom is another form or figure of speech that is similarly used both in oral and written literature. An idiom is a form of expression that is peculiar in the sense that it has a meaning other than its grammatical or logical one. Idioms are usually peculiar to a language or people, and their subtlety makes extrapolation into another language or media almost impossible to achieve as happens in riddles. Proverbs make frequent use of idioms. You have also come across ideophones and onomatopoeia.

Characterization

As you will notice in the respective sections, there are characters who play the role of actors in oral narratives. These may either be identifiable animals, or ogres, who behave like human beings but have indistinct physical features.

There are also real human characters displaying common human qualities and weaknesses. But despite this apparent distinction between the various characters, they exist in a similar world.

The choice of monsters and animals for narratives enables the narrator to ridicule and scorn any unbecoming behaviour without necessarily having to point a finger at any individuals. Yet it is obvious that whatever type of behaviour is referred to, it is associated with characters with behaviour and characteristics known within the community. Since there are many stories where characters are human beings, the effort to disguise their identity does not always seem necessary. Thus while Hyena almost always plays the role of the gluttonous and selfish fool, a similar theme is presented in another narrative with an old man acting Hyena's role. Characterization is dealt with in greater detail later.

Review Questions

i) With reference to your own community, explain the social setting of story telling and the posing of riddles, taking into consideration the ages and social status of the participants.

ii) Describe the role of the audience in any two forms of oral literature.

iii) Discuss the following features of style: symbolism, metaphors, imagery, similes and personification, giving examples of each.

CHAPTER THREE

Narratives

Narratives are often classified according to their function. While this kind of classification is convenient, it does not prevent an inevitable overlap of categories. For this reason, no classification of narratives, and other forms of oral literature, should be adhered to rigidly.

Narratives included in this book include myths, legends, ogre tales, trickster and other animal tales, and man stories. Under myths, we have narratives that explain the origin of various phenomena. As explained in *Oral Literature: A School Certificate Course* by Akivaga and Odaga, these are narratives that contain explanations about a community's origins and early history. Story **1** is an attempt to explain the origin of a most intriguing eventuality, death.

The story goes that the first man was granted a password by which to avert death. But either through forgetfulness or malice, he reversed the password, thereby placing man in a vulnerable position, in relation to death, and endowing moon with the ability to survive it. In narrative **2** we are offered a socio-cultural explanation for the reason why the sun shines brightly, but the moon does not: the sun beat the moon "in the same way husbands beat their wives". Even an irregularity like the wife fighting her husband is explained in cultural terms: the moon is one of those short-tempered women who beat their husbands.

Explanations offered in these myths are imaginative; most of these narratives could be described as aetiological. They are also called "the how and why" stories because they explain the origin and characteristics of various animals, plants, features of the landscape, or different social customs. In such explanations, there are often cultural additions and some rather marvellous and anachronistic colourings that make it almost impossible to separate the true element from the traditional or socio-cultural. Thus the cause of the embarrassment felt by the sun, but not by the moon in story **2** is based on the traditional norms and expectations of the society. A husband would not walk about undaunted with a wound that was inflicted by his wife!

A common feature of myths is their reference to emotions and experiences that are universally understood and felt. In narrative **3** we are told that the fight between the gods is based on the difference in their respective natures: while the black god is kind and loving, the red god is malevolent and cruel. Sacred beings are by no means set above human beings; they fight and are preoccupied with petty jealousies; and the fact that an essential commodity such as water becomes the bone of contention is significant and expected in a semi-arid region.

Some myths embody customs that are still very strongly observed. Others serve the interests of the community by justifying good as well as evil practices, or illustrating the consequences of good as well as bad behaviour. In story **4** the Dorobo hunter, through no fault of his own, expresses surprise on seeing cattle descend from a thong, and for this he is cursed to hunt game forever. This myth, therefore, justifies subjugation of the hunters by the pastoralists even to the present day. Another myth (**5**) explains how women irresponsibly let their cattle wander away and get lost. This illustrates not only why women do not own cattle, or any property, but also justifies their maltreatment. The same is true of narrative **6** where marriage is said to have been caused by woman's lust. It implies that if marriage has evolved into a necessary evil for women, it was brought about by one of them. The significance of this myth rests in the fact that voluntary celibacy does not exist traditionally among the Maasai.

The belief system and social values of a community are conveyed in some of its myths. Some stories (not included) explain the appearance, shape and behaviour of insects. We are told that Louse disobeyed her grandmother, was cursed by her, and became paralysed enabling even a blind person to catch her. Flea, for his part, was obedient, and for this he was showered with blessings, which made him swift and able to manoeuvre between the fingers of human predators. The consequences of the curse and blessing in the respective cases is a way of saying that the young have to obey their seniors in order to receive blessings. Failure to obey could result in the young being cursed, which would in turn lead to grave consequences.

In another narrative Louse, envious for not possessing the much admired sword, tricks her friend Termite into tightening his sword belt to the extent of almost cutting through his waist, and ending up with a ridiculous shape. But the mischievous trick makes Louse laugh to the extent of splitting her nose. Therefore, while Termite suffers from an ugly shape, Louse, who bears responsibility for it, consequently loses perhaps a very valuable part of her body. The explanatory element is a common feature in myths, although the explanation does not necessarily have to be stated explicitly. The function of the above myths in illustrating the consequences of good and bad behaviour is only made by implication.

Most myths are simple to follow. Each myth often illustrates the consequences of one or two aspects of social behaviour. There are, however, other narratives in this category that are relayed in a complex manner to encompass multiple facets of a myth. Narrative **7** is a fine example. The dog defies god's orders and betrays the sheep. For this he loses favour with god, is sent down to earth, where he becomes a servant of man, who in turn obtains god's favourite creature, the sheep.

Both animals get re-named: Dog requests qualities he needs for survival in his new and unpleasant environment. These he is given. The myth illustrates his peculiar characteristics and the establishment of the triangular relationship between god, dog and man. This is a complex narrative since it contains several myths within it, and various illustrations of differing behaviours.

Legends

Stories **8** and **9** are legends. They are about events and people in a historical context within a particular community. They also revolve around historical figures, characters or events. The basic difference between myths and legends is that while a legend is told as if it is true, and is often based on true events or characters the veracity of a myth is based on the beliefs of its hearers. In narrative **8** the present clan system among the Maasai is explained in very precise detail; this makes it sound like a simple description rather than a story. But the fact that the clan system, as explained here, conforms to the present system in all detail removes the mythical element and makes it a legend.

Narrative **9** is an example of a hero legend; these are common in many communities. The hero always has super-human qualities. The Arinkon leader is said to be mighty and strong like a giant; Lwanda Magere, a legendary character from among the Luo community had a body made of rock and strength was in his shadow. It is significant, however, to note that the giant in story **9** is not a Maasai hero, and that his strength and bravery only go to indicate how clever his conquerors were. The heroism is interestingly shifted to the clever boy who kills the giant. This is a David and Goliath type legend, and it is intriguing to imagine how it would have been told by the Arinkon themselves.

Animal Stories

The animal stories included in this book fall into two categories. First, there are those that revolve around adventures of weird creatures and their encounters with the human beings. These creatures, like the warrior with two mouths or a crow-like suitor, are formless and are not easily visualized or described. Some have names like **Mbiti, Konyek, Ntemelua**, but they are all lumped together in Maa as **nkukuuni** or **ng'wesi**, which translated means some fearful monster or ogre. The second category includes trickster tales and tales of other animals with clearly identifiable animal characters.

In the first category of narratives, one can identify common features in the monster characters. Although this is not stated in each case, these ogres are all unusual in one way or another. Each has some outstanding characteristic. The warrior in story **1** has two mouths and is also strikingly handsome; the crow in **13** is also an attractive young man; **Mbiti (11)** alone of all other monsters has a cowrie shell on the tail that eventually betrays her; **Konyek (12)** has protruding eyes from which he got his name; and **Ntemelua (15)** is significantly portrayed as a new-born baby in order to highlight the marvellous nature of his grotesque behaviour.

Another aspect that is evident in ogre tales is their portrayal as greedy and cruel creatures. Mbiti's monstrosity is seen in the way she makes the girl choose whether to be eaten or spared. The girl chooses the latter, and the monster indeed brings her up like a beloved daughter. But when she grows fat Mbiti begins to view her as potential food, and keeps pricking her to determine whether she is ready for the table. Konyek kills his aunt and takes his twin cousins to be roasted for kidneys. The crow taunts his bride instead of eating her immediately, and the ogre (**14**) does the same to the young woman.

Ogres are also portrayed as potentially intelligent, but their intelligence is never utilized at the right time. The warrior monster has suspicions that he was betrayed by the warrior who had put on a squint and a limp. **Mbiti** is suspicious of the girl who called herself "a skin of ashes" and questions her a second time about her identity before dismissing her; **Konyek's** premonition is quite outstanding, but the presence of his father in the story as a perfect dupe is a deliberate stylistic feature to prevent his eventual triumph. The crow tricks both of the girls' parents and succeeds in obtaining the bride; he is about to succeed when unexpected rescuers are introduced. This technique, stylistically known as *deus ex machina*, is commonly employed in ogre tales when a sure end seems imminent for the hero or heroine.

Another interesting factor in ogre tales is their beginning and the way the would – be victim starts by forgetting something, or having one reason or another to return in order to recover it, and ends up by being a victim of the ogre. The girl in story **12** forgets her beads on the monster's bed; when she goes to recover them she puts herself into the hands of the monster. In story **11** the youngest of the girls, having been tricked by the others, picks unripe berries; she returns for ripe ones, in anger and determination, only to become a victim of the ogre; again the young woman (notice how most victims happen to be women!) in pursuit of her warrior lover (**14**) confuses the left with the right path, takes the wrong path, and consequently meets the monster.

Another interesting aspect is the way songs are introduced into monster narratives, initially as laments, but at the same time signal an alarm that results in the rescue of the victim. The crow's bride (**13**) having resigned herself to a fateful end sings out her last wish (if only her stubborn parents were there to see for themselves!). Although she is much too far away from home and has no hope whatsoever of being rescued, the girl's song alarms the passers-by who immediately come to her aid. In story **14**, the woman composes a song that flatters the ogre, keeps the audience in suspense, but also brings forth the desperately needed help.

Finally, the ending of ogre narratives is significant. There are numerous Maasai monster stories, and many of them have different endings. The commonest is the one in which the monster gets killed, or opened up, and the victim is rescued. Others normally request that some part of themselves – thumb or little finger – be cut to let out all the victims **(15)**. Yet others bring about their own deaths. Mbiti **(11)** collects all the other monsters to feast on her victim, but she ends up being the victim of her friends; Konyek **(12)** and his father find "kidneys" which they bring up, not knowing that they will be the cause of death for both of them; the crow **(13)** lights a big fire in which to roast the bride, but he gets roasted in it instead; and the ogre **(14)** prepares a bed of sweet smelling leaves on which his flesh (not his victim's) is laid after his death. Yet again mysterious creatures like **Ntemelua (15)** disappear in equally mysterious ways.

These types of narrative entertain as much as they teach, but as they do so, their grotesque characterization, coupled with suspense, strike great fear into the audience.

Trickster and Other Animal Tales

Stories in this category are of a more humorous and light-hearted nature than ogre tales, myths or legends. But beneath this humour are subtle commentaries on social activities. A child is, therefore, taught important lessons through pleasant entertainment.

The most outstanding feature of these narratives is characterization. The role of the trickster and his foils is a well-established feature in many African narratives.

Among the Yoruba, Edo and Ibo of Nigeria, for example, the tortoise is the primary trickster; but in other parts of West and East Africa, his role as trickster is secondary. The spider plays this role in Liberia, Sierra-Leone, Ghana, and Jamaica, where he is referred to by his Twi name, Ananse. In South Carolina, he is called Aunt Nancy, obviously a corruption of his

Twi name. In East Africa, Hare, Tortoise and Mongoose play the role of tricksters in different communities, in varying degrees. But while it is evident that small animals are generally preferred for tricksters and large ones for their dupes, it is also true that the choice of animals more or less depends on geographical and topographical factors.

In Maasai narratives, Hare plays the role of primary trickster, a role she plays by manipulating all the big animals in turn. There are, nevertheless, several other animals that play the role of secondary tricksters. Mongoose, Chameleon and Tortoise are some of these. Of the dupes, Hyena stands out as a primary one, while Elephant and Lion are secondary foils. But as is evident from these narratives, many other animals are involved as foils, not so much to portray their foolishness, but to highlight the ingenuity of the trickster.

In the many incidents involving tricksters, Hare feigns fatigue or helplessness in order to ride a powerful animal such as Elephant as if he were her horse; or she will ask to be carried on the back so that, while everyone else wades through water she is perched above, dry and smug, scheming ingenious schemes (**17**); Mongoose tricks the king of all beasts to wait for him until he is starved to death (**18**); Chameleon rides on the back of a swifter animal, so that she gets ahead in the race without competing; Tortoise stations his friends along the course so that he always appears ahead with a confident and faster animal.

As is the case with animal tales in many communities, there is a fixed conceptualization of the qualities and characteristics for each of the major animal characters in the tales. Hare's name in Maa (Enkitejo) means "the utterer" or "the speaker", for she is always speaking for herself and the rest of the animals during meetings. She is regarded as clever, cunning, shrewd and unscrupulous. She takes maximum advantage of her small size to feign helplessness or incapacity so as to get others working for her.

In narrative **18**, we see her using one animal against the other, eliminating them all, and ending up by owning all the cattle. To get the animals to participate in this elimination exercise, she plants fear in them, by making them believe the victim has some advantage over the other members of the group and, therefore, poses a threat. But in the end, when the job has been done, instead of commending the animal which has eliminated the victim for the good deed, he in turn is eliminated for posing a threat to the others. And so the exercise is repeated until all the animals are eliminated. Having led Hyena to get his cattle stuck in the mud, Hare pretends to be kind and offers to share her remaining herd, but in the process tricks Hyena to kill his mother, to reduce the number of mouths to feed, while at the same time using Hyena's labour and feeding her mother with the best meat. In the end, Hare drives Hyena to get himself roasted.

In narrative **17**, after making Elephant carry her a long distance, Hare gets him to fill up his own honey bag with stones, in the pretext that she is using the stones, and by the time this trick is discovered, it is too late: the honey is all gone and elephant, in a bid to punish the culprits, ends up with nothing but a skin from her tail. In another narrative (**19**), Hare gets people and animals involved in an uproar against each other, merely because of her string of beads.

In another story, Hare obtains two rams and having no proper place to slaughter them, goes to tell Lion that she has taken the two rams to him to aid in his recovery from an eye ailment. On hearing Hare's story, Lion quickly plucks his eyes out to justify the reception of the rams. But all Hare wanted was some comfortable and secure residence in which to feast on her rams. From these incidents, it is evident that all of Hare's tricks are contrived to enable her to obtain something or to get services from the bigger animals. Nevertheless, there are occasions when she plays tricks just for the sheer delight of proving to herself and others that she is cleverer than all of them.

Through Hare's antics, we witness the triumph of brain over brawn and of brilliance over steadiness. Despite her cruel tricks, she is still admired and even loved for her intelligence. For instance, though she maliciously tricks Hyena to get rid of his mother (**16**), the audience cannot help but sympathize with her when her own mother is eaten. And when she seeks support from others to aid her in recovering her beads (**19**), the audience once more shares the anxiety and the hope that she succeeds in the end. Although it is only in a few instances that the trickster finds herself tricked, she is by no means infallible or immune to tricks. This is shown in narrative **16** when Hyena eats Hare's mother.

For his part, Hyena is portrayed as an insatiable glutton who constantly gets himself into trouble in his search for food. In one story, he gets so carried away by the supply of food at the cave of the lioness that he forgets the password thus getting himself caught. And when lioness employs him as a baby sitter, he cannot keep the job due to his inborn weakness for cracking bones, thus killing the baby and subsequently getting punished. In another story, convinced that the moon is fat juicy meat, Hyena gets his friends and relatives to climb one on top of the other to get to it.

In the process, they all come tumbling down, each breaking his hind-leg; that is why hyenas limp.

In narrative **21**, Hyena unashamedly displays his ravenous nature by expressing the amount of food he is capable of containing without in the least getting satisfied. A mighty big ox to him is but a speck in the teeth. When the tails of his cattle come off as he struggles to pull them out of the mud, without in the least being deterred by the tragedy of losing all his cattle, he eats the tails one after the other **(16)**. Hyena's decision to eat the donkeys in narrative **19** is induced, neither by his sympathy for Hare nor his desire to see justice done, but merely by his gluttonous nature. He is not the kind to let such an opportunity slip.

Apart from his gluttony, Hyena is also famous for his extreme gullibility and stupidity. He is at once unkind and selfish, and these weaknesses are liabilities to him. Being selfish he is too concerned about his own safety to notice that by choosing "hornless cattle" he ends up with donkeys. The same weakness makes him avoid the dusty path to the river, only to end up getting all his "cattle" stuck in what he thought was the better of the two paths. With the hope of obtaining more cattle, he collaborates with Hare in eliminating the other animals **(16)**, only to end up with the worst deal disinheritance, the loss of his mother and an eventual roasting.

Hyena's encounter with cow in story **21** summarizes all his bad qualities. In the song he expresses his greed in stating the amount of food that does not satisfy him; his selfishness is evident from the fact that he does not share food with his poor mother; his disregard of all entreaties from a helpless, thirsty, suckling cow is a clear indication of his extreme cruelty; and the crude and indiscreet manner in which he hangs the hind leg of Hare's mother at the gate post is an act that can only be associated with an inhuman character.

Mongoose and Tortoise, on the other hand, are seen as sages whose "reasoning" not tricks to extricate themselves and others from intricate situations. Aware of their physical limitations in the face of the insurmountable might of the bigger animals, they avoid any physical combat and instead rely on reason. Mongoose uses his oratorical talent, coupled with a little trickery, to retrieve the chicks of the ostrich from the bullying lion **(18)**. The astute manner in which he conducts and eventually resolves the dispute is commendable. Notice how he, of all the other richly-endowed animals, succeeds in winning the much desired daughter of Tiyiogo **(20)** without saying anything spectacular.

Tortoise on his part often relies on chance. In one story, he is unanimously chosen to be Lion's dinner, and having no means by which to defend himself, cleverly extends his speech in expectation of rain, which falls and forms a puddle, into which he jumps and disappears after declaring that god was not present when the fateful decision was reached and had, therefore, come to his rescue. When, in another story, Elephant loses his temper after Tortoise tricks and beats him in a race, he throws Tortoise into the river, from where he happily swims along to meet his friend.

Chameleon also beats Lion in a race by perching herself on his back, and then quickly jumps on to the tree that was to act as finishing post and camouflages herself immediately, so that Elephant fails to locate her.

The role of the Chameleon, Mongoose and Tortoise further brings out the contrast between brain and brawn. Their brilliance and steadiness give advantage over physically stronger opponents. Elephant and Lion are both strong, but are not very intelligent. But while the lion represents power and authority which tricksters strive to bring down, the elephant breeds no malice, but his mere size and little brain is a cause for constant ridicule. From these adventures we are taught many lessons, one being that brains are often more useful than simple physical might.

Man Stories

While ogre and trickster tales discuss human qualities indirectly by use of animal characters, stories in this category are direct commentaries on the life of the people. In these stories, we are presented with situations and characters that are so real that one can easily visualize and identify with them. We get a complete picture of a society from the social setting, dietary and other social habits and taboos, kinship, and other relations, sex roles, customs, beliefs, values, attitudes and philosophy of life.

Despite their apparent clarity and their apparent reflection of a people's life, it must be stressed that stories alone should not be used as a criterion to determine a people's culture, philosophy or history. The mind has after all, an interesting way of manipulating ideas and creating what seems unimaginable. For instance it is impossible to imagine a normal person with two heads or a moon that eats grass! One needs to have a grasp of the totality of a people's life to develop the expertise to analyse, judge and make conclusions about their behaviour.

As manifested in some stories in this category, greed is not only unacceptable, but can also lead to very grave consequences. The old man in story **22** steals his mother-in-law's sausage and because he is in a hurry, he does not notice the live coal that is stuck on the sausage, as he shoves it inside the quiver and tries to conceal the truth about the cause of the smoke. His mother-in-law escorts him, as custom demands, only to be embarrassed at seeing the sausage drop in front of her. Both are extremely embarrassed, but the old man is greedy enough to remember to beg his mother-in-law not to eat the sausage. He is so greedy that he disregards all the rules of social decorum.

Another greedy man almost goes hungry for turning down the offer of milk, in the hope of getting what he thought was meat, but alas, he finds it was only some medicinal herb.

Cruelty is another ill that society scorns. In each of the incidents in these narratives where cruelty is manifest, it is displayed in unusual circumstances and in extremity. The step-mother in story **31** buries her step-son and leaves him to die; the foster mother (**32**) hates the shepherd boy; the old man (**33**) overworks his pregnant wife to death. The lessons contained in these stories are shown by the consequences suffered by the cruel characters. The cruel step-mother is killed by her own son to avenge the maltreatment received by his friend and half-brother. Although we know that by killing this woman both boys remain motherless and possibly worse off than before, the fact becomes irrelevant, and the audience is satisfied that the cruel woman suffers for her sins.

The same fate befalls the foster mother and, as a contrast, the life of the kindly foster father is spared and he is rewarded. The father of "the girls of the knee" (**33**) in the end loses his wife and is deprived of the children which he struggled so hard to bring up. In story **28** the twins' mother suffers for many years looking after donkeys through the evil designs of her co-wife but eventually her sons appear and the truth is revealed. And although the malicious co-wife is not killed, the audience is once more satisfied that she takes the place of the "donkey woman" for the rest of her life.

Robbery, selfishness and maltreatment of the weak by the strong are not condoned by society. This is shown in story **24** when strong sturdy warriors disregard the helplessness of the old man and his young wife and their inability to defend their property from robbers. But fairness and justice triumph when the culprits are brought to book in the end. Here, the calm disposition of the old man is contrasted with the rough and arrogant behaviour of the warriors.

A similar contrast is brought out in story **29** when the patient, persevering warrior is rewarded, but his rash brother returns with nothing but weapons. The raiders in narrative **31** are all exterminated.

In narrative **28** we learn that society scoffs at ungratefulness, but from story **32** we learn that fertility and the need for children is such an overpowering desire that fruit turn into children and men become pregnant! Good behaviour is usually rewarded but bad conduct is either punished or disregarded (**29**).

Feelings of love and affection are brought out in story **25** where the warrior's love for his parents, siblings, girlfriend, and even for his cows is quite intense. Great affection also exists between the two stepbrothers in story **30**. But this kind of affection is more obviously brought out in songs and poetry.

The role of birds in these stories is of special significance. Certain birds, such as Dove and Eagle, are portrayed as kind and benevolent, and their role is to rescue man from difficult situations.

Myths and Legends

1. Enkiterunolo e keeya

Ore apa tenkiterunoto nemeetae apa Keeya. Inji oshi eikununye keeya enkop.

Eetae apa oIlung'ani oji Leeyio Iaa ninye apa eiterie Naiteru·kop enkop. Nejoki apa Naiteru· kop Leeyio. "Nchoo ake peyie eye oItung'ani iwa auIuo nilo ajo, 'Apa tua nilotie, tung'ani tua niitu'. Tenijo neijia nepok ilo tung'ani otua."

Nelusoo ilapaitin kumok meetae oltung'ani otua. Ore kenya peyie elo enkerai e likae marei aye neipoti L.eeyio meshomo aiturraa. Neya ake L.eeyio enkerai auluo neidang' ajo. "Apa tua niitu, tung'ani tua nilotie." Nelotie enkarai ina.

Ore peyie elusoo ilkuti apaitin nelaiy enkerai e L.eeyio. Neya menye ong'ata nejo. "Apa tua nilotie, tung'ani tua niitu". Nening' Naiterukop. Nejoki, "Meekure ebaiki amu enotoki apa keeya peyie eye enkerai elde marei." Ine taa oshi eimua keeya. Ina paa teneye oltung'ani nelotie kake tenemuta olapa neitu anaake menyaakini aashil.

1. The Origin of Death

In the beginning there was no death. This is the story of how death came into the world.

There was once a man known as Leeyio who was the first man that Naiteru-kop* brought to earth. Naiteru-Kop then called Leeyio and said to him: "When a man dies and you dispose of the corpse, you must remember to say, 'man die and come back again, moon die, and remain away.'"

Many months elapsed before anyone died. When, in the end, a neighbour's child did die, Leeyio was summoned to dispose of the body. When he took the corpse outside, he made a mistake and said: "Moon die and come back again, man die and stay away." So after that no man survived death.

A few more months elapsed, and Leeyio's own child went missing**. So the father took the corpse outside and said: "Moon die and remain away, man die and come back again." On hearing this, Naiteru-kop said to Leeyio: "You are too late now for, through your own mistake, death was born the day when your neighbour's child died." So that is how death came about, and that is why up to this day when a man dies he does not return, but when the moon dies, it always comes back again.

*Literally 'the beginner of the earth'.

** The Maasai never refer to a dead man as 'dead', they talk of him as being 'missing' (*etalaki*) in the case of young people, or 'having slept' when referring to the old. I believe this is so to ameliorate the grief that bitter truth elicits.

Review Questions

i) In this narrative, we are presented with the Maasai conception of the deity.

Before the advent of Christianity and Islam in your community, what was the people's concept of God, and in what ways was it different or similar from those of the other religions you may have come across?

ii) In other lessons, you have discussed myths that relate to the origin of death. Referring to these, and to any other similar myths, discuss the major points made about death in these narratives.

2. Enkolong' o lapa

Ore apa tiapa neyam enkolong' olapa. Niaku keirukuruko anaake eituruk enkolong' nesuj olapa. Naa keya nenauru olapa neyeng'iyeng'a nenap enkolong' inkolong'i uni tolapa. Ore tenkolong' e ong'wan neji etoduaa isirkon olapa. Neyoki iltung'ana aadol.

Ore nabo olong' neitarruo olapa niar' enkolong' anaa oshi ake peyie ear ilpayiani nkituak. Naa idol apa olapa naa inoshi kituaak naatolo naing'ar ilpayiani. Ore peyie eari niarisho sii ninye. Neosh enkolong' enkomom nebor. Niar sii ninye enkolong' olapa, nekokot enkomon nekurtu enkong'u nabo. Nedol enkolong' ajo ebora nekurru oleng' nejo toongoso kutiti, "Kailang' taa iltung'ana oleng' peyie maatum aatisipu." Newang'u oleng niaku meidim tukul iltung'ana aing'ura. Metaa ina oshi peyie ewang' enkolong'.

Ore ninye olapa neitu edol enkurruna niaku eitu ninye ewang'u. Ore o taata tenisipu olapa nidol inkiporo naatipika apa enkolong' tenapa ara.

2. The Sun and the Moon

In the beginning, the sun married the moon. They travelled together for a long time, the sun leading and the moon following. As they travelled, the moon would get tired and the sun would carry her* for three days every month.

On the fourth day the donkeys are said to be able to see the moon. People can only see the moon on the fifth day.

One day the moon made a mistake and she was beaten by the sun in just the same way women are beaten by their husbands. But it happened that the moon was one of those short-tempered women who fight their husbands. When she was beaten, she fought back, and wounded the sun's forehead. The sun also beat the moon and scratched her face and plucked out one of her eyes.

When the sun realised that he was wounded, he was very embarrassed and said to himself, "I am going to shine so hard that people will not be able to look at me." And so he shone so hard that people could not look at him without squinting. That is why the sun shines so brightly.

As for the moon, she did not feel any embarrassment and so she did not have to shine any brighter. And even now, if you look closely at the moon, you will see the scars that the sun inflicted on her during their fight.

*The word for moon (*olapa*) carries the masculine gender form '01' in the prefix and so I would have referred to it as "he" as has been done in other narratives but here I have used the feminine form "her" in order to conform to its role as the "wife".

Review Questions

i) What social norm do we learn from this narrative relating to the position of women in this particular society? Why do you think the sun was embarrassed but the moon was not?

ii) Myths such as the one above are part of a community's search for explanations of the existence and formation of the universe and other natural phenomena. Can you think of a similar myth from your community?

3. Enkikurrukur o nkaitin

Eetae apa nkaitin are: enkai narok o enkai nanyokie. Naa ore ena ai narok naa kebor, naa supat oleng' nenyor iltung'ana. Kake ore enkai nanyokie naa ketolo nemeikenu olorere. Naa keshula apa kuna aitin te shumata kake enarok natii abori enkae ataaniki iltung'ana.

Ore nabo olong' niaku enkop pooki olameyu. Nelau nkishu nkujit naanya nelau sii enkare niaku keya iltung'ana esumash. Nejoki nabo olong enkai narok enanyokie: "Matayoki aaisho olorere enkare peyie memut olameyu."' Neng'as enkai nanyokie aany eishori olorere enkare. Nesai enkai narok o metonyorrai. Neji kebolori enkare; meshomo enkop. Ore peyie ebolori enkare nesha oleng' nkolong'i kumok.

Ore peyie elusoo nkuti olong'i nejoki enkai narok enanyokie. "Taluana taa taata enkare amu eidipa ina olorere". Nejoki enkai narok: "Maishoo eitoki asha nkuti olong'i amu etoyio oshi enkop oleng'." Neishori eitoki asha nkuti olong'i. Ore peyie eitoki enkai nanyokie ajoki enkae meiboo enkare neibok enkae, neguar.

Ore toonkuti olong'i neitoki enkai narok ajoki enanyokie menyaaki aisho iltung'ana enkare.

Niany enkai nanyokie. Neiteru taa aaishankarra. Nejo enkai nanyokie kemut olorere amu etapashipashita. Nemitiki enkai narok. Niaku ore-os hi o taata tenedar naa enkai nanyokie najo agiru enkae ejo peyie emut iltung'ana. Naa teneikurrukur akiti nemedar naa enkai narok ina natem aibooyo enkae peyie memut olorere.

3. Thunder and the Gods

Once there were two gods: the black god and the red god. The black god was very humble, kind and loving, while the red god was malevolent and did not care about people at all.

These gods lived together way up in heaven, but the black god lived below the red god, and therefore closer to the people on earth.

One day, famine spread all over the land, cattle could find neither grass to eat nor water to drink and they were almost dying from starvation. Then the black god spoke to the red god and said "Let us give people water for they are about to starve to death", the red god was at first reluctant to let people have water, for he had no liking for them, but after much pleading from the black god, she relented. It was then agreed that water was to be released from heaven to earth. When this was done, it rained very hard for many days.

After some time, the red god said to the black god: "You can now hold back the water, for the people have had enough." The black god answered: "Let us leave it for a few more days for the earth had been parched dry."

This was done, and when the red god again told the black god to hold back the water, she did so and the rain stopped falling.

A few more days elapsed and the black god once more asked the red god to release some more water for the people. The red god refused, and there ensued an argument between them, with the red god threatening to wipe out all the people, whom she described as having been spoilt, and the black god struggling to prevent her from doing so. And so, up to this day, when one hears loud thunder, it is the red god who is trying to get past the black god to wipe out the people on earth. But when the sound of thunder is not very loud, it is the black god who is trying to prevent the red god from killing the people.

Review Questions

i) Discuss the qualities of the two gods.

ii) Summarise this narrative in less than 50 words.

4. Eneimua enkiteng'

Ore apa tiapa nemeeta apa Ilmaasai nkishu. Ore nabo olong' neipot Naiteru-kop Maasinta, aa ninye apa oltung'ani oiterie Naiteru·kop enkop nejoki: "Maasinta lai, ayieu niyoki aitobir enkang' sapuk oleng'. Ore ake peyie indip nikilotu aliki," Ore pee eidip nelo alikioo. Neitoki Naiteru.kop ajoki: 'Tayooki nyio tolakira shomo ntasho tesuntai e boo amu kaayoki aisho entoki naji enkiteng'. Naa tenining' anaa tenidol toki nimiputukuny ake, ti-girayu."

Ore tenkakenya nedumunye Maasinta alo aanyu entoki duo naishori. Ore teina kata nening' peyie edar neikurukur .neitadou Naiteru·kop enkeene naado 'aitadoiki olosinko lenaduo ang'. Nedou nkishu aaporu ena keene aadoiki enkang'. Neikirikira enkop oleng' o metaa kejo enkaji aurori. Ina peyie eirut Maasinta oleng' kake eitu ejo ae. Ore eton edou nkishu neputunye Torroboni oshulare apa Maasinta tenkaji. Ore ena naipang' nemaniki nkishu nemeeta esiana erukunye aaimu enkeene. Neiputukuny oleng' nejo: "ayieyieyie. '" Ore ake peyie ening' Naiteru·kop nerriny enkeene, nedung'o nkishu. Nejo ninye Naiteru·kop tenaa ke Maasinta otejo neijia, nejoki: "Amaa. kenkaraki kindipa kuna? Mmaaitoki aikata aikonji metaa tonyorra kuna kishu anaa peyie aanyor nanu iyie". Ina taa oshi peyie enyor Ilmaasai inkishu.

Oo naa ninye oltorroboni? Emeiba naa Maasinta ena natudung'oki enkeene? Nedek ajoki: 'Torroboni. keyie oewuo adung' enkeene Enkai? Taa aisinani anaa apa ake peyie ira. Iyaku iyie onkera inono isinkan lainei intarasi. Nchoo metaa ng'wesi eong'ata inchuyie, niaku enduaran kule oonkishu ainei teninchiam." Ina taa oshi peyie aa entim emanya Iltorrobo okinya kulo, nemeishori aikata kule.

4. Origin of Cattle

In the beginning, the Maasai did not have any cattle. One day God called Maasinta, who was the first Maasai, and said to him: "I want you to make a large enclosure, and when you have done so, come back and inform me." Maasinta went and did as he was instructed, and came back to report what he had done. Next, God said to him:

"Tomorrow, very early in the morning, I want you to go and stand against the outside wall of the house for I will give you something called cattle. But when you see or hear anything do not be surprised. Keep very silent."

Very early next morning, Maasinta went to wait for what was to be given him. He soon heard the sound of thunder and God released a long leather thong from heaven to earth.

Cattle descended down this thong into the enclosure. The surface of the earth shook so vigorously that his house almost fell over. Maasinta was gripped with fear, but did not make any move or sound. While the cattle were still descending, the Dorobo, who was a house-mate of Maasinta, woke up from his sleep. He went outside and on seeing the countless cattle coming down the strap, he was so surprised that he said: "Ayieyieyie ....!", an exclamation of utter shock. On hearing this, God took back the thong and the cattle stopped descending. God then said to Maasinta, thinking he was the one who had spoken: "Is it that these cattle are enough for you? I will never again do this to you, so you had better love these cattle in the same way I love you." That is why the Maasai love cattle very much.

How about the Dorobo? Maasinta was very upset with him for having cut God's thong. He cursed him thus: "Dorobo, are you the one who cut God's thong? May you remain as poor as you have always been. You and your offspring will forever remain my servants. Let it be that you will live off animals in the wild. May the milk of my cattle be poison if you ever taste it." This is why up to this day the Dorobo still live in the forest and they are never given milk.

Review Question

"This is a stereotyped myth that serves to justify the subjugation of the Dorobo (hunters) by the Maasai." Discuss.

5. Nkishu oo nkituaak

Ore apa ng'wesi entim naa ninche nkishu oonkituak. Ore nabo olong' neyieng'i enkiteng' tadekenya, enoshi kata eton eirrag nkishu ontare. Neirrag ake duo nkishu o metalaari aapuo daa. Nelaari sii ninche ntare. Nejoki entasat nabo enkerai: "Nyio shomo mboo nkishu."Nening' ake ng 'otonye enkerai nejoki ina tasat: "Ai a-ah, melo ninye enkerai ai eton eitu enya olairakuji." Naa kejokini ake ae kerai meshomo arrinyu nkishu nemitiki ng'otonye elo eton eitu eonyu enkiti toki.

Neikoni neijia o meshomo nkishu o ntare entim, nepuo aaimin. Ore. kenya peyie eidip nkera pooki aainosa nkiri neji maape aaleenu nkishu neinepuni etaapishote. Neiturrarrie apa nkituaak nkishu ina. Neidur aapuo aashula o ilewa leitu ninche eitololoiki nkunenye. Ina oshi paa ore nkishu naa inoolewa, kianyu ake nkituaak meishori pooki toki.

5. The Women's Cattle

Long ago, wild animals used to be women's cattle. Then, one morning before the cattle were taken out to graze, a cow was slaughtered. Soon, the cattle started moving away to graze by themselves and wandered off. One woman told one of the children to go and drive the cattle back before they went too far. When the child's mother heard this she said: "Oh, no, my child is not going until he has eaten the kidney." It followed that whenever a child was asked to go, his mother forbade him to go until he had had a bite of the meat.

This went on until all the cattle, sheep and goats wandered away into the bush and got lost. When all the children had eaten the meat, they tried to bring the cattle back, but they found that they had all gone wild. And so that is how it came about that women lost their cattle. They then went and lived with the men who had all along taken good care of their cattle. This is why up to this very day, all the cattle belong to the men and women simply wait for the men to provide for them.

Review Question

This myth is similar in certain respects to the one before. Identify the similarities and discuss their significance in any society that discriminates according to sex, occupation, race or any other factor.

6. Enklterunoto enkiama

Netii apa, nebau enkat:i naa olameyu enkop pooki. Nelau inkishu inkujit neeku keye anaake. Nelau iltung'ana eneas. Ore nabo olong' nedoli emotonyi naata inkujit naanyori. neyiolouni aajo etii enkop nanoto empilili. Neoshi iltung'ana oopuo eleenore. Nepuo taa ninye lelo tung'ana nepuo aatum enkop naa olari aike. Nerik olmurrani obo entito nang'arie kina, nereu endung'ori oonkishu, nepuo aamanyisho teina kop. Netoni apa ake ometoisho inkishu. Neisho enkiteng' nabo ele murrani neiu enkashe sidai oleng'. Naa keiro ena ashe. Naa keisho ake ele murrani tenelo shoo, neikenoo ena ashe tolale liaji. Neturoki enkanashe enkumoto tiatua aji, neeku atua enkumoto ninye etii endama pooki o metushukunye ade olalashe te shoo. Nepising' ena kumoto tosoit sapuk, nelo ninye shoo.

Netoni apa :ike ore nabo olong', neponu ilmurran ena ang' dama. Nejing' ena aji natii ena tito.

Netoni aaleen enkaji nedol ajo metii toki. Nepuo. Ore ake ae olong' neitoki aaponu. Netonie olmurrani obo ele soit opising'are enkumoto natii entito. Neud ena tito toltidu. Nejo olmurrani, "Shye, Ke irpidila toi; laaonyita?" Nedumunye ajo aing'uraa nemetii sii toki, neitoki aton. Ore kiti kata, neitoki :ike entito arem. Nedumunye olmurrani akur osoit ejo tenaa kelpidila oonyita, paa keitoki aton. Kake eitu :ike epal entito eitu erem. Neinyiototo olmurrani nejo duo mbeloi osoit neinepu entito neme esidano eeta etii atua enkumoto.

Nepuku entito aderrie ilmurran. Nenyae taa ilomon. Ore ake peyie edol entito ajo emuto nejoki ilmurran meshomo peyie eponu likae kekun, amu etaa keshukunye olalashe teshoo. Nepuo ilmurran neaku keponu anaake dama airorie ena tito. Ore toonkuti olong'i nenyorru entito olmurrani obo tekulo neaku meitudutie ninye olalashe.

Nelusoo taa inkolong'i, neaku keing'oru kulo murran eneiko peyie ear olmurrani ong'arie ena tito kina peyie etum aawaita ena anashe. Kake etii ena ashe naena tolale naa keisho ake peyie edol araki ening' enkiti toki nelotu ade aliki olmurrani teipa. Naa keisho ake peyie ening'u inkishu nedung' enkeene nekwet alo anang'are nkishu neinosaki olmurrani ilomon. Naa keng'as aomon olmurrani eton eitu enak. Nejoki, "Olmurrani lai Ie nkai," Nejo olmurrani, "enkashe ai enkai", nejoki enkashe, "Kang'as anak anaa kaang'as aliki ena?" Nejoki olmurrani, 'Tang'asa tanaa." Ore ake peyie eidip enkashe atanaa neliki olmurrani pooki naatadua nening'. Neaku keliki pooki naajo kulo murran o ena tito neliki sii pooki najo peyie eas. Neitu aikata ninye eliki ena tito olalashe ajo keponu oshi ilmurran.

Ore nabo olong' neji keishori ele murrani esayiet. Neyau ilmurran esayiet aaisho entito metipikaki kule. Nelepu ake entito kule, nepik esayiet, neshum tenkutuk erruat. Kake eituruko duo enkashe nelo ajoki olmurrani, "Olmurrani lai Ie nkai, kang'as anak anaa kaang'as aliki ena?" Nejoki olmurrani, "Tang'asa tanaa, enkashe ai enkai."

37

Ore ake peyie eidip atanaa nejoki olmurrani peyie meok ilo kekun kule amu etipikaki esayiet. Nejoki metudumu enkukuri natii kule ashum tenkalo olale peyie ero enkashe aibukoo. Neas anaa enatiaka enkashe. Nero enkashe kule aibukoo. Neitoki entito aisho olmurrani kulie Ie nemetii esayiet. Nelo ilo kekun.

Ore peyie ekenyu neponu ilmurran aaleenoo tenaa ketua olmurrani peyie etum aawaita inkishu nerik entito. Nejo maetu neliki entito ajo eibukoyie enkashe kule pooki metaa eitu eok olalashe. Neitoki kulo mang'ati aadamu ae naas. Neyau imbaa naatii esayiet, neun tekishomi paa tenelotu ade olmurrani amu ninye oshi oituruku ang' nerem. Ore peyie eponu inkishu ang' nekwet enkashe nelo ajoki olmurrani eneas. Nejoki peyie eng'as aimie isirkon kishomi neitoki aimie inkishu ore peyie aatukurroki entulugumi neitoki sii ninye aim. Neas olmurrani anaa enatiaka enkashe neitoki ilo kekun alusoo eishu.

Ore peyie ening' ilmang'ati aajo eitu sii eye olmurrani ilo kekun neing'asia nejo, "Shye eeta pae oshi entoki naliki enikijo'" Nejo, pooki enaikash teneshirrakino aar. Nejoki entito, "Ore taa amu kepi negol oleng' enchoo metang'asa alep enkiteng' natii ene naata kule oleng' ore peyie ining'ining'i aipot mayaki enkee niyiolouu ajo meekure eeta engolon naing'arrie intae, nibaikiki aar." Ore oshi ena keene naa enaenie olmurrani enkoriong' tenelep enkiteng' ng'otonye ena ashe nairo amu keeta kule oleng' naa kenaur tenelep. Neji taa ina easi ina olong' teipa.

Ore ake peyie eponu inkishu ang' teipa nedung' enkashe nairo enkeene. Nejoki olmurrani, "Olmurrani lai Ie nkai, kang'as anak anaa kaang'as aliki ena?" Nejoki olmurrani. "Tang'asa tanaa enkashe ai enkai." Nenak ake enkashe nejoki olmurrani, "Ore taa amu etejoki ekiari taata, intaakunoyu ake ilepisho kake mikilep peyie minauru, nijoki. entito meyau enkeene." Nerretana olmurrani paa keton aanyu enoshi kata peyie eipotu enkeene. Ore ake peyie ening' ilmang'ati neidu enkang' aajo kiar. Ore naa amu eitu enaura neterretene near pooki metuata. Nerik enkanashe.

Ore peyie eidip olmurrani ataparipara ilmang'ati neidur tolakira arrinyo enkop enye. Kake ore tenkoitoi nedamu ajo etorikine olng'oret. Nejo arrinyo alo ayau nejoki enkashe, "Totona iyie mashomo nanu ayau." Nelo ake ore eshukunye neng'or iltorrobo tembae natii esayiet. Nelo enetii olmurrani erumisho embae. Nejoki olmurrani: "Ore taa amu etaa ae, teying'aki ake nikipej nkiri pooki, nimionyu ake oldung'oti Ie nkiring'o osesen lai, kake minkenu tenaye amu aikiiki yieyio ae ashe nijo ake nanu."

Neas olmurrani enetiakaki kake eishirita aishiraki ena ashe enye natua nanyor. Nepuo nkituaak ooladuo Torrobo aanya nena kiri. Ore ake peyie·eidip aainosa nejo naboo; "Ijo kayieu nanu nanya enkerai ai". Nejo enkae: "Kayieu sii nanu." Ore ejo pooki neijia nenya nkera enye. Ore peyie emut inkera neitoki aanya ate o metuata pooki teine.

Ore ake peyie ebaya olmurrani ang', neipot olkiu. Neinosaki iltung'ana pooki inaitaasa entito e ng'otonye. Nejoki, "Ore ebaiki taata enoto enchooi intoyie, emintoki aiook amu imang'ati.

Imeitudutie oleng'otonye olang'ata." Neeku ina oshi pee etaa keyami intoyie. Ina apa enkiterunoto enkiama.

6. The Origin of Marriage

There was once a time when the whole world was all dry. The cattle could not find any grass to eat; they kept dying day after day and the people did not know what to do. One day, a bird carrying a blade of green grass was spotted and the people were curious to find out from where it had obtained the blade, for they knew that there was an area that had got some rain. Some people were sent out on a reconnaissance mission and found a country that had plenty of lush vegetation.

One of the warriors took a small herd and together with his younger sister, went to settle in the new country. After staying there for some time, the cows began to give birth. One of the cows belonging to this warrior gave birth to a very beautiful calf and this calf could speak. Whenever the warrior went to herd the cattle, he would lock up the calf in the pen inside the house. He also dug a hole inside the house where his sister would stay until he returned home from herding. He covered this hole with a big stone before he and the cattle set off for the day.

They stayed there for a long time. One day, two warriors from another country came to this village during the day. They went inside the house where the girl was hidden; after inspecting the hut they reached the conclusion that there was nobody and so they left. They came again another day and this time one of the warriors sat on the stone that was used as a cover for the hole that contained the girl. The girl pricked the warrior with a needle, whereupon he jumped up quickly, saying, "Is it the fleas that are biting me?" He checked, but on failing to see anything, he sat down again. After a little while, the girl pricked him again.

The warrior stood up and cleared the stone of any possible fleas or whatever might have been biting him. After brushing them away, he sat down once more, but the girl did not stop pricking him. The warrior got up this time and on rolling the stone away, he found this very beautiful girl inside the hole.

The girl then came out of the hole to talk with the warriors. They spent the whole day talking, and in the evening the girl advised the warriors to leave in case her brother found them, but to come another day. So the warriors left, but after that day, they made it a habit of visiting the girl every day. Within a short time, the girl had fallen in love with one of the warriors and her love for him surpassed that which she felt for her brother.

So the days went by and the warriors, in collaboration with the girl, began to look for ways and means of killing her brother so that they could take his sister away. But the calf in the pen reported everything that she saw or heard to the brother as soon as he came back from herding the cattle. She would always ask the man whether she should suckle first, or whether she should first relate the day's news. She would say, "My warrior of God"', since that was how she referred to him, and the warrior would say in response, "My calf of God." "Shall I suck, or shall I first tell you something?" And the warrior would always say, "You may suck first." When she had finished sucking she told the warrior all that she had seen and heard. She told him all that had transpired between his sister and the newcomers and all they had planned to do. But the girl had never talked to her brother about the warriors' visit.

One day, a decision was reached that the warrior of God was to be poisoned, so the visiting warriors brought the poison which the sister would put in her brother's milk. When the milking was done that evening, the girl mixed the poison with the milk and left the gourd leaning against the bed post where she normally kept it.

But the calf had by this time informed the warrior of the plan and advised him to move the gourd and lean it against the pen so that the calf could kick it and make it appear as though it was by accident. The warrior did as he was told, and so the calf kicked the gourd and spilled all the milk. The girl then gave her brother some more milk, this time without any poison, since she had no more of the poison left. And so that day passed.

The next day, the warriors came to check whether their enemy had died so that they could take his cattle and his sister away. The girl informed them how the calf had spilt all the milk accidentally before her brother could drink any. The disappointed enemies had to conjure up another plan. This time, they got some poisoned arrows and stuck them in the ground at the entrance to the village gate so that as the warrior entered before the stock, as he normally did, he would step on them. But as the cattle approached the village that evening, the talking calf broke off its harness and ran to inform the warrior of everything that had transpired between the girl and his enemies. She advised the warrior to let the donkeys go in first that night, followed by the rest of the cattle, and he should go in last, when the arrows had been covered by the animal's waste. The warrior did as he was bid and so another day passed with no casualties.

When the warrior's enemies learnt that he was still alive, they were very surprised and they said: "There must be someone who informs him of our plans!" They were very intrigued. They decided that the best thing was to conduct a bold attack against the warrior. The sister thought it wise to warn the attackers of her brother's bravery. She said to them, "Now because he is very brave and strong, you must wait until he has milked one of the cows that has a lot of milk and when you hear him calling for a strap you can then attack him since he will be too weak to fight with you." The warrior used the strap to tie his back since the mother of the talking calf had plenty of milk and on milking her he got exhausted. So that plan was to be carried out that evening.

That evening, when the cattle approached the village, the talking calf broke off the harness as usual and ran to meet the warrior. She said to him, "My warrior of God, shall I suck or shall I first tell you something?" The warrior said to her, "You may first suck, my calf of God". When she had sucked, she said to the warrior, "Since they have planned to kill you today do not do any milking, just pretend to be doing so because if you do, you will get tired, and when the usual time lapses you can call out for the strap." The warrior then prepared his armour, waited for the normal length of time to pass, then called out for the strap. When the enemies heard what they had been waiting for, they jumped over the fence intending to carry out their plan. But since the brave warrior was not tired and was well-armed, he killed them all and prepared to take his sister away.

After his victory with the enemy, the warrior set off with the earliest flickers of dawn for his country. But on his way, he remembered that he had forgotten the arrow that he used to puncture the jugular vein of cattle to draw blood. As he was about to return for it, the calf volunteered to do so instead. She went, and on her way back, she was shot with a poisoned arrow by some Dorobo hunters. She arrived with the arrow stuck in her side and said to the warrior, "Since I am about to die, skin me and roast all the meat without taking even a single bite and leave, but don't you worry for my mother will bear you another calf just like me."

The warrior sorrowfully did as he was bid, weeping for his beloved calf who was no more. The wives of the Dorobo hunters came and found the meat and ate it. As they did so, they felt like eating their own children. One of them said, "I feel like eating my own child." "So do I," answered another, and another. They ate all their young ones, after which they ate each other, until they were all dead.

On reaching home, the warrior convened a meeting and he related what his sister had done to him. He said, "So, from now on, I beseech you to marry off the girls, never keep them at home because they are your enemies. If they have to choose, they will prefer a lover to a brother." Since that time, the girls have been given out in marriage. That was the origin of marriage.

Review Questions

i) What aspects of the girl's personality does this narrative highlight?

ii) In what ways would you agree or disagree that the circumstances in which she found herself led the girl to betray her brother?

7. Eneikununye oIdia enkop

Ore apa oIdia naa entoki kirotet olong' te Nkai. Nemeji naarri oidia. ekeji apa Lenanu aitapashipash. Ore tenkaraki nanyika shumata o enkop niaku kelo ake Lenanu aparan Maasinta tenkop neshuko shumata amu ine apa namanya.

Ore nabo olong' neipot Enkai Lenanu nejoki, "Lenanu. irorie taa Maasinta anaa eniyieu kake milikioo aikata Namaae ai amu mayieu naishooyo." Nejo Lenanu, "Malikioo." Ore ake peyie ebaya enetii Maasinta nelaikino atigirayu. Nejoki, "Maasinta, aaliki ena? Eeta oshi Enkai entoki nabo neitu apa kincho najo namaae napir oleng' nebor naa ninye kenya ake itum nelo osina enelakua. Shomo toomono amu mikimitiki."

Ina peyie edumunye Maasinta alo aomonu Namaae. Nejo, "Naai, nchooki taata Namaae." Neing'asia Enkai peyie ening' enetejo oltung'ani. Neikilikuan ajoki, "Aing'ae nikitolikio ina toki naji Namaae?" Nejoki Maasinta, "Oloji Lenanu laatolikio." Neipaaya Enkai Maasinta meshomo aipot Lenanu. Ore peyie elotu Lenanu nejoki Enkai: "Lenanu, ke Namaae ai ishomo alikioo naaitanapa apa ajoki milikioo ake?" Negira Lenanu amu etukurrua niaku mijo ninye eirorieki. Nejoki Enkai: "Ore tenkaraki ena nitaasa ekaaitaa oidia. Ore ebaiki taata mintoki atti enkang' ai ilo abik tenkop aaku osinga le Maasinta niaku nkik intaa endaa." Nening: ake Lenanu enatiakaki neitoki esirai, paa keton eeta enabaiki? Nejoki Enkai: "Papa ore naa amu kitediaa nchooki ntokitin ong'wan ake peyie atum sii nanu atopuaa.

Nchooki enkume nemeikenu olng'usillo onkik tenetaa naa ninche naaku endaa ai; Nchooki enkume naing'uaya ndaiki toonkadoru peyie miaku naa kaaya olameyu; Nchooki sii ilpapit oinyiari nabo alo peyie tenaamutiki alilita naidim atulutoi ilpaashien eitu aibung' ilkiku amu iyiolo ajo meeta entoki nayieu nebolu osinga kewarie; Ore entoki nabayie aaomon naa osesen ronkai neneneng' oidim atalang'a nkariak nelutoo ineepirik etaa naa kinturrayie." Nejoki Enkai oidia, "Aishoo nena tokitin pooki nimpoto nimijo ae amu keon intayio tenkaji nasheta."

Niaku neijia oshi eikuna Lenanu peyie eitemena keon Enkai neponunui aajo "oidia" nenang'uni enkop meeu aisiaai oltung'ani. Ina kias oshi oidia eimua endung'et-e-rashe naji, "Ore peyie einosa oidia nkik mme oliki etaia, kiok ming'ani einosa." Inie sii oshi enotie oltung'ani entoki naji Namaae nelotu adung'oki ae arna ajo "Enker."

7. The Fall of the Dog

In the beginning, the dog used to be one of God's favourite creatures. He was not called dog as he is called now, but was called Lenanu, * for he was very much pampered. And since heaven and earth were not as far apart as they now are, Lenanu used to pay frequent visits to man, after which he would return to the heavens, where he resided.

One day, God called Lenanu to him and said: "My favourite one, you may talk to man as you please, but don't you ever tell him of the gentle-one, for I do not want to part with her." Lenanu said: "Very well, I will never tell him." But as soon as he was in the company of his friend, man, Lenanu could not keep God's secret. He said to him, "Man, shall I tell you something? God has one thing that he did not give you, and which he calls the gentle-one. This creature is very fat and humble but if ever you manage to procure it, all your problems will go away. Go and ask for it, for he will not deny you."

Thereupon man went to request God for the gentle-one. "Oh God," he pleaded, "I have come to ask you to give me the gentle-one." God was startled by this request and asked man, "Who told you of that gentle creature." "It is Lenanu who told me," man answered. God then sent man to go and call Lenanu, and he spoke to him thus: "Lenanu you have indeed let out the secret of my gentle-one which l bid you never to tell!" Lenanu kept mum out of shame as though he was not the one who was being spoken to. "Because of what you have done," God continued, "I will make you a dog. ** From this very day you will not reside in my home, but you will go to earth and be servant to man, and for your food you will feed on excrement." On hearing this, Lenanu regretted his actions very much, but was it not too late?

Lenanu then said to God, "Oh father, now that you have indeed cursed me, I have four things to request of you, so that I can at least survive. Grant me a nose that can withstand the distasteful smell of excrement now that you fate it to be my food; grant me a nose that can detect the scent of food from long distances, so that I do not die from starvation; grant me too hairs that face one direction so that if I am delayed at the hunt I can manoeuvre through the thorn fences without my hairs getting caught between thorns, for, as you know, no one wishes to let servants in at night. And the last thing that I shall ask of you is an agile and light body that can go across waters and squeeze through narrow spaces now that you have disowned me." God then said to dog, "I have granted you all that you asked for, but blame no one, for you have removed yourself from a house that was already built."***

That was how Lenanu fell out of favour with God and earned the name "dog", and was thrown down to earth to serve man. The dog's behaviour became the origin of the saying: "The reason why the dog ate excrement is not for lack of sound advice, it is because he ate the deaf ear." This was also the time when man procured the gentle-one, which he later renamed 'sheep'.

* Literally, "that of me" or "mine". Used as an endearment name, just as children are named after parts of the body, e.g., eyes, mouth, legs,. etc. Children are, however, never referred to as "Lenanu" .

** Generally associated with the unreliability of character as well as improper eating habits. To the Maasai, the food one eats, the company one eats with (in the case of warriors) and the way one eats, are all significant in determining one's reputation. See the tales of "greedy old men", below. It is rather difficult to determine whether the dog earned the name from the apt description of his behaviour or vice versa.

*** A saying that is used to refer to one who rejects goodwill.

Review Questions

i) Consider the dog's four requests and discuss ways in which he could be said to be endowed with the qualities essential for his survival in a traditional Maasai environment.

ii) Comment on the narrative style of this story.

iii) How would you describe the relationship between:
   a) God and the dog;
   b) God and man;
   c) Man and dog in this narrative?

8. Ilgliat Ie Maasai

Eoro oshi Ilmaasai are, eatae odo-mong'i neetae orok-kiteng. Neisho kuna kishomin neitoki aaoro imiet. Naa kuna orot imiet oshi eimutua ilgilat Ie Maasai. Naa inji eikununye ena oro.

Ore apa tenkiterunoto neetae Naiteru-kop. Neyam Naiteru-kop inkituaak are. Ore enkitok edukuya neisho nkishu naanyokioo nedung'okini enkarna oolpayiani aajo Nado-Mong'i. Neishori metesheta enkaji enye tentaloishi e tatene e kishomi. Ore enkitok e are neishori ninye nkishu naarok neshet sii ninye enkaji enye tentaloishi e kedianye e kishomi. Nedung'okini sii ninye enkarna aajo Narok-Kiteng'.

Nebik apa ake o metoisho kuna kituaak. Neiu enedukuya ilayiok okuni. Ore olayioni Ie dukuya neji Lelian aa ninye oiterua Ilmolelian. Neji olikae Lokesen, neiteru sii ninye Ilmakesen. Ore oliokuni neji Losero, naa ninye apa oiterua Iltaarrosero. Kulo gilat oshi eji ilenkaina e tatene tenkaraki netii enkaji enye entaloishi e tatene e kishomi.

Neisho sii runye Narok-kiteng' neiu ilayiok aare; oloji Laiser laa ninye oiterua Ilaiser oloji Lukum laa ninye oshi eipotieki Ilukumae. Niaku sii ninje kulo ilgilat Ie kedianye. Neitayu olgilata pooki olponoto lenye peyie etum aatoor nkishu. Neeku ina oshi peyie epiki nkishu olponoto lenkishomi ololgilata o taata.

45

8. The Maasai Clans

The Maasai people are divided into two moieties, the one called the house of the red oxen and the other of black cattle. These moieties are further subdivided into five, this latter subdivision being the origin of Maasai clans. This is how the division came about.

In the beginning, there was Naiteru-kop, the beginner of the earth. He married two wives. To the first wife he gave red cattle and she was given the elders', name Nado-Mong'i the owner of red oxen. She built her house on the right-hand side of the gateway. The second wife was given black cattle and she built her house on the left-hand side of the gateway. She was given the name Narok-kiteng', the owner of black cattle.

After a while, these wives gave birth. The first wife gave birth to three boys, the first of whom was named Lelian, who began the Ilmolelian clan. The second son was called Lokesen and he began the clan of Ilmakesen. Losero was the name of the third boy, who began the clan that is now known as Iltaarrosero. These clans are said to be clans of the right hand, since their mother's house was situated on the right-hand side of the gateway.

The second wife, on her part, gave birth to two sons. The first was called Laiser, who became the progenitor of the Aiser clan; and the second one was called Lukum, who in turn started the Lukumai clan. The latter two formed the left-hand clans. Each clan invented its own branding system in order to distinguish its cattle from the other clan. And ever since that time, the cattle are distinguished by the moiety brand as well as by the clan brand. This is still done up to this day.

Review Questions

i)   This narrative is a legend in the sense that it explains the historical development of the Maasai clan system that is still adhered to to this day. From what you have learnt of legends, describe their other qualities, using this narrative, as well as any other that you are familiar with, to illustrate your points.

ii) For Maasai readers:

In later years, there have been developments that have slightly modified the veracity of this legend. Find out what they are. What is their significance in the present clan system?

9. Olarinkoi

Eetae apa olorere oji llarinkon laa ninche apa ilopeny enkop naidurrakitia llmaasae peyie eilepu tendikir e Kerio. Ore ele orere neeta olaiguenani lenye Ieme esapuko eeta. Niaku keurei oleng' keyopareki peyie miaku keitagori memut ake iltung'ana. Neiba naa kulo Arinkon ena kop enye naibulutua llmaasae muj nemeyieu sii niaraa pesho. Neirriwaa olkilikuai aajoki metayoki aidur.

Nemeyieu naa llmaasae neidur tena kop amu mme esidano eeta neton sii aa enayagie tenapa aidurra enkilepunoto tendikir. Nemeyieu sii niarare olorere lemeyiolo empijan naata neisulaki edolita engolon naata elaiguenani lenye. Nenya eng'en. Neiteru aaku kerop ele orere toonkishu o toontare o tekulie masaa peyie eing'uraa tenaa keishori metobiko. Neisho sii ninche ele orere niaku keisilisil Ilmaasae peyie eing'uraa tenaa kesi nepuo eneing'ua apa anaa epuo ae wueji.

Ore nabo olong' neirriwaki Olarinkoi Ilmaasae olkilikuai ajoki. "Pooki ake peyie kipal intae tenipuopuo aayau kule naitokitok neton etii olaburra." Nejoki Ilmaasae, "Nchoo naa iyiook inkolong'i isiet peyie kiyau." Naa kelakua apa ene nemanya Ilmaasae metaa keiropiju ade kule teneitudung'i enkop aayaki Olarinkoi. Nerrinyo ake Ilmaasae ang' nepuo aibung' enkiguana. Ore tembata ele shani oiguanareki netii enkayioni nairrita ilasho. Nening' enejoito ilpayiani, nejoki: "Loopapa emintanyamal ate, enchom entereu enkiteng' kipeke ninchosho ake peyie eiturrurro ilmang'ati nipuopuo aalep nikwetietie kule eton eitokitok."

Neisho ake Ilmaasae enoshi kata peyie edol aajo eiturrurrote ilmang'ati eanyu duo metara amu mejo ketum kule naaitokitok, nelep enkiteng' nekwetie kule. Oo naa peyie eiputukuny Ilarinkon! Neyiolou aajo etii lejet. Nejo Olarinkoi, "Aaidimutua tena!," Nejoki Ilmaasae, "Enchom naa peyie iitutu olkekun oje," Nepuo, ore ake peyie ebau enkata nayieunyieki nerrinyo enetii Ilarinkon.

Eshomo taa sii ninche Ilarinkon aaiguena. Ore peyie epuo Ilmaasae nejoki olkitok, "Ayieu taata niyauu enamuke naju nchot pokira." Negoliki taa Ilmaasae amu kang'ae aikata natadua olchoni oju poki alole? Ore amu etejoki apa merisio nyuaat o nkidimat, nejoki ilkulikae 'ayia'.

Nepuoi olapa ake shani. Ore peyie elikini enkayioni nejo, "Elelek, enchom eng'oru osikiria, entudung' enkiok nishetishete anaa enamuke niyakiki!" Neji, "Etisipa." Oo naa peyie eyakini Ilarinkon entoki nemejo apa ketum aikata Ilmaasae. Neiputukuny. Nejoki, "Enchom naa peyie tenaitoki ayieu ae toki naipotu ntae."

Ore ake peyie errinyo ilpayiani neibung' Ilarinkon enkiguana aing'oru entoki nagol najoki Ilmaasae meshomo aing'oru ejo peyie tenelau neiterunyie ine olarrabal. Ore kenya peyie eitoki Ilarinkon airriwaa olkilikuai neipoti Ilmaasae nejoki, "Enyaai taa emputa enkoti ilpidila eyakaki eton eipidipid."

Nerrinyo ilpayiani enetii enkayioni amu etaa apa keji 'ntang'enoi' neinosaki enetejo Ilarinkon. Ore ake peyie ening' nejo, "Ai egol elelek kake loopapa eminkenu amu aiking'uraki ilpidila." Nejoki, "Enyaai embung'a osikiria entudung'u ilpapit lolmelil entikitiko te entakeita nipikipiki enkoti ore peyie iyakiki nibolibolo aing'orie enchoto naimu osiwuo." Nias taa ninye ilpayiani enatiaka enkayioni. Neitabaikini taa ninye. Ore ena naitarasaki olpayian Olarinkoi enkoti, neikonji aisegel aing'orie enchoto naimu osiwuo neisardakie osiwuo ilpapit pooki nejoki Ilarinkon, "Lelelo entasaru embung'a!" Paa kesarunoyu naa eisardaka? Eitu aikata eiputukuny tung'ana anaa Ilarinkon ilo kekun.

Nelusoo taa sii ilo kekun meyiolo Ilarinkon eneitaas Ilmaasae tenkaraki eng'eno sapuk naata. Neitoki Ilarinkon aaigwena nejoki, Ilmaasae, "Enyaaki taa eng'urakaki tokitin are ake, eyakaki enkike olmishire niking'urakiki enkoitoi nalo enkai." Neibung' ilewa nkutukie. Nejoki, "Nchoo naa yiook ilapaitin okuni peyie kipuo aing'oru nena tokitin." Neshukoi taa nepuoi aaigwena. Neigwenae o memuto. Nelikini enkayioni enetejoki. Nejo: "Enchom eng'urakaki oringa peyie alotu aliki ntae enkike olmishire enaikununi." Nepuoi aaing'oru. Naa keyakini ake enkayioni neineneng' ilo negil, neineneng' olikae negila sii ninye ilo. Negil iringan kumok. Nejoki ilpayiani: "Enchom Oletukat eng'oru orinka lologol-tim otoonyo emuny elukunya meshomo enkare entonata, eyakaki." Nepuoi Oletukat, neiposhae o menoti enaduo shani, neidosuni. Neyakini enkayioni, nejo ineneng'a neitu egila. Nejo: "Enyoito taa emaape enetii Ilarinkon peyie alo alimu enkike olmishire teine."

Ore tolakira nedumunye olorere, nepuo o metabai enkop oolmang'ati. Netii ena ayioni ejapita oringa tenkitikiti. Neinepu eiturrurrote duo Ilarinkon aang'amu entoki nayakaki. Neng'asi duo aanya ilomon.

Nedumunye menye ena ayioni ng'en. Etayioloki taa duo enejo enkayioni peyie eas. Nedumunye menye ena ayioni ng'en Nejo: "Neilo sukudi ntonat orok enchata emperinta oiba ndueta yiook.

Tenira ee, nilimu peyie kigil olkung'u, niimu tenchumata enkaluena meimu oloipirnyiny ising'eta. Tenira m-mh nilimu peyie kiar oloboru ng'otonye." Neitu ening'u Ilarinkon enetejoki. Nejo maikilikuanu aajo, "Shye' kejaa iltung'ana?" Nejoki olpayian: "Aikitejo kiyautua enkike olmishire." Neinyiototo enkayioni anaa oloitarasaa enkike. Neosh ake Olarinkoi nedou inkonyck, neimu oloipirnyiny inkumeishin. Ore eeri Ilarinkon nejokini, "Arinkon 'inko enoshi niyieu." Ine taa oshi etumutieki Ilarinkon neeli ilooelaki. Naa ina sii peyie eji Arinkon inko eniyieu. Ine eimu ina walata.

9. The Arinkon

There was once a people known as Ilarinkon who were the owners of the land that the Maasai occupied after their ascent from the Kerio escarpment. These people had a leader who was a mighty giant. Since he was very much feared, it was deemed wise to avoid him for fear that upon the slightest provocation, he might decide to wipe out the whole Maasai population. But the Arinkon remained resentful of the Maasai occupation spreading over their land. He sent messages ordering them to leave.

But the Maasai were unwilling to leave the richly-endowed country, having just recovered from the formidable ascent of the escarpment. At the same time, they were reluctant to fight people whose might they were unsure of, especially after having observed signs of great physical might in their leader. They instead played tricks on them. They started by bribing them with gifts of cattle, sheep and various other items, with the hope of being permitted to stay on. But these people developed a habit of pestering the Maasai with the intention of getting them fed up, hoping to make them leave, either to wherever they had come from or elsewhere.

One day, the Arinkon chief sent a message to the Maasai saying: "We will only let you stay if you bring warm frothing milk." The Maasai said: "Very well, give us eight days and we will bring it." Since the Maasai lived a long way off, the milk would without doubt have cooled before they got to the Arinkon chief. As soon as they got home, the Maasai called a meeting. Close by the meeting place, there was a little boy who was tending calves. He heard what the elders were discussing and said to them: "Fathers, do not worry yourselves, go and drive away that cow whose calf is dead and when the enemies have assembled, milk it quickly and take the milk while it is still frothing."

The Maasai waited until the enemy had assembled waiting to kill them, not at all expecting them to procure the milk. They milked the cow and quickly took the milk. The Arinkon were staggered with shock. They immediately knew that they must have been tricked. Their ruler said: "Very well, they have beaten me on this one." He then told them to go and return on a certain day. On the arranged day, they returned to the Arinkon.

By the time the Maasai returned, the Arinkon ruler said to them, "I now want you to bring me a sandal with hair on both sides." The Maasai were in a fix, for who had ever seen a hide that is hairy on both sides? As the saying goes, "*menyaanyuk inyuat o nkidimat*" "abilities and determination are not equal", the Maasai said: "Very well."

Back at the same meeting place, the young boy was briefed on what had transpired. He quickly said: "It is a simple matter, go and find a donkey and cut off one ear, make a sandal and take it to him!" The elders replied: "He has spoken the truth." The Arinkon received the sandal with great consternation, for he had not expected the Maasai to obtain it at all. The ruler then said to the Maasai, "You may now go back and when I need something else I shall send for you."

As soon as the Maasai departed, the Arinkon held counsel to figure out the most difficult item to request from the Maasai, so that failure to procure it would lead to a fight.

When the Arinkon chief next sent for the Maasai, he said to them: "Go and fill up a gourd with fleas and bring them to me when they are still hopping about."

The elders went back to the clever boy, who had, by then, been nicknamed "clever one", and informed him of what they had been told. When he heard it, he said: "Oh fathers, this is difficult, but it is easy at the same time, but do not worry yourselves for we will find them fleas. Take hold of a donkey and cut off some hairs from the mane and crush these in a buffalo horn container and put them in a gourd. When you hand the Arinkon the gourd, you must make sure you face the windward side." The elders did as they were directed and soon delivered the "fleas". As they were handing over the gourd, they tilted it so that the hairs were blown about by the wind, creating the impression that fleas were dashing about. "There, get hold of them!" the Arinkon shouted. But could they be got hold of when they had already dispersed? The Arinkon had never before been so flabbergasted!

Another day passed, and still the Arinkon did not know what to do with a people that was proving too smart for them. They again held counsel, and when they next summoned the Maasai, their leader said to them:

"I want you to bring me only two more things. Bring me a metal toothbrush and find me a way that leads to heaven." The Maasai drew their hands to their mouths in amazement.* They requested him to give them three months to find those items. When they returned home, they held a meeting that lasted the whole day. When the clever boy was informed of what had been requested, he said: "Go and bring me a club and I will show you how to make a metal toothbrush." They went in search of it.

Several clubs were taken to the boy, but each time he tried to use one, it would break. Many clubs got broken.

Eventually, he said to the elders: "Go to a place called Oletukat and get me a club from the Ologol-tim tree, whose stem had been bitten off by a rhinoceros and the water has gone down to the roots." After a long search the tree was found, uprooted and taken to the boy. When he tried, it did not break. He said: "Now let us go to the Arinkon where I will tell you of the metal toothbrush."

At the first flickers of dawn, the people started off to the enemy country. The boy was among the rest with his club tucked under his armpit. They found the Arinkon having gathered to receive what was brought. The meeting was opened with the exchange of news. What the boy was going to do was by now obvious to the Maasai. The father of the clever boy stood up and said: "There he is in a crouching position with the notorious one** whose shaft is black and whose organs of sight detest us. If you are for the affirmative confirm so we can fold the knee*** and approach above the organ that is bent *** so that the brain may pop out through the nostrils. If you are for the negative confirm so that we beat a retreat." The Arinkon did not understand what was said, and started asking themselves: "What are these people saying?" The elder answered: "We have simply said that we have brought the metal toothbrush . . ."

The boy stood up as though he was going to hand over the toothbrush. He hit the Arinkon chief and the eyes popped out and the brain oozed out through the nostrils. While they were being beaten, the Arinkon were being told: "Arinkon, here, have what you have always sought."

That was when the Arinkon race was exterminated and some were adopted and assimilated. That was also how the saying, "Arinkon have what you have always sought" originated.

* A common gesture of amazement stressing that one is lost for words .

** The spear.

*** One often half kneels down in preparation to spear an object.

*** The ear.

Review Questions

i) Discuss the character of the Arinkon chief as portrayed in this narrative.

ii) Discuss the figures of speech contained in the speech of the old man as he was giving instructions to his son.

iii) Compare and contrast this narrative with the Biblical one of David and Goliath.

OGRE TALES

10. Olmurrani oota Inkutukle are

Netii apa, netii ele murrani oota inkutukie are. Naa entim namanya. Naa sidai apa ele murrani enenking'asia. Neeta ilpapit, enkoriong' ebaiki enchada. Ore nabo olong', neing'oru iltualan, neeniki ilkeel paa tenening' iltung'ana nejo inkishu natii ilmong'i naadaa. Neeku kemanaa tentim aisulisho anaa oltung'ani oirritisho.

Ore nabo olong', neponu ilmurran ooreuta olkiteng' opir oleng'. Netoni aamanaa tentim aing'oru olchani sidai oitaa olpul. Ore epuopuo, neinepu ele murrani etii enkiti wueji neisiaja nalamita penyo ene wueji nening'ore iltualan. Neirorokino taa, "Supa olmurrani!" - "Ipa!" "Supa olmurrani!" "Ipa!" "Keninono nena kishu naaning'o iltualan?" Nejoki ele murrani, "Ee ninche nena naadaa tenkalo e kuldo tepes adoru paa ketim ine imeimayu." Keniyie ng'ieng'ie olkiteng' ing'oruru?" Nejoki ilmurran, "Ee." Nejoki ele murrani, "Kolpul osira iyieuu anaa kolooliatuani?" Nejoki olmurrani, "Ai! Olosira osidai pee etoni ilmurran aapeipeenore." Nejoki ele murrani ilkulikae, "Entotoni taa tene matang'asa alo aleenoo olotii ene tenaa kesidai peyie alotu aliki intae." Netoni ilmurran. Neituruk ele murrani alo aoroki ilkulikae olpul. Neor aoroo iloik apa looltung'ana pooki oinosa. Ore peyie eidip, nelotu arik ilkulikae. Neinepu ilmurran olpul leme esidano eeta.

52

Nesisini eneirragi, nesotuni ilkeek, ore peyie eidipi neyieng'i olkiteng'. Neishori oladuo murrani osarge o enkiring'o nanya. Neng'amu ake nelo aigara ilkeek anya. Neen ilpapit tenchumata elukunya peyie etum aishoo inkutukie pokira.

Ore einosita, naa keisho ake ena kutuk natii empiding' peyie enya olmurrani enkiring'o nejoki, "Nchooki maalikio." Neigil, "Loolgirgir," neng'amaa enkae ajoki, "Laitondolie," "Nchooki maalikio." Nenang'aki. Nejo neijia ometumuta enkiring'o. Neisho olmurrani obo neleliari alo aing'or edaa nedol ajo enkukuu.

Ore peyie eidip nejoki ilkulikae looleng' amu etaa enalo airrita inkishu.

Neisho ele murrani duo otadua, nelo ajoki ilkulikae metisipu ilo murrani amu eng'ues. Neing'asia sii kuna kishu naa nebo ade edaare memuto. Kake eitu eiruk ilkulikae. Nejo olmurrani obo, "Oi emoda ilbarnot, olmurrani sidai aikonji ilo ajo eng'ues!" Neanyi ening'i.

Ore ake peyie eaku kewarie, neirura ilmurran. Neisho ele duo murrani otadua olikae edaa nelo aked shumata olchani otii embata olpul. Ore ake peyie eitorito enkewarie nelotu omurrani ele pul otii ilmurran. Neiken, "Obo, aare, okuni, oong'uan, ... isiet! Ooudo duo kulo murran, koree olioudo?" Neitoki ake aiken nera isiet. Nenya pokira isiet. Ore ake peyie edol oladuo murrani otii enchumata olchani neirut oleng'. Neureyu airisha. Nedou maakutiti tolchani, neisik alo ang' alikioo.

Ore peyie ebaya ang' nelikioo pooki natadua. Neing'oruni kulie murran isiet oiriamariyie ele murrani enapa wueji. Neishop ninye ele murrani enkila narok, neitong'ojinuo, negil enkong'u paa kerik ilkulikae. Ejo peyie meyiolou olmurrani oota inkutukie are. Nepuo ometabai enapa wueji netii olmurrani.

Neinepu olmurrani tenapa wueji. Nirorokino taa anaa oshi ake. Neikilikuan ele murrani ilkulikae, "Kolpul oigisa iyieuu anaa kolooliatuani?" Nejoki ilmurran, "olosira osidai peyie etoni ilmurran aapeipeenore. Neng'as alo aoroo iloik paa kelotu arik ilkulikae.

Ore ake peyie eidip ilmurran eyiang'are neisho olikae osarge o enkiring'o. Neiko anaa oshi ake, nelo aigara entim, neen ilpapit tenchumata elukunya peyie etum aishoo inkutukie pokira endaa. Ore peyie eidip, nejoki ilkulikae sere paa kelo. Etoduaa taa ilkulie kuti murran edaa. Neisho ake ilmurran peyie elusoo, nedung'u ilkeek sapuki, neitoosh olkereri terruat, neitoip toolkarash. Neaku ijo iltung'ana oirura. Nepuo ninche aisudori.

Ore peyie eaku kewarie, nelotu olmurrani oota inkutukie are. Neiken iladuo keek oimulumula ejo ninye kelmurran, nera ooudo. Nejo, "Elulung'a taata." Ore enoshi kata ejo tabolu oledukuya neishimakini iremeta. Ore etaa keye nejo, "Oi atayiolo duo ake, egil enkong'u megil, neitong'ojinuo meng'ojine!" Nejoki ilmurran metudung'o olkimojino sapuk aitayu iltung'ana apa pooki oinosa. Ore peyie edung'i nepuku iltung'ana pooki onkishu pooki apa nainosa. Neishunye enkatini teine.

10. The Warrior with two Mouths

Once upon a time, a long time ago, there lived a warrior who had two mouths. This warrior was strikingly handsome and had nice long hair that rested on his back. *He lived all by himself in the forest.

At one time he assembled some cattle bells and tied them on trees so that they would be heard jingling when tree branches were swayed by the wind. He did this so that when people heard the bells ringing, they would think that a herd of cattle with many oxen was grazing. **The warrior would walk around whistling like one herding his stock.

One day, a team of nine warriors came to the forest. They brought with them a fat ox for slaughter and were searching for a suitable tree under which to make a camp. As they were walking around, they found the warrior with two mouths at a little clearing. He was not very far from the place where the jingling sounds could be heard. After exchanging greetings, they enquired about the jingling sounds, that could be heard from nearby. "Are those your cows?" they asked. The warrior replied, "Oh yes, they are grazing over there near the tall acacia trees but the thicket there is too thorny for one to walk in. Are you looking for a place to slaughter the ox?" The others said, "yes", in unison. He then asked them: "Which kind of meat-camp would you prefer, one with wall paintings or one with compartments?" The others replied, "Oh! the one with the paintings is better so that we can idle about with the paintings." Then he said to them, "Wait for me here while I check on one nearby then I will come and let you know." So the others waited.

The warrior with two mouths went and swept the camp. He swept it clean of all the bones of the people he had eaten. When he had finished, he went back for the other warriors. The warriors found the neatest camp they had ever seen. They prepared a place for a bed and gathered firewood. The ox was then slaughtered and skinned. The host was given meat and blood. He took the food he was given and went behind the bush to eat it.

It so happened that each of the two mouths had a name. The normal mouth was called **Loolgirgir** and the one at the nape of the neck was **Laitondolie**.

As the warrior was eating, each of the mouths would ask for food threatening to expose the warrior if they did not get fed. They kept talking back and forth until the food was finished. As the two-mouthed warrior was eating, a young warrior walked stealthily behind him and watched him eat. He realised that he was a beast. When he had eaten, the warrior with two mouths bade the others goodbye, since he was going to look after his cattle.

The young warrior who had watched him eat went and told the others what he had seen. He warned them to watch out because their host was a beast. He also expressed surprise at the cows that grazed at one spot all day long. But none of others paid any attention to this observation. One of them admonished the young warrior for making such a fool of himself. He said to him, "How could you call such a handsome warrior a beast!" They refused to believe him. When night came, the warriors folded up for the night, but the one who had witnessed the warrior with two mouths feeding did not sleep with the rest. He climbed up a tree near the camp and kept watch.

In the middle of the night, the warrior with two mouths came to the camp. He counted the sleeping warriors, "One, two, three, four, five ... eight! They were nine, where was the ninth?" he wondered. He counted them a second time and again he found them to be eight. He ate them all. When the warrior at the top of the tree saw what was happening, he was filled with fear. He knew better than to attempt to fight the two-mouthed warrior single-handedly. He gently climbed down the tree and went home to convey the news of this strange encounter.

At home, when the incident had been discussed, a group of eight warriors were chosen to accompany the lone survivor back to the camp. The leader of the team, who happened to be the survivor himself, clothed himself in a black calf-skin, walked with a limping gait and put on a squint so as to disguise himself. Then they set off.

On arrival at the camp, the warrior with two mouths appeared to the warriors as he had done the first time and asked them, "What kind of meat-camp would you like, one with wall paintings or one with compartments?" The warriors answered just like before, "Oh the one with wall paintings is better so that we may idle around watching the paintings."

As he had done the first time, the two-mouthed warrior proceeded to clear the bones away and led the others to the camp. As usual, he went behind the bush, tied his hair up so he could feed both mouths and began to eat. As soon as he finished eating, he bade the others goodbye and left. This time a few more warriors had observed him eat. The warriors then collected large logs of wood, arranged them on the places they had prepared for their beds and covered them with their sheets, so that they looked like sleeping men. Then they hid away.

At night, the warrior with two mouths came along, counted the logs, assuming them to be warriors, and happily said to himself, "They are all in order." Just as he was about to uncover the first one, spears rained on him. But before he died he said: "Oh! How I had known it, that put-on squint and limping gait!" He was referring to the leader of the team. He then told the warriors to cut his big toe for all the people he had eaten to come out. When this was done, all the people and animals he had eaten emerged. The story ends there.

*In Maasai it is men who keep their hair long while women shave their heads clean. Long hair is considered a sign of beauty.

**It is prestigious to own a herd with many oxen that can be seen by everyone. But it is even better if the oxen can be heard. Bells are, therefore, tied on to straps or twines and suspended on the necks of big oxen.

Review Questions

i) Summarize this story in two short paragraphs.
ii) What qualities did this handsome young man have that betrayed him as an ogre?

11. Mbiti

Netii apa, nepuo inkera aanya ilamuriak. Nera apa kuna toyie uni, are botorok o nabo kiti. Nejo kuna botorok, "Emaikeno sii intae inkonyek peyie kidol enaitayu ilamuriak ooto medolita." Neiken ena kiti kake eitu ninche eiken kuna botorok. Ore; ake peyie eidipi aitayu ilamuriak, neboluni inkonyek paa kepuoi ang' eton eitu eing'urari ilamuriak oitayioki. Nepuo ake intoyie, ore pee ebaya auluo nejo emaing'urai ilamuriak nenyorrikiaa iloojon ake ninye eeta entito kiti. Negoro oleng', neishir nejo, "Imayaki ake ninye nini lai ilamuriak oojon, ekarrinyo ake enaduo shani aitayu ilooto." Nesai inkulie aajoki peyie melo amu emuto peyie eoriki ilkulenye, niany tukul eton.

56

Nerrinyo entito kiti enaduo wueji. Ore duo ejo aitayu ilamuriak, nejoki enkukuu, "Nakerai mikidany enkong'u." Neirut ena tito oleng'. Neikilikuan enkukuu, "Iyieu naanya tenaa iyieu naitaa enkerai?" Nejoki entito, "Oi intaaki enkerai." Nerik enkukuu enkerai omeitabai enemanya oshi. Naa keji apa ena kukuu Mbiti. Neeku keitoti Mbiti ena tito oleng'. Neyiang'aki ilkerra anaake. Naa keisho ake peyie eyieu neing'uraa tenaa ketopiro entito, neud lolkikuei. Nedol ajo osarge oimu. Naa tenejo entito aikilikuan ajo kainyioo peyie kituudo, nejoki Mbiti, "Oi eitu aaotiki enkerai ai." Neitoti apa o metasapuka entito oleng' kake kejo ake aud neimu osarge. Neitoki ake .aitoti oleng'. Ore akenya peyie eitoki aud, neimu eilata. Neyiolou taa ninye ajo etopiro entito etaa keinosayu.

Ore nabo olong', nedumunye Mbiti alo ariku inkulie ng'uesi peyie elotu ang'arie entito. Kake ore etioyo, nelotu olkurruk ene wueji netii ena tito. Neinepu entito ekitito endapana olker. Nejoki olkurruk entito, "Natito nchooki empalai peyie aaliki ena." Nejoki entito, "Shomo amu meeta enikiliki." Nenang' tosoit meshomo. Neitoki ake olkurruk amanu tiae alo. "Natito nchooki sii empalai peyie aaliki ena." Neton duo entito emitiki ake olkurruk empalai ometanang'aki ade nejoki, "Inosa esepe hoo nemeeta enikijoki." Ore ake peyie eidip olkurruk ainosa esunyai, nejoki entito, "Ore taa amu eshomo duo Mbiti ariku inkulie ng'uesi pee kiponu aanya, inyio ielare inkuruon niim ena oitoi naimu inkukuuni, isika shomo enkang' inyi. Naa tenikinkilikuan inkukuuni ajo ira eneng'ae nijoki, "ara enchoni oonkuruon nalo ake." Neinyiototo entito aas enatiaka olkurruk. Neishop enchoni musana, neelare inkuruon paa kelo aim ena oitoi naimu ade ing'uesi amu ina oitoi ake nalo enkang' enye.

Ore ake peyie elo entito enkiti wueji nenang'are eluata e dukuya oong'uesi. Neikilikuan aajoki, "Natito ira eneng'ae?" Nejoki entito, "Ara enchoni oonkuruon nalo ake." Nejoki inkukuuni, "Elioo ajo mira enatito e Mbiti nagila engelemian isiet nikipuo ade pooki aapukorie." Nepuo ing'uesi, nelo sii ninye entito. Neitoki ake entito anang'are ae luata oong'uesi. Neikilikuan ing'uesi, "Natito ira eneng'ae?" Nejoki entito, "Ara enchoni oonkuruon naloolo ake." Nejoki ng'uesi, "Shomo amu mira ena tito e Mbiti nagila engelemian isiet nikipuo ade pooki aapukorie." Neishori entito meshomo.

Nelo taa ake entito enang'are ake nkukuuni neikilikuan pooki aajo keneng'ae, nejoki ake entito, "Ara enchoni oonkuruon nalo ake." Negiroo inkukuuni pooki. Nelo ake entito o metanang'are inkukuuni naabayie naa ninche etii Mbiti. Neikilikuan Mbiti ena tito ajoki, "Natito ira eneng'ae?" Nejoki entito enetiaka inkulie ng'uesi pooki, "Ara enchoni oonkuruon naloolo ake." Nejo ayiolou penyo. Neitoki ake aikilikuan, "Eji itejo ira eneng'ae?" Neitoki ake entito ajoki enaduo ake natiaka: "Ara enchoni oonkuruon naloolo ake."

Nejoki entito, "Elioo ajo mira ena tito ai nagila engelemian isiet nikipuo ade inkukuuni ena kop pooki aapukorie." Neisho inkukuuni pooki entito meshomo, nepuo sii ninche enkang' e Mbiti.

Ore peyie ebaya ang', nejing' duo Mbiti aji aitayu entito. Oo naa pee ejo inkuna inji metii entito! Neyiolou ajo einosa enkop. Neyiolou ajo ninye enaduo najo keon enchoni oo nkuruon. Neyiolo ajo anaata etalakuana entito meekure ejo meinepua.

Nesotu inkulie ng'uesi ilkeek ooinokie enkima, neinok enkima sapuk oleng'.·Netoni aanyu Mbiti meitupuku entito o metumuta lelo keek enkima. Neitokini aasotu ilkulie. Neji taa ake, "Mbiti intupuku toi ade entito." Nejoki Mbiti, "Entasho toi amu isekenke alaku." Nesotu taa ake ng'uesi ilkeek emut ake enkima. Ore peyie eitoki aajoki Mbiti meitupuku entito nejo, "Entasho amu elukunya olker aarita." Etoning'o taa inkulie eidong'isho Mbiti tiaji, aa enkumoto najing' eturito. Ore ake peyie egutu enkumoto, nejing' ake Mbiti nenukaa keon amu eyiolo ajo tenelau ade ng'uesi entito nedoiki ninye.

Ore peyie edol inkulie kukuuni ajo meekure duo eitupuku Mbiti entito netumuta iladuo keek ootasotuoki enkima, mijing' aji aing'oru. Neer enkaji pooki aaing'oru Mbiti o metalaita. Netoni tengoro sapuk. Neetae duo eng'ues nabo naata enkerai kiti. Neiteru ena ketai aishir aa esumash eeta. Nejoki ng'otonye: "Yieyio nchooki olkina peyie aaliki ena." Nejoki ng'otonye, "Idol iyie kitalaita Mbiti nijo nchooki olkina, inchira amu mijo maishoo." Neitoki ake enkerai aomonu olkina, "Yieyio nchooki olkina peyie aaliki ena." Nejoki inkulie kukuuni ng'otonye ena kerai: "Aha, nchoo amu etejoki apa edol enkerai ilainyiamok eitu edol menye!" Neisho.

Ore ake peyie eidip enkerai atanaa nejo: "Neidia entikiyai e Mbiti!" Eeta apa Mbiti enkiti sikirai naenikino enkidong'oe, ore peyie ejing' enkumoto, neing'uari entikiyai erumisho. Neitayuni Mbiti tenkumoto, neisuyusui tenaduo kima, nepukorie inaduo ng'uesi pooki. Neiting' sii ninye Mbiti teine.

11. Mbiti

Once upon a time, there were three children who went to the bush to pick some berries. There were two older girls and one who was slightly younger. One of the older girls said, "Let us all shut our eyes and see who can pick ripe berries without seeing." The youngest of the girls shut her eyes but the older girls did not. When they had gathered enough berries, the girls headed home without checking the berries they had picked. On approaching the village and upon checking the berries, the younger girl noticed that while the other girls had only ripe berries, hers were all green. She was angered by the trick her friends had played on her; she told them that she would not take unripe berries to her mother so she would have to go back for ripe ones. The other girls urged her not to go because it was getting late, promising to share some of the berries, but she remained adamant.

The young girl went all the way back to where they had been picking berries. As she was reaching out for some berries, a big monster said to her in a deep voice: "Hey, do not pock my eye little girl." The little girl was beside herself with fear. The monster then asked her: "Shall I eat you or make you my child?" The girl answered, "Please make me your child." So the monster, whose name was Mbiti, led the girl into the forest to where she lived. Mbiti then fed the girl with rams that she stole from people's homes until the girl grew very fat. And whenever Mbiti wanted to check how fat the girl had grown, she would prick her with a needle, and when she complained of this treatment, Mbiti would comfort her saying: "Oh, I didn't mean to do it my child." She continued feeding her until she grew very fat indeed, but on pricking her, Mbiti found it was still blood that oozed from her skin. So she continued feeding her until finally some fat trickled out of her skin. Mbiti was then convinced that the girl was good enough to eat.

One day, Mbiti went to invite all her animal friends to come and feast on the girl. But while she was away, a crow went to visit the girl. She found her tanning a hide, discarding the fleshy parts of it. He said to her: "If you give me one of those strips, I will tell you something nice." The girl said to the crow, "Get away, you have nothing to tell me!" She threw a stone at him in a bid to chase him away. The crow circled the area and reappeared from another direction. He again begged the girl for a piece of fleshy strip of hide, promising to tell her something. The girl eventually grew impatient with the bird, and she angrily threw a strip of hide at him, saying as she did so: "There you go, you glutton, though you have nothing to tell me."

When the crow had eaten, he said to the girl: "You know, Mbiti went to fetch some other animals to come and feast on you. So you had better apply ashes to your body and go as quickly as you can back to your home, and if the monsters ask you who you are, you must answer: 'I am only a wandering skin of ashes.'" The girl did as she was instructed. She put on an old tattered skin and applied ashes to her body, then walked along the path that the monsters were going to follow on their way to Mbiti's home, since that happened to be the only way to her village.

It was not long before the girl met the first group of monsters who asked her: "To whom do you belong, little girl?" The girl answered, "I am only a wandering skin of ashes." The monsters let her pass, saying, "It is obvious you are not Mbiti's girl with her fat eight-layered belly that all of us are going to have for our evening meal!" As the girl continued on her way, she came across yet another group of monsters who also wished to find out who she was. She answered in the same way she had answered the first group; the monsters dismissed the girl as the others had done, telling her: "You may go since you are not Mbiti's girl with her fat eight-layered belly that we will all have for our evening meal."

The girl went on meeting many other groups of monsters, all of whom enquired of her identity and she told them that she was "only a wandering skin of ashes". Finally, she met the last group among whom was Mbiti herself. When Mbiti asked the girl who she was, the girl answered, "I am only a wandering skin of ashes." She threw a second glance at her, as though she was about to recognise her, and she once more asked: "What, who did you say you are?" The girl once more repeated her answer. Thereupon Mbiti dismissed the girl, telling her: "It is obvious you are not my daughter with eight layers of fat on her belly whom all the animals in this country are going to have for the evening meal!" This way, all the monsters let the girl pass while they continued on their way to Mbiti's home for the promised feast.

When the monsters reached home, Mbiti proudly and quite unsuspectingly went inside to get the girl. But alas, the girl was not there! She knew that was the end of her; the visiting monsters would surely feast on her. She recalled that her daughter must have been the girl who was calling herself "the skin of ashes", but she must by then be too far gone to be caught and brought back.

Unaware of what had happened the other monsters gathered firewood and lit a large fire outside. They all made themselves comfortable, eagerly waiting for Mbiti to bring out the girl, but soon the firewood got burnt up and some more had to be collected before Mbiti brought out the girl. So the monsters took turns calling Mbiti and telling her to hurry up and bring the girl out. Mbiti told the monsters to give her time, for she was only removing the girl's arm coils.*After a while, the monsters heard

Mbiti hitting at something inside the house, and on enquiring what was going on, Mbiti said, "I am preparing the head of a ram **, but I'll be out immediately." Mbiti was by this time digging a hole in which to hide, since she knew that when the monsters failed to get the meal they had been invited for, they would eat her instead. So when the hole was deep enough, Mbiti got inside and covered herself with the soil.

When the other monsters realised that Mbiti was taking far too long in bringing out the girl, and that the firewood that had been collected had by then been burnt up, they all rushed in angrily to find out what was going on. They searched everywhere in the house, but Mbiti was nowhere to be found, so they all sat down sulking.

It so happened that one of the monsters had a small child. The child felt hungry and started crying wishing to be fed. She said to her mother, "Please let me suckle then I shall tell you something." The mother furiously scolded her saying, "You can see that we have failed to find Mbiti and you dare ask for the breast! You can go on crying because you will not get it."

When the child asked to be suckled, once more promising to tell something, the rest of the monsters intervened saying to the mother, "Do give it to her, because as the saying goes, 'the child might see thieves before the father does'." So she did.

After the child had suckled she said, "I can see Mbiti's cowrie!" Mbiti used to wear a little cowrie shell on her tail, and this cowrie was left on the ground when Mbiti got into the hole. Mbiti was then pulled out of the hole and barbecued on what was left of the fire. All the animals had her for their evening meal. And that was the end of Mbiti.

* These are worn by girls as part of their ornaments.

**The head of a ram is normally split in two halves before it is ready for roasting.

Review Questions

i) Describe the personality and character of Mbiti in one paragraph.

ii) Discuss the role of the crow in this story and state the ways in which his character would be said to be consistent with or different from the role he plays in narrative **13**.

12. Konyek

Netii apa nemuratishoe tenkang' nabo, nepuo iltung'ana kumok osinkolio. Nepuo taa ilmurran ontoyie kumok ina masho. Netii ele murrani sidai aisul ilkulikae neyiolo ataranya entorrono. Netil intoyie kumok nabo olong'. Ore peyie emutu eidipate ntaleng'o nepuoi inkang'itie. Netii kuna toyie uni naayieu nerubare ele murrani aapuo aayiolou enemanya peyie etum aashom likae kekun. Naa ore duo ele murrani naa enkukuu natoole aaku oltung'ani kake eitu eyiolou oltung'ani hoo obo.

Nerik taa olmurrani intoyie, nerik, nerik o meitabai enemanya oshi amu kelakua apa ina kop oleng'. Ore etaa kebaya neduaya ntoyie intokitin naibor tolosho. Neikilikuan entito nabo olmurrani ajoki, "Kainyioo nekua naijo ntare?" Nejoki olmurrani, "Ai eme ntare ainei nena naibor muj!" Kake ore enasipa naa iloik looltung'ana apa oinosa lelo. Nejoki olmurrani ntoyie, "Enchomishom sii ntae amu kalo aboinaki nekua tare emuatata peyie ainepu ntae." Neutaa taa olmurrani intoyie meima enkoitoi naado neeim ninye eng'usur alo asotu iladuo oik apik erruat aitaa isisineta neshukunye ainepu ntoyie. Neiriamari pooki aapuo ang'.

Oo naa peyie ebaiki ntoyie enaduo ang' naa enkaji nabo ake natii! Neiteru aing'asia kake meitieu aaikilikuana olmurrani. Neitoomon olmurrani ntoyie ayiang'aki olker opir oleng' nepejoki nkiri neing'ua meinosa. Nejoki ntoyie, "Enosa taa entaraposhoto amu kalotu tenakata."Neipang' ninye eng'ues alo anya imauti oshi naanya, nelo aisudori peyie miaku keyiolou intoyie.

Ore ake enaipang'ie olmurrani nening' intoyie enkiti toilo nairo torungu lerruat naa penyo nening'o enejo. Neun intoyie inkiyiaa ainining' enejo. Nejoki intoyie: "Inkera ainei, kainyioo nayaua ntae ena kop mitil aikonji?" Nejoki ntoyie, "Olmurrani openy enkang' otorikuo yiook." Neitoki ina toilo ajoki ntoyie: "Oi ketelejua ntae eng'ues? Enyieito enchom amu mme oltung'ani ele etoole apa aaku olowuaru nenya iltung'na lenye pooki ebaiki elatia. Ore nanu ena nairo nara ng'otonye enkorrok kake ainosa apa naaku loik ake, kake ore peyie iyiolouu ajo asip entabolu sii ntae isisineta peyie kidolidolo." Oo naa peyie ebolu ntoyie sisineta neinepu iloik lentasat moruo. Nenyorriki aa iloik ake oorupa tenaduo rruat. Neutaa iloik lentasat intoyie metuudu elusie tenaduo aji naaim aaisik eton etioyo olmurrani. Nias taa ninye ntoyie enatiakita iloik, neposh enkaji aaim neisik aapuo. Ore tenkoitoi nedamu entito nabo ajo etalaa toi duo ninye keon alaku masaa pooki neing'ua imankek enyena eiteleikino erruat tenkaji enaduo tiamasi. Nejo, "Auui aatorikinote masaa ainei!" Nejo meeta nchere keitu eshuko alo ayau masaa ainei." Niapare nkulie aajoki 'milo siake peyie kioriki iyie, milo siake amu eikilo enkukuu anya! niany tukul aning'. Ore peyie elaikino nkulie tukul nejoki, "shomo naa peyie kianyu iyie tene."

Neina entito, neina nelo ometabai enaduo ang'. Neim enaduo lusie naimutua, nedumu mankek enyena, ore ena najo aipang' nejing'u enaduo kukuuu olmurrani. Eyieu eya entito olkiruroto. Nejoki olmurrani, "Asa nilo, ou amu iyie taata apukorie!" Nesioki entito asai ajoki, "oi mikinya siake ntaaki ng'utunyi!" Nejoki olmurrani, "Ainosa apa yieyio toolarin lenchumbi!" Neitoki entito ajoki, "Ntaaki naa siake enkanashe ino." Nejoki olmurrani: "Ainosa sii nena metunuki nkarn." Neitoki ake entito asaisho nejo: "Oi mikinya naa ntaaki enkitok ino." Nejo olmurrani: "Ina taa tejo." Ina taa oshi peyie eyam entiamasi entito. Kake ore naa amu menya ninye entito ng'uesi oltung'ana oonya ninye niaku keyaki ilkerra onkineji, neyaki sii inkishu naalep. Nebik tenebo enkata naado. Etaanyutua taa apa nkulie toyie enkae o metisiaita nepuo ninche ang'.

Neton apa ake ena kitok o metunutayu. Neton o metoisho neiu enkayioni. Neisho ena ayioni naa kepoku nkonyek nedung'okini enkarna aajo 'Konyek'. Naa aing'en apa Konyek oleng'. Ore ina olong' naini neinyiototo airiamariyie menye osero aapuo aing'oru iltung'ana oonya.

Ore nabo olong' etioyo Konyek o menye tosero nelo enkanashe ng'oto Konyek abaiki enkanashe. Etuutaitie taa apa inapa toyie nejoki: "shomo ake iyie ng'urai tenaa keton eishu." Naa entua apa ena anashe ng'oto Konyek natabayie. Ore peyie eidip intomonok pokira ainosa lomon neitanap ng'oto Konyek enkanashe ajoki, "Shomo taa kake tenikinepu elopiro tenkoitoi mishur ake tolchani turrur otii empolos emurua amu ninye oshi eyeng'iyeng'are Konyek o menye." Nejoki enkanashe 'ayia', neishoro elesere, neoro. Nelo enkae, ore ake peyie ebaya enaduo murua nedany olopiro, naa ele shani ake oshur. Ore ake peyie edamu enaduo natiaka enkanashe negiroo olchani alo. Ore ake ena nagiroo olchani nedolu Konyek o menye eponu. Nenyamalu entasat, nekwetiki oladuo shani neked alo ilng'osil. Neponu taa ninye ilowuarak aatoni tentonata oladuo shani. Ore ake ena nadol en tasat kulo owuarak neirut o meisirisira nkulak. Neitong'akino nkulak Konyek o menye ilukuny. Nejo Konyek, "Shye! anaijo toi taata keo ele shani nemeo oshi ake!" Nejoki menye, "Ai enchan natenetua." Nejo Konyek imariria ele shani nedol enaduo tasat anashe ng'otonye. Nejo, "Oi aishoo sii taata enkai endaa nao!" Neitadouni entasat aanya, nedanyi enkoshoke nedanyuni ilmao ayiok. Neisho olpayian Konyek lelo mao nejoki, "iyaki ng'utunyi mikitapejoki kulo airakuj." Neya Konyek.

Ore ake ena nadol ng'oto Konyek inaduo kera neyiolou ajo enkanashe duo enotito ilowuarak niar nedanyu nkera. Neng'amu ake lairakuj nejoki Konyek, "Shomo naa ngurana ore peyie eoku ilairakuj naipot." Neisho ake entasat meipang'a Konyek nedumunye aing'oru indero are niar nepej apejoki Konyek. Ore ake peyie eoku neipotoki Konyek. Nedol ake Konyek nejo: "Yieyio anaijo toi etaa kuna ayakuj ainei kutiti naa sapuki duo?" Nejoki ng'otonye: "Kanya oshi nanu inoshi mauti ninyanya ntae?" Nening' menye neisikong' Konyek nejoki entasat: "Minya otiake entomononi ai."

Neitoti ng'oto Konyek ilmao o metaa ilayiok botoro oleng'. Neyoki nabo olong' entasat ajoki olpayian lenye, "Olee lai, ore amu manya oshi nanu iltung'ana linyanya ntae tayooki ng'urakaki olkiteng' layieng' sii akenya nanu aitoki aok imotori." Ore peyie ening' Konyek ina nejo: "Eitu aikata kining' eng'oroyioni nanya olkiteng' openy naa ore eikununo neijia eton oshi nanu amen eneima nkayakuj ainei." Nelo ninye olpayian alilita aing'oru olkiteng' sapuk neyiang'aki entasat. Neyieng' entasat ele kiteng' ayiang'aki ilayiok lenkanashe naisho meinosa aaraposho, neitaiki olpurda omooki aanya. Ore peyie emutu nejing' enoshi ake wueji netii aaisudori.

Ore nabo olong' nedol Konyek iroruat kumok kutiti tekutukaji nejo: "Yieyio, amaa kenkuneng'ae toi kuna roruat kumok kutiti anijo mme nainei?" Nejoki ng'otonye: "Ai ininono ake enkerai ai, kang'ae naa enkae kerai natii ena aji? Nabo, amaa tenaipang' naitu, naipang' naitu emiaku ade kumok iroruat?" Nening' olpayian lenye nejo: "Eee itisipa entomononiai." Niar Kenyok neijoo. Ore kiti lele Konyek oton toltiren. Nejoki menye: "Konyek kaji iimua?" Nejoki, "Kaji duo itunuka?"

Nebulu layiok, netum engolon sapuk oleng'. Neinosak'i entasat ilomon le kulo owuarak ooboitare. Neikilikuan tenaa keidim naaji aataar. Nejo ilayiok, "Ai, ee pae." Ore ilo kekun peyie ebau menye Konyek nejoki entasat: "Olee lai, inkuna peyie kiyoki aing'uraki iremeta are olong'oi are o lalema aare peyie teneyoki ilmang'ati aaponu naidim sii nanu atomitu keon." Nejoki olpayian: "Ee itisipa entomononi ai!" Nening' ake Konyek nejo: "A-ha! eitu aikata kining' te Maasai entasat nayieu inareta oolewa naa kajo nanu inapa ayakuj ainei eing'urakini." Neyoki ninye olmoruo ayaki enkitok inareta.

Ore tenkakenya nejoki entasat Konyek o menye metulutoi olchoni peyie eshe ninye peyie eing'uraa tenaa keidim naaji aatomitu ate teneponu ilmang'ati. Nelutoo Konyek o menye olchoni, neshe entasat paa kejoki Konyek: "Konyek kaji naaji inko tenimitu iyiook?" Nejo Konyek, "Kaikonji ake naikonji ake, namitu yieyio, naikonji ake naikonji ake, namitu papa!" Neipushupusho taa' ninye entiamasi o metoposha olchoni aimu. Neitoki ake entasat ajoki menyaaki aalutoo olchoni neitoki ashe aitobiraki. Neitoki aikilikuan Konyek eneiko naaji tenemitu enkang' enye. Nejo konyek aipushupusho nelaikino atoposha olchoni. Ore peyie edol entasat ajo eta iaikinote ilowuarak aatupuku nebuaku ajo 'uui' aipotu ilayiok. Neponu ilayiok aaparripar Konyek o menye. Ore peyie eeku kedung'o Konyek tau nejo, "Oi atayiolo apa ake ajo eitu anya nkayakuj ainei naa ninche kuna." Niaku enapa naji, 'edol enkerai ilainyiamok eitu edol menye.' Ore ake peyie eye Konyek o menye nerik ilayiok enkanashe ng'otonye ang'.

12. Konyek

It once came to pass that an initiation ceremony was held at a certain village and many people converged there on this occasion. Many girls as well as young men attended the festivity. Among the distinguished guests was a strikingly handsome warrior who danced most elegantly, thus attracting the attention of many a girl. The celebrations continued until evening when the guests started departing to their respective homesteads. The handsome warrior found himself in the company of three girls who wanted to accompany him to his home, for he was irresistibly handsome. In reality, the warrior was a beast that had transformed himself into a human being, though no one knew it at the time.

So the warrior went off with the girls, and they travelled a long way to his home. On nearing the warrior's home, the girls spotted some white objects on a ridge, a little distance away. When one of the girls asked what the objects were, the warrior boastfully replied, "Those white objects are my own sheep." But the truth was that the white objects were the skeletons of human beings he had eaten. The warrior then directed the girls to follow a long path, while he himself took a short-cut to the village on the pretext that he was going to drive the sheep into their enclosures. What he did was clear away the bones which he stuffed under the bed. He then caught up with the girls, whom he had brought home with him.

So the girls arrived at a homestead with only one house. This surprised them, but they were afraid to ask the warrior, who was by then playing such a fine host.

He slaughtered a fat ram for the girls, roasted the meat, and as they were eating, he excused himself, promising to return immediately. He then went elsewhere to eat whatever he used to feed on, without the girls finding out.

As soon as the warrior left, the girls heard a faint voice from under the bed. On listening closely to what the voice was saying, they heard a woman's voice ask: "My dear children, what brings you to this lonely place?" The girls replied: "Why, it is the owner of the homestead who brought us." "Oh, how you have been tricked by a beast! Get up and leave immediately for this is no human being, he transformed himself into a beast and ate all his relatives as well as neighbours. Even I, the one who now talks to you, am his own mother, but he has reduced me to a mere skeleton, and if you want to prove the truth of what I am telling you, you may check under the bed and you will see for yourselves." And were the girls shocked to see the skeleton of an old woman!

The skeleton then advised the girls to make an opening in the wall, through which they could escape before the return of the monster. The girls did as they were instructed and succeeded in getting away. On their way home, one of the girls remembered that she had removed her beads and left them on the bed at the monster's house. She exclaimed to the others, "Oh dear! I have forgotten my necklaces and I must go back for them." Her friends, in a bid to persuade her not to return, promised to contribute some beads for her. They warned her she might get eaten by the monster. The girl, refusing to heed the warning, proceeded to the monster's homestead. Realising that she would not be persuaded not to go, her friends wished her good luck and promised to wait for her.

The girl retraced her steps back to the warrior's homestead, manoeuvered through the opening they had made, recovered her necklaces, and was about to exit, when in came the warrior turned monster! The girl was about to collapse from fright, when the warrior said to her, "Come, come, you have nowhere to go, for you will be my supper tonight!" The girl, in a bid to save herself, quickly pleaded with him saying: "Please do not eat me and I will be your mother." The warrior said to her: "I ate my mother many years ago". The girl pleaded further, "Then don't eat me and I will be your sister," she cried. The warrior retorted, "I ate those too until their names were buried." The girl further begged the warrior, saying in desperation, "Oh please don't eat me, oh please make me your wife." "That sounds better!" cried the monster. And that is how it came about that the monster married the girl. From then on, while he ate people and wild animals, he brought rams, goats and milk cows for the girl. They lived together for a long time. By this time the other girls had waited for their companion until they had given her up for dead.

After a few months, the girl conceived and later gave birth to a baby boy, with protuberant eyes, on account of which he was called 'the bulgy-eyed-one', or 'Konyek'. Konyek happened to be a very clever boy. On the day he was born, he accompanied his father to the wilderness to hunt human prey.

One day, as Konyek and his father were out hunting, his mother's sister came to visit her. The girls who had returned had given her directions to the monster's home, bidding her to go and check what had happened to her sister: "Just go and find out whether she is still alive," they pleaded. This woman was pregnant, just about to give birth. When the two women had finished their conversation, Konyek's mother advised her sister: "You may now leave but if the rain finds you on the way, do not shelter under a leafy tree in the middle of the plain, for this is where Konyek and his father rest." Her sister said, "Very well." They bade each other farewell and parted.

The sister left, and as soon as she got to the plain that her sister had talked about, it started raining, and there was only one tree she could shelter under. She was quick to remember that that was the tree under which she was advised not to shelter. As she was about to bypass the tree, she saw Konyek and his father approaching. She ran back to the lone tree and climbed up to its thick foliage, hoping against hope that the monsters could not see her. On arrival, the two monsters crouched at the foot of the tree, sheltering from the rain. On seeing them below her, the woman was so much overcome by fear that she started urinating, and the urine dripped on Konyek and his father. "Why! This tree is letting in rain today and it never does!" exclaimed Konyek. "Oh! It is the rain that is rather heavy today," replied his father. But as Konyek raised his eyes, he saw the woman who was a sister to his mother and said: "Oh! What luck! I have found some ready food!" And so the woman was pulled down to be consumed and when her womb was opened, there emerged two healthy twin boys. His father handed them to Konyek saying, "Take these kidneys to your mother to roast them for you." Konyek happily did as he was bid.

On seeing the two babies, Konyek's mother was quick to realise what had happened to her sister. She asked Konyek to go and play outside. "You can go and play outside and I will call you when your kidneys are ready," she said to him, while thinking of her next plan of action. As Konyek walked out, his mother quickly killed two rats and roasted them, at the same time hiding the twins under the bed. Konyek was soon told to come for his kidneys.

On seeing the two shrivelled up rats Konyek said, "Mother, why, my kidneys are now small, yet they were bigger than this!" His mother answered by asking him a question, "Do you think I eat the strange things that you people eat?" When the father heard this, he reprimanded Konyek for being mean to his mother, and consoled his wife saying, "I know you don't eat them, my dear wife."

So Konyek's mother looked after the children until they grew into big boys. One day, the woman said to her husband, "My dear husband, since I do not eat your kind of food, I would like you to get me an ox, so that I too may for once make bone soup." Konyek heard this and said, "I have never heard of a woman eating an ox all by herself, and I am still suspicious about the disappearance of my kidneys!" The man, nevertheless, went ahead to hunt for a fat ox which he brought to his wife. The woman slaughtered the ox, which the boys ate until they had had their fill, after which they returned to their usual hiding place.

On another day, Konyek saw many little footprints by the doorway, and he asked his mother suspiciously: "Mother, whose footprints are these, I know they are not mine." His mother told him, "Oh, they have to be yours my son, for which other child is in this house? Furthermore, when I keep going in and out of the house, don't the footprints become many?" On hearing this, her husband supported her saying: "You have indeed spoken the truth my dear wife." He thrashed Konyek, then swallowed him up. In an instant Konyek reappeared seated at the hearth, and when his father asked him, "Konyek, where did you come through?" he in turn asked him: "Where did you block?"

The boys grew and became big and strong. Their aunt confided to them that the people she was living with were monsters. On enquiring from them whether they would be able to kill them, they replied in the affirmative. So when her husband arrived that evening, his wife said to him, "My dear husband, please find me two spears, two shields and two swords so that I may be able to defend myself in case I am ever attacked by enemies." Her husband said in agreement, "You have spoken the truth my dearest wife." But when Konyek heard of his mother's request he exclaimed: "We have never heard of a woman asking for men's weapons among the Maasai and I suspect they are being sought for my kidneys." Even so the husband procured the required items for the wife.

Early the next morning, the woman asked Konyek and his father to go under a cow hide which she would peg down and ask them to try and get out as a way of proving their powers in defending the family in case of attack. When the two monsters were under the hide, the woman pegged it down tightly and said to her son: "Konyek, show us how you would defend us." Konyek said, fidgeting, "I would do this and that and rescue my mother, and do this and that and rescue my father." And so the monster managed to squeeze out between the pegs. His mother asked Konyek once more to go under the hide, and this time she pegged the skin more tightly and again asked Konyek to demonstrate his ability to defend the family. Konyek struggled to free himself, but was unable to. The woman then made a loud cry, "uui" to summon the boys, who at once set upon Konyek and his father, killing them instantly. As Konyek was dying he said, "Oh how I have always known that I had not eaten my kidneys and here they are!" And so the saying goes, "the child sees thieves before the father does." When Konyek and his father died, the boys took their aunt to their home.

Review Questions

i) "The child sees thieves before the father does." Explain this proverb with reference to Konyek and his father.

ii) What is the theme of this story?

13. Entito nayama olkurruk

Netii apa, netii ele kurruk oyieu oleng' entito naayam. Neisho nabo olong' nedumunye neishop enkila narok, nepika masaa shaati nekuso peyie eji koltung'ani netil intoyie. Nedumunye nelo enkang' nabo aing'oru entito.

Nelo taa ninye atum entito natisira. Ore peyie eirorie menye entito nejoki, "Aishoo entito kake shomo taanyu metubulu peyie ilotu arik." Memus olkurruk peyie etum entito, kejo ake kanu kenya ebulu peyie erik. Niaku kelo ake abaiki enkang' enkaputi aleenoo entito tenaa ketubulua. Kake ore eleenoo ejur sii ninye entito o metodua ajo meisiriri irregiei loltung'ani, ijo makurruk empukunoto.

Negirakino apa entito inaataduaa o meeu kenya aliki ng'otonye. Nejoki, "Nini, emikinchosho ele tung'ani amu ijo olkurruk." Nejo ng'otonye, "Eji olkurruk! Nchoo naa kinya." Negira entito. Neitoki aiki papaai lenye. Nejo sii ninye, "Eji olkurruk! Nchoo naa kinya! Tenaa koltung'ani imba tolimu kake minor olpayian leme esidano eeta." Eitu eitoki entito aimaki olung'ani peyie miaku kejo menye aimeeta oldau. Ore peyie ebau enkolong' nariki nesuj olpayian lenye maakutiti eishirita anaa peyie eishir ntoyie pooki eriki.

Nepuo, nepuo, nelang' ilkejek, neked ildoinyio nedung' entim aapuo. Nelusoo nkolong'i kumok etii enkoitoi. Nejoki entito olkurruk, "Amaa, emeekure toi kenya kibaya?" Nejoki olkurruk: "Eton elakua enkop". Neitoki aapuo, nepuo nejoki olkurruk entito, "Keton kiporito ilojong'a lenkop inyi?" Nejoki entito, "meekure." Neitoki ake aapuo neitoki ajoki, "Keton idolita modiok oonkishu nyi?" Nejoki entito, "meekure adolita." ore peyie eitoki aapuo eneedo neitoki olkurruk aikilikuan entito, "Keton elioo ildoinyio lenkop inyi?" Nejo entito anang' silig atalu neitu edol Nejoki: "Meekure elioo, eimiso."

Neisho ake olkurruk peyie ebaya empolos entim naripa nedol ajo etalakuana enkop nejoki entito metakedo olchani. Ore ake peyie eked entito olchani neitayu olkurruk enaduo kila narok o masaa muj. Ina peyie eiting'ie taa ninye entito ajo olkurruk abaraki. Neirut oleng' nelau eniaas. Nejoki olkurruk entito, "Nairo ena, nchiru taata minyi o ng'utunyi amu tene apa aalotu anya." Nelo ninye asotu ilkeek oolutu apejie entito.

Ore ake ena naimis olkurruk tentim nerany entito ajo:

"Yieyio, papa

Keitu apa ajoki Mikincho ele tung'ani

Amu olkurruk

Nijo kukuny aisho!

Neigil entito arany katitin kumok.

Ore teina tim netii duo ilmurran oing'ua olamayio looshukori inkang'itie. Netii kulo murran olong'arie kina ena 'tito, netii olang'ata olkulikae aare ooboitare. Ore erany entito nening' olang'ata nejoki olalashe entito: 'Shye anaijo enkanashe ino ina naning'o erany tentim?" Nejoki olalashe: "Ee pae sii apa kinyial ena tito e yieyio elukunya, ketaa tenining' imotonyi nijo ninye itoning'o?" Nejo ilkulikae mainining'o nesipu taa ninye aajo ninye ina, nepuo aing'oru. Ore peyie etum neinosie ilomon neliki entito ajoki eishooyioki apa" aisho olkurruk laa ilkeek eshomo asotu oolotu apejie anya. Neisho ilmurran entito oringa nejoki metooshie olkurruk elukunya tenejo akedoki nepuo ninche aigara inkeek teine.

Ore peyie ebau olkurruk neinok ake enkima sapuk nejoki entito metadou teina kata. Nejoki entito, "madou." Neiputukuny olkurruk oleng'. Neikoroj entito ajoki, "Ae pae sii duo itum ilkulinyi likimitu!" Nejo takedoki newuap ake entito oringa neosh elukunya. Ore ina kata ake neipang'u ilmurran tentim neparripar olkurruk teine. Nerik entito ang'.

70

13. The Girl Who Married a Crow

Once upon a time, there was a crow who wanted a woman to marry very much. One day, he wore a calf-skin garment and adorned himself with many fancy ornaments in order to disguise himself as a man and to attract the girls' attention. He then set off to a certain village in search of a bride.

He succeeded in finding a girl to whom he became betrothed. During the marriage negotiations, her father said to him: "I have given you the girl but you will have to wait until she is old enough to be married before you can take her." The crow was elated with the prospects of getting a bride and could not wait to take the girl for his wife. He made occasional visits to the family of his prospective inlaws and kept a check on the girl's growth. The girl was also observing him and taking note of his crow-like peculiarities.

The girl first kept this observation to herself, then one day she confided to her mother, saying: "Dear mother, please let me not be married to this man for he looks like a crow." On hearing this, the mother said: "Did you say a crow, then let him eat you!" After sometime, the girl made the same complaint to her father, who also said the same thing. "What, a crow! May he eat you. If you do not like him it is better to say so instead of smearing the reputation of such a handsome man for nothing."

Not wishing to appear disrespectful to her parents, the girl never brought up the subject again. On her wedding day, she meekly followed her husband, slowly, bobbing away as she did so in the same way girls do on their wedding day.

They kept on walking across rivers, over mountains and into dense forests. They were on their way for many days. Feeling tired, the girl finally asked: "Tell me, when are we ever going to get there?" The crow answered: "Oh, it is still a long way off." As they walked on, the crow asked the girl, "Are flies from your country still on you?" The girl answered; "No, not anymore." As they walked a little further on, the crow again enquired of the girl: "Do you still see the dung of your cattle?" "I see no more of it," answered the bride. And as they walked further and deeper into the forest the crow asked the girl: "Are the mountains of your country still in view?"

The girl, squinting her eyes as she looked back, replied: "I do not see them any more, they are out of view." The crow led the girl on, and when they got to a very thick forest a long distance away from her home, he ordered her to climb up a tree.

When she got to the top of the tree, the crow discarded his garment and all the other ornaments and revealed his true nature. The girl, having confirmed the truth of what she had always feared, was very shaken, but she did not know what to do. The crow said to the girl: "You can now call out to your mother and father because it is here that I shall eat you up." On saying this he went about gathering firewood to make a fire to roast the girl. On seeing the crow disappearing behind the bushes, the girl started lamenting and sang:

> Mother, father
> Had I not told you
> Not to marry me to this man
> For he is a crow
> And you said, "Let him eat you"?

She repeated this lament over and over again.

And it so happened that at the same forest there were warriors who were on their way home after a lion hunt. Among these warriors were the girl's brother, her lover, and two others. As the girl sang, the lover heard her voice and said to her brother: "Ssh that sounds like your sister singing in the forest!" The girl's brother said to him: "Oh how that daughter of my mother has turned your head! When you hear the singing of birds you think you are hearing her voice!" When the others listened intently, however, they realised that it sounded like the girl, indeed, and so they set off in search of her. On finding her, the girl told them how she had been married off to a crow, who had gone to fetch firewood to roast and eat her. The warriors gave the girl a club and told her to hit the crow on the head with it if he tried to get at her, and hid themselves behind the nearby bushes.

On his return, the crow lit a big fire and commanded the girl to come down immediately, at which the girl replied boldly: "No". The crow was utterly shocked to hear such impudence from a helpless creature.

"What! You must have found some relatives to rescue you!" said the crow sarcastically. When he tried to climb the tree, the girl swung the club and hit him hard on the head. Thereupon, the warriors immediately emerged from the bushes and crushed the crow. They then led the girl back home, and she was married to her lover.

Review Questions ◼

i) In what way(s) is the character of the girl's parents in this story similar to that of Konyek's father in story **12**?

ii) What do we learn from this story about the girl's role in the choice of a spouse? Is there some similarity to what takes place in today's society in your community or any other?

14. Esiankiki o Enkukuu

Neti apa, netii ena siankiki natopolosari. Neutaa ele duo murrani olo apolosakino, neliki enkoitoi naaim. Nejoki: "Nchoo taa ake peyie eoro nkoitoi tadamayu tatene." Nelo ninye olmurrani aton tentim aanyu. Nelo ake esiankiki ore peyie eoro nkoitoi nepal enaaim enkoitoi e tatene neim ena natii kedianye.

Nelo ake esiankiki. nelo. o meinepu enkukuu Nejoki: "Siankiki, kaji ilo tene? Ijo aa amu kaanya?" Neranyaki esiankiki ajoki:

"Mme tene entureishi ai

Maape iyie embata enkare

Peyie kinya niokisho

Le long'o lai. kaji duoo?"

Naa tim ena kop oleng.' Nerik enkukuu esiankiki, nerik, ore peyie ebaya ae wueji nejoki: "Ekaanya tene." Neitoki esiankiki aranyaki enkukuu ajoki peyie menya teine.

Neitoki taa ake aapuo, nepuo, ejo taa ake esiankiki kening' olmurrani. Ore peyie eitoki aapuo eneedo nejoki enkukuu esiankiki: "Aanya tene?" Nejoki esiankiki:

"Mme tene entureishi ai

Maape iyie embata enkare

Peyie kinya niokisho

Le long'o lai, kaji duo?"

Ore taa ejo entito 'Ielong'o lai kaji duo,' olmurrani eikilikuan ajoki kaji toi duo itejo peyie kitumore. Kake meekure duo ening' olmurrani.

73

Ore ade peyie epuo aabaya enkapune natii embata olkeju nelo enkukuu adung'u mbenek duo naaiteleiki nkiri entito. Naa kedung'u ake inaadung'u neyau. Nejoki entito: "Ore engelemian ena tito oolmurran imeitepetari nkulie benek inolmatasiai ake eitepetari." Naa keyau ake nkulie nejoki: "ke kuna?" Nejoki entito: "Mme ninche." Neyau kulie nejoki mme ninche. Omeyau ade inolmatasiai. Nejoki entito: "Ee ninche." Nesisin ewueji ade neiteleiki nkiri, neinok enkima sapuk. Eranyita taa ake entito oladuo sinkolio. Ore enoshi kata ejo enkukuu aidaki esiankiki neipang'u olmurrani tentim. Nejoki esiankiki enkukuu: "Inchudat inono taata eiteleikini nena benek." Niar olmurrani enkuu neiteleiki mbenek, nerik esiankiki. Neishunye.

14. A Young Woman and an Ogre

Once upon a time, there lived a young woman who eloped to meet her warrior lover out in the wilderness. The warrior directed the young woman to a place in the forest where he would meet her. He said to her: "If you get to a fork along the path take the right path." Then the warrior went ahead to await her arrival in the forest.

The young woman took off, and when she got to the fork that the warrior had mentioned, she followed the left path, forgetting which path the warrior had instructed her to follow.

As the girl walked on, she came upon an ogre who said to her: "Hey young woman, where are you going; do you have anything to say, now that I'm going to eat you?" The girl answered in song:

> Not here my bead*
> Let us go to the water hole
> Where you can eat me
> And have a drink
> Oh my dear warrior, where was it?**

And it so happened that this was very bushy country. The ogre led the young woman on, and when they got to another spot, he said to her: "I am now going to eat you here." The lady again broke into song, urging him not to eat her yet.

They went farther on, and the young woman kept hoping that the warrior would hear her voice. As they walked on, the ogre asked the young lady: "Shall I eat you here?" The girl sang again:

Not here my bead
Let us go to the water hole
Where you can eat me
And have a drink
Oh my dear warrior, where was it?

But the warrior had still not heard her.

When they got to a cave by a river, the ogre collected branches and leaves on which to place the young woman's flesh after he had slaughtered her. When he brought one type of leaf, the girl objected to having her flesh laid on ordinary leaves, preferring the sweet-scented leaves of the matasia plant. The ogre brought another kind of leaf, but the girl rejected them, until eventually the sweet-scented leaves of the matasia plant were brought. When the ogre asked the girl whether those were the right type of leaves she said: "Yes, these are the ones." The ogre then laid the leaves down on the ground and lit a big fire. All this while, the girl was continuously singing the same song.

Just when the ogre was about to jump on the young woman, the warrior suddenly emerged from the bush. The young woman said to the ogre: "It is now your skinny flesh that will be laid on those leaves." The warrior killed the ogre and placed him on the bed of leaves and took the lady away. And that is the end.

* An oval shaped type of bead. Often people exchange these and name each other by them.

  The girl, by using the term was flattering the ogre.

** Talking to the warrior and asking where they were supposed to meet.

Review Questions

i) The young woman in this story spoke to the ogre in a sarcastic manner. Substantiate this statement, quoting the appropriate line(s) in the story.

ii) Describe the nature and character of the young lady in this story.

iii) What do you think led the young woman to elope?

15. Ntemelua

Netii apa, neisho entasat neiu enkerai, nedung'okini enkarna aajo Ntemelua. Neyieng'i olkiteng' oitaikinyieki entomononi eilata. Neyier entasat ironkena neipang' alo aramatisho neing'uaa eyiara. Neing'uaa sii ninye enkerai eirura.

Tudumunye ake enaduo ng'oki nedou oltiren paa kejo:

"Moti, tinyikinyiku

Kipiye, tinyikinyiku

Naitayu ironkena, napik imboyo."

Neyet emoti nenya ronkena pooki, nepik emoti ilboro neilep alo airura anaa enkerai kiti.

Nejo entasat alotu akurt emoti neinepu emoti naa ilboro ake ootii. Neiputukuny kake eitu eliki likae tung'ani. Neitoki ayier kulie ronkena neipang'. Neisho ake metulusoi enkiti kata neleleunye ajing' olale. Nedol enaduo ng'oki, neyet emoti anya ronkena, nedumaki emoti ilboro. Nedol entasat, neitoki aleliari aipang'. Ore kiti kata nening' enkerai eishir. Nelo entasat adumu.

Nelo enkitok ainosaki olpayian lenye pooki toki. Niany olpayian eiruk tukul. Nejo meteyieng'i olker neyieri ironkena. Ore ake peyie eikoni neijia nejing' olpayian o kulie tung'ana olale aaisudori aarreshu tenaa kesipa enatejo entasat. Neinyiototo Ntemelua nejo:

"Moti tinyikinyiku

Kipiye tinyikinyiku

Naitayu ironkena, napik imboyo."

Nepalari taa ninye olpayian. Nejoki pooki ng'ae meteena lolan peyie eidurri teina ang' ina kata ake.

Neeni ake ilolan, neiroti isirkon, neidurri. Neing'uari Ntemelua eirura. Eitu ninye eyae toki tena rruat natii peyie miaku keputunye nening'oo iltung'ana. Ore peyie miaku keliyioyu enkang' anaa enaidurrieki neji keing'uari enkiteng', o enkine oosikiria. Neing'uari, neorito enkiteng' o enkine, neru osikiria anaa oshi ake.

Oo naa peyie ejo Ntemelua aputunye neinepu aa ninye ake entung'ani natii enaduo ang'! Nedumunye neosh enkine pau! Neorito enkine ajo mee! Nejoki Ntemelua, "Anaijo mee, neitu duo ijo Ntemelua inyio amu kitung'ayioki'!" Neitoki alo aosh osikiria neru sii ninye, neitoki Ntemelua ajoki enatiaka enkine. Neitoki abaiki enkiteng' neosh pau! Ore peyie eorito enkiteng' nejoki Ntemelua: "Pesho ijo moo neito duo ijo Ntemelua inyio amu Kitung'uayioki."

Nereu Ntemelua enkiteng' enye neibung' orregie le naidurra. Ore elo nenang'are ilmurran. Neisho ake meitayu enkiteng' imodiok neim osiadi alo enkoshoke. Nebau ake ilmurran nejo matatalu olopeny enkiteng' nelau, nereu enkiteng'. Naa keosh ake nening' entoilo najo: "Tapala enkiteng' naata olopemy!" are peyie eitoki aaosh ae wueji neitoki aaning' ejo: "Shye! kaji toi ireureo enkiteng' naata olopeny?" Netalu ilmurran ina toki nairo ore peyie elau nereu ninche enkiteng' eilepilep ake Ntemelua o meitabai olpul opuo duo aayieng'ie.

Ore tolpul neiteru duo ilmurran aayieng' enkiteng', naa kedung' ake enedung' nejo Ntemelua: "Ooi eyieu kidung'!" Neing'oru duo ilmurran entoki nairo nelau. Neton taa Ntemelua ailepilep o meitaini enkiring'o nabayie. Nejo purjuk' nemanikini etii olmurrani obo enkoriong', nerepaa. Naa keji ake maitayu nelaikinoi. Neji matudung'u etaa duo nabo osesen lolmurrani nedung'i olmurrani. Ore peyie epali neeku kekedito ake anaa enkiti kerai nanapitae. Neyieng'isho ake ilmurran neisho Ntemelua ironkena, neisho eilata sapuk metooko. Ore ake peyie eok neiliar eilata, nelepoo, netir injo, neirura. Neirrag sii ninye olmurrani. Ore ake peyie eitumurru Ntemelua njo neinyiototo ilmurran aluarie.

Ore ake peyie elusoo ilmurran nelo olng'ojine olpul asotisho aing'oru iloik. Ore ebel iloik neputu Ntemelua. Neitiamu ake Ntemelua neidaki olng'ojine enkoriong', nerep. Neton ankata naado enapita olng'ojine. Niaku meidim olng'ojine ashomo atililitayu oing'oru endaa kekwetita ake. Nesasu oleng'. Ore Kenya, nelo olng'ojine ajing' enkumoto neshurtaa Ntemelua te kutukaji. Neya olng'ojine esumash meitieu atupuku, nemeyioloi oshi enetaasa Ntemelua ebaiki ina kata.

15. Ntemelua

Once a woman gave birth to a child who was given the name Ntemelua. As is the practice, an ox was slaughtered to obtain fat for the new mother. The mother cut up the fatty parts of the meat and left it cooking while she performed other duties outside. She left the baby sleeping.

The mysterious little baby then got out of bed, sat by the fire, took a spoon and started removing the meat from the pot, saying:

Draw near little pot

Draw near little spoon

I fish out the meat and put in boulders.

He ate all the meat and replaced it with hardened moulds of dung. When he had finished, he went back to sleep like a new-born baby.

When the mother returned to stir the pot of meat, she found it full of moulds of dung. She was startled but told no one what had happened. She prepared some more meat and left it cooking. After a short while, she stealthily stole into the calf-pen and observed the baby perform his uncanny tricks of eating the meat and replacing it with moulds of cow dung. She then stole away softly. After a few minutes, the baby was heard crying and the mother went to pick him up.

The woman related the incident to her husband, who absolutely refused to believe it. He ordered that a ram be slaughtered and the fatty pieces of meat be left cooking while the old man and a few others hid at the calf-pen to wait for the baby to perform the alleged tricks. It was not long before Ntemelua awoke, and was soon at his usual tricks:

Draw near little pot

Draw near little spoon

I fish out the meat and put in boulders.

What the old man saw convinced him about the character of his child. He immediately ordered everyone to pack and leave that home. All the packing was done and loaded on to the donkeys. Ntemelua was left sleep. To avoid waking him up, nothing had been touched at the bed where he lay.

It was further decided that a cow, a goat and a donkey be left behind so as to give the impression that the village was not deserted. The cow mooed, the goat bleated and the donkey brayed as they had always done.

On waking up, Ntemelua realised that he was the only being in the village. He got up and hit the goat pau! The goat bleated: mee! Ntemelua said to the goat: "Why do you now bleat and you never said 'Ntemelua, get up for you are being left behind!'" He then went and hit the donkey which brayed. Ntemelua told it what he had told the goat. Soon, he was at the cow whom he hit pau! When the cow mooed, Ntemelua said: "You moo for nothing since you never said 'Ntemelua, get up for you are being left behind!'"

Ntemelua then drove his cow following the hoofprints of the caravan. As he was walking along, he came across some warriors. At the same time, the cow defecated. Ntemelua quickly went through the cow's anus into its stomach. The warriors came, looked around, and finding no one, they assumed that the cow had no owner, so they drove it along. When they hit it, a little voice was heard saying: "Leave this cow alone since it has an owner." On hitting it for the second time, the voice again said: "What! Where are you taking a cow that has an owner!" The warriors searched the whole place for the source of the voice, but on failing to find it, they drove the cow up to the meat-camp, where they were to slaughter it. From inside the cow's stomach, Ntemelua continued making noises all the way.

At the meat-camp, when the warriors were cutting up the cow, the little voice said: "Oh, how you almost cut me!" But still the warriors could not see where the voice was coming from. This continued until they had removed the last piece of meat from the dead cow, when Ntemelua suddenly slipped out, sprang on to the back of one of the warriors and clung to it.

The other warriors tried to pull him down, but he clung even tighter. When they tried to cut him down, they ended up cutting the warrior, for the two had merged into one. But when they stopped pulling or cutting Ntemelua, he remained on the warrior's back like a child that was being carried. Eventually the warriors came up with an idea: they gave him a lot of fatty meat as well as liquid fat to drink. This made him limp and drowsy. The warrior lay down with him for a while and when slumber overcame Ntemelua, all the warriors stole away leaving him asleep.

When the warriors had disappeared, the hyena arrived at the camp and rummaged through looking for bones. As he cracked a bone, he woke up Ntemelua, who immediately jumped on to the hyena's back and stuck there. He stayed there for a long time and hyena was unable to go hunting for food, since he was constantly on the run. He became very thin. After a long time hyena got into a hole, leaving Ntemelua sitting by the entrance. Hyena finally died of hunger, too scared to come out and no one knows what happened to Ntemelua from that time.

Review Questions

i) In what ways could Ntemelua be referred to as an anomaly?

ii) Can you think of narratives with weird creatures in your community?

iii) Compare and contrast the character types of Ntemelua and Konyek.

TRICKSTER AND OTHER ANIMAL STORIES

16. Enkitejo o kulie ng'wesi

Netii apa netii enkitejo, oltome, olasurai, oloikuma olng'ojine neeta pooki emboo oonkishu osirkon tenebo. Niaku keiloikino pooki shoo.

Neisho nabo olong' enkitejo etii oltome shoo neipot nkulie ng'wesi, nepuoi olkiu, nejoki. "Ore amu kaisapuk oltome naa keyoki aimag iyiook aoru iyiook kuna kishu. Eamaing'oru enikingo peyie kiar." Nenyorraa nkulie aajo'ee kiari oltome. Nejokini olasurai metarresho ore ake peyie edol elo olkeju aok enkare neituruk atua enkare paa kianyu aony enkaina.

Neiko neijia olasurai. Neduaya ake oltome elo olkeju nemurut alo aanyu. Neng'amaa enkaina aony. 'Nedung'o oltome tau teine. Neiwuang'a ilo.

Ore peyie eyoki akenyu niaku olkekun lolasurai peyie elo shoo. Neitoki naikitejo aigwenaki nkulie ngwesi ajoki: "Itadua eneikuna olasurai oltome? Ninye taata opi alang'u iyiook pooki naa keyoki aoru iyiook nkishu pooki. Emaing'oru enikingo peyie kiar."

Nejo nkulie pooki: "Ai, ee itisipa!" Neji taa pooki eneikoni ekepuoi aaigwena tenkoshoke oldoinyio paa keishori oloikuma meitaakunoyu kesulari nesulakino olasurai elukunya.

Ore peyie ereu alasurai nkishu ang' neipotokini enkigwana. Ore ake peyie eitiring'a pooki ng'ae nedumunye oloikuma alo enchumata endoinyio anaa oloshi loota esapuk naliki inkulie. Ore kiti leilo oik,ururumunye o metusulakinoyu olasurai elukunya kas! Nedung' tau. Neitoki sii ninye ilo aiwuang'a.

Etaa taa uni ake etung'ayioki, Enkitejo, olng'ojine, oloikuma.

Neyoki naikitejo ajoki nkulie, "maidurra aing'oru enetashaikia" Neidur. Nejoki enkitejo olng'ojine: "are taa amu meidimari oloikuma nimikibaya aikata enikipuo tenikirubare, kainyioo peyie mikiluarie?" Nejoki' olng'ojine: "Itisipa".

Nepuo ake enkitejo olng'ojine omenotito emarti nemiraki nkishu osirkon neilep sii ninche aapuo. Oonaa ninye oloikuma? Neing'uari eekenya ajo ailepaki emarti asuj nkishu. Ina oshi peyie eton ejo oloikuma 'uu', ina marti oshi eton eekenya ajo ailepaki.

Neosh ninye enkitejo olng'ojine enterit aapuo. Nepuo o menyaaki enkitejo aing'oru eneiko tenelej olng'ojine. Nejoki: "Leng'ojin, ore taa amu etaa nkunaang' ake oyie nkishu matoor nikincho nanu nkishu rumai amu kaure nanu tenaar inkishu, niya iyie nkulie. Nejoki olng'ojine:

"Eeyia! ijo nanu peyie aar! Nanu oya irumai niya iyie nkulie." Nenyorraa Enkitejo. Neya ninye nkishu oomowuarak negelaki olng'ojine nkishu rumai, aa isirkon taa.

Nepuo taa pokira eshepari eirritaa ake enkae nkishu enyena neiritaa olikae inenyenak. are nabo olong' nelo enkitejo aleenu enetii enkare tolkeju. Neshukunye ajoki olng'ojine. "Anoto taa ninye ewueji neetii enkare, netii nkoitoi are naapuo ine; Etii enkoitoi naa enterit ake naa keitamodok nkishu teneim, netii enkae oitoi naa esarng'ab ake." Ore eton eitu eidip enkitejo enejo duo leilo olng'ojine omirta sirkon lenyenak olkeju ejoki enkitejo: "Ai, mijo duo materewa nkishu ainei meshomo aamodoku, tuutakaki enkoitoi e sarng'ab." Neimie olng'ojine, sirkon lenyenak enkoitoi natii esarng'ab neonyori pooki. Naa kejo ake awuapu osikiria nedotu olkidong'oe. Nenya ilo. Nejo awuapu olikae nedotunye olkidong'oe, nenyaal sii ilo. Neiko neijia o metaa meetae osikiria hoo obo oota olkidong'oe, netoonyori pooki te sarng'ab. Nebaraki ake ninye enkitejo aitook nkishu enyenak neilepie tolkeju. Neshuko ajoki olng'ojine metung'uai nkishu enyenak tenetalaikine aitayu peyie eng'ar inenyenak neiloikino shoo.

Neikoni neijia enkata naado·. Neeta apa pokira noong'otonye. Ore nabo olong' nejoki enkitejo olng'ojine: "Leng'ojin ore amu ijo meekure edupa yiook endaa maape aasulaa nooyieyio tendikir paa ore enkiti daa nikitum nebaiki iyiook pokira." Nenyorraa olng'ojine. Leilo, nelo aikururumoo ng'otonye tendikir. Nedumunye ninye enkitejo nelo ashetaki ng'otonye enkaji tentim, neisudoo.

Ore nabo olong' nepuo aayieng olkiteng' tembata ene wueji apa neisudorie enkitejo ng'otonye.

Naa kedung' ake enkitejo isunya nenang'aki ine nejo: 'Tim inosa ine neitondol." Nedumu ng'otonye anya. Neiko sii neijia tenedol olng'ojine ejo anya ineepir: "Oi olngarng'arri ilo minya!" Nenang'aki ng'otonye tentim. Neitoti naikiteji ng'otonye o metaraposhoyu.

Ore peyie ekenyu nelo olng'ojine shoo, nelo enkitejo metabarno ng'otonye. Neyela, nekuso. Ore peyie edol olng'ojine teipa neikilikuan ajoki: "Naikitejo ang' kainyioo nikinkuna nji? Nejoki: "Osoit ake atalama naosh katitin isiet natiu nji." Nerik olng'ojine alo autaki enetii osoit neliki eniaas. Neikum ake olng'ojine osoit katitin are neimu enkiti sarge. Neelie ake naikitejo enkiti wueji osoit ereko nejoki: "Idolita ajo etaa peyie etiu anaa nanu'" Neikum ake olng'ojine osoit katitin ong'uan nening" emion oleng' nepalie. Neyiolou ajo eteleja enkitejo.

Neyoki akenyu aa olkekun le nkitejo peyie elo shoo. Nelilita olng'ojine aing'oru ng'otonye enkitejo o menoto, nenya. Neik emuro te kishomi. Ore teipa neimaa enkitejo enetii ng'otonye. Nelau ake nereu nkishu ang'. Oo naa peyie ejo tabaiki kishomi neduaaya enkeju e ng'otonye! Nebuaku aishir. Neishir o metabai aji. Nejoki olng'ojine: "Naikitejo ang' kang'ae nikitaara? Nejoki enkitejo: "Empuyio naainosita." Nejoki olng'ojine: "Shomo naa olale peyie mikintoki anya." Nelo. Nedol olng'ojine ejut ilkiyio neitoki ajoki: "Naikitejo kainyioo sii neton kinosita?" Nejoki enkitejo: "Enkijape nainosita". Neisho olng'ojine olkarasha oitoipore. Neitu ake egira. Nejoki ade olng'ojine: "Ayiolo entoki nikinya, ng'utunyi duo ainosa'"

Netoni. Neing'oru enkitejo eneiko peyie eitalaku olng'ojine. Nejoki nabo olong: "Ekalo taata oloiboni." Nelo ake eneshomo nelotu ajoki olng'ojine:

"Ashomo oloiboni naajoki peyie kinok enkima naid nanu ong'uan eton epuru niid iyie ong'uan teneyupuyup." Neinoki ake enkima neid enkitejo katitin ong'uan eton epuru. Ore peyie eilep olang'at nejoki enkitejo olng'ojine meida. Neid ake olng'ojine katitin ong'uan nedoiki atua. Nejo: "Naikitejo ang' intayioki!" Nejoki enkae: "Eji imbeibeekenyaki'" Neibelibelekenyaki toltarge o metumuta olng'ojine enkima. Neiting'.

16. Hare and Other Animals

There were once Hare, Elephant, Snake, Tortoise and Hyena who owned a herd of cattle and donkeys collectively. They took turns to take them out grazing.

One day when Elephant was out tending the herd, Hare called the rest of the animals together in counsel and said: "Now, since Elephant is very big and might one day cheat us out of our cattle, let us find a way of killing him." The others agreed with her: Elephant must be killed. Snake was instructed to keep watch and if he saw Elephant going to the river to drink, he would go ahead of him and get ready to bite his trunk as he drank water. Snake did as he was bid. As soon as he saw Elephant strutting towards the river, he ran ahead and lay in wait for him. He got hold of his trunk and bit it. Elephant collapsed and died instantly. He was kept out of the way.

The next day it was Snake's turn to tend the herd. Hare called the other animals together again and said: "Did you all see what Snake did to Elephant? He is now the bravest of us all and he will soon take all our cattle for himself. Let us find a way of killing him." The other animals nodded in agreement, and said: "Oh yes, you have indeed spoken the truth." An agreement was reached that a meeting would be held on a hillside, and that Tortoise was to roll down and fall on Snake's head as though by accident.

When Snake brought the cattle home that evening, he was called to the meeting. When everyone was seated, Tortoise went to the top of the hill as one who had something important to tell the others. Within a short time, he was seen rolling down the hillside and falling on Snake's head, *kas!* and killed him. So Snake too was out of the way. There remained only three, Hare, Hyena and Tortoise.

The following day Hare told the others to move homes and search for greener pasture. She said to Hyena: "Since Tortoise is very slow we will never reach our destination if we keep his pace, why don't we leave him behind?" "You have spoken the truth," answered Hyena.

Hare and Hyena continued on their journey until they found a cliff. They drove the cattle together with the donkeys and went on their way. And what happened to poor old Tortoise? He was left behind struggling to climb up the cliff to follow the cattle. That is why Tortoise makes the sound UU; he is still struggling to climb the cliff.

Hare and Hyena continued on their way until the former contrived a way of cheating the latter. She said to him: "Hyena, now that all the cattle belong to just the two of us, let us divide them. You let me take the cows without horns because I'm afraid of being butted with horns and you take the other ones." Hyena replied: "What! You want me to be butted! I will take the ones without horns while you take the other ones." They settled on this, and while Hare took the cattle with horns, Hyena was given the cattle without horns. The latter were the donkeys.

They went on side by side, each herding his/her cattle. One day Hare went to survey for water at the riverbed. She came back and said to Hyena: "I have managed to find a place with water and there are two paths leading to this place. One of them is so dusty that the cattle might go blind if they were driven along it while the other one is only muddy ..." Before Hare could finish what she had to say, Hyena was already driving his donkeys towards the river saying: "I sure don't want my cattle to go blind, direct me to the muddy path!" Hyena drove his donkeys right into the mud where they all got stuck. When he tried to pull the first one out, he broke off its tail. He ate them.

He tried pulling the next one out, but again broke off the tail, which he chewed. This went on until none of Hyena's donkeys had tails, and all were still stuck in the mud. Hare watered her cattle and drove them out of the river. She later went and told Hyena not to worry if he could not pull his cattle out for she would allow him to share hers on condition that he assisted in taking them out to graze.

This went on for a long time. Both were staying with their mothers. One day Hare said to Hyena: "My friend, since food is getting rather scarce, let us go and throw our mothers over the cliff, so that the little we get will be enough for the two of us." Hyena agreed and went off to the cliff over which he thrust his mother. On her part Hare went and built a house in the bush where she hid her mother.

One day, they went to slaughter an ox near the place where Hare had hidden her mother. As they ate the meat, Hare would cut the best bits and throw them to the place where her mother was hidden; she told the bush to eat the "bad" parts. Her mother ate them. When Hyena tried to eat the good parts of the meat, Hare would stop him, saying, "Oh, that is a gland, don't eat it." She would throw the piece to her mother. This way, Hare fed her mother until she was satisfied.

The next morning, as Hyena took the cattle for grazing, Hare remained at home. She had her head shaven, applied ochre to her body, and made herself up.

When Hyena saw this he asked: "Oh, Hare who made you up like that?" Hare told him that she had hit her head against a rock eight times until she had become like that. She offered to take Hyena to the same rock and to instruct him on how to go about it. Hyena thrust his head against the rock twice and a little blood started coming out. Hare smeared a little red ochre over the blood and said: "See, you are just about to become like me!" Hyena continued knocking his head against the rock until he could no longer bear the pain. He suspected foul play.

The next day, it was Hare's turn to take the cattle out grazing. Hyena spent the day looking for Hare's mother, whom he found and ate up. However he took one of her hind legs which he hung up at the gate. In the evening, Hare passed by her mother's hiding place. Not finding her, she took the cattle home. But alas, what met her eyes but her own mother's leg! She burst out crying and did not stop sobbing even when she had entered the house. When Hyena asked her why she was crying, Hare replied that smoke was hurting her eyes. She was told to go into the calf-pen where it was not smoky. This she did, yet she did not stop crying. When asked for the second time why she was still crying, she said she was feeling cold. Hyena gave her a sheet to wrap herself in, but she still did not stop crying. Eventually Hyena blurted out his secret: "I know why you are crying, I ate your mother!"

As time went on, Hare thought of a way to avenge her mother, One morning, she said to him: 'Today I am going to the diviner." She went wherever she went, and on her return she said to Hyena: "I have been to the diviner who said that we should light a big fire which I should jump over four times when it is still smoking and you should do the same when it starts burning." This they agreed to do, Hare did her part of the jumping whilst the fire was still smoking and told Hyena to jump when it was in flames. Hyena jumped over the flames three times, and on the fourth time, he plunged into the it, writhing in pain, he begged Hare to rescue him from the fire, but Hare turned him over and over with a rake saying: "Did you ask me to turn you over!" And that is the end.

Review Questions

i) Hare has been named "The utterer" or "the one who speaks". How apt is this description with regard to the role she plays in this story?

ii) Hare has ingeniously duped all the animals in this story. Describe the way she succeeds in doing so, and give your own opinion on whether or not this trickery was deserved in each case.

iii) What is the theme of this narrative?

17. Oltome o Enkitejo

Netii apa, netii kulo tomia. Neyoki aapuo erutore aarutu enaisho naya enkang' enkaputi, Ore epuoito nejo matalang' oreyiet neinepu enkitejo. Nejoki enkitejo obo Ie siadi, "Mpapa intalang'aki ele reyiet." Nejoki oltome, "Takedoki naa enkoriong.'"

85

Neked enkitejo enkoriong' oltome. Nedol Naikitejo ilbenia oobore enaisho oolotorok tenkoriong' oladuo tome. Neiteru anya ena aisho; ore peyie emut tolbene obo nejoki ele tome, "Mpapa nchooki sii iyie osoit laiguranie." Neisho oltome. Neitadoiki oladuo bene lemeekure etii toki. Neitoki anya enaisho natii olikae bene. Ore ake peyie emut nejoki oltome, "Mpapa nchooki taa ake yie likae soit lanang'ie enda motonyi amu etadoyie oladoi." Neisho oltome. Neton taa aiko neijia aomonu isoito oonang'ie motonyi nelej oltome ajoki imotonyi enang'ie omeiputa isoito ilbenia pokira aare. Ore ake peyie edol ajo etaa kebaya iltomia enkang' duo napuo nejoki enkitejo oltome, "Mpapa, ntadowuoki taa amu atabawua." Nelo ninye enkitejo. Nejo oltome taleenoi ilbenia nenyorriki aa isoito ake ootii. Nejoki ilkulikae, "Uui, etumuta enkitejo inaishi ainei'" Nejo kinkonji aatalisho neduaya enkitejo elo teidie. Nemir aajo mainepu. Nejo mbung'a nepaashare enkitejo nejing' enkumoto. Neitoki ake ajo mbung'a neibung' enkidong'oe neidoso, neibung' enkeju. Nejoki enkitejo, "Hae oloibung'a entonai ejo nanu!" Neing'ueiki, neng'amaa entonai. Nejo enkitejo, "Oi mpapa kitigila enkeju!" Ore eerare oltome entonai ayietu ejo kenkeju enkitejo nepurjukare ninye enkitejo aipang' alo. Naidosu oltome entonai nenyorriki naa mme enkeju enkitejo. Ore kiti neduaya enkitejo elo eid inkeek. Nemir ajo ainepu.

Nekwet enkitejo nelo ainepu ilchekuti. Nejoki, "Loshekuti kulo, idolitata elde tome okwetu tende?" "Esika amu ntae elotu aar." Neisardak ilchekuti aaim inkaloli pooki. Ore peyie eduaya oltome ilchekuti ekwet nejo tenaa kenkitejo emirta. Nemir omeinepu embata, neikilikuan ajoki, "Loshekuti kulo, itadua ake enkitejo naidoso kidong'oe naima ene?" Nejoki ilchekuti, "Itapaashare eima idia ae alo." Ore emirta oltome ilchekuti netum ninye naikitejo oloigute nerrinyo alo idia alo duo naing'ua.

Nekwet taa ake naikitejo o meshomo ainepu intasati naaripisho tiauluo. Nejoki, "Nooyieyio kuna naaripisho, idolitata lido tome okwetu teidie enyeito amu intae elotu aar." Neinyiototo intasati aing'ua eripare nesar inkajijik. Ore peyie einepu oltome nejoki, "Natomonok kuna, koree ake enkitejo naidoso kidong'oe naima ene?" Nejoki intasati, "Neidia naima idie."

Neina enkitejo, nekwet nelo ainepu inkoiliin naadaa. Nejoki, "Nooiliin kuna, esika amu intae elotu lido tome aar." Neidiyiadiy inkoilii. Neipirri aapuo. Neinepu oltome nejoki, "Nooiliin kuna, itadua ake enkitejo naidoso kidong'oe naima ene?" Neutaa inkoiliin oltome metusuja enkitojo.

Neina naikitejo, nelo ainepu inkulie kitejon nejoki, "Nakitejon kuna, idolitata elde tome okwetu tende? Endoso pooki inkidong'o amu inkitejon nemeidoso kidong'o elotu aing'oru." Neidos inaduo kitejon pooki inkidong'o. Ore ake peyie eidos nebau oltome. Neikilikuan ajoki, "Nakitejon kuna,'itadua ake enkitejo naidoso kidong'oe naima ene?" Nejoki inkitejon, "Emidol ajo keidoso iyiook pooki?" Neikonji inkitejon pooki aitodol oltome inkidong'o amu kejo ninche anaa kembae sidai etaasa metaa meekure ear oltome.

Neisirng' ang'a oltome. Nejo ng'ura kuna kitejon nedol ajo keidoso pooki inkidol)g'o neyiolou ajo eeseka enkitejo. Nelau oltome enkitejo naar o enapal anaa kenyaanyuk pooki. Neishunye enkatini eba neijia.

17. Elephant and Hare

There was once a herd of elephants who went to gather honey to take to their in-laws. As they were walking along, they came upon Hare who was just about to cross the river. She said to one of them: "Father, please help me get across the river." The elephant agreed to this request and said to Hare: "You may jump on to my back." As Hare sat on the elephant's back, she was quick to notice the two bags full of honey that the elephant was carrying. She started eating honey from one of the bags, and when she had eaten it all, she called out to Elephant saying: "Father, please hand me a stone to play with." When she was given the stone, she put it in the now empty bag of honey, and started eating the honey from the second bag. When she had eaten it all, she again requested another stone saying: "Father, please hand me another stone for the one you gave me has dropped, and I want to throw it at the birds." Elephant handed her another stone, and then another, as she kept asking for stones on the pretext that she was throwing them at the birds, until she had filled both bags with stones.

When Hare realised that the elephants were about to arrive at their destination, she said to the elephant who was carrying her: "Father, I have now arrived, please let me down." So Hare went on her way. Soon afterwards, the elephant looked at his bags, only to realise that they were full of stones! He exclaimed to the others: "Oh my goodness! Hare has finished all my honey!" They lifted up their eyes and saw Hare leaping away at a distance; they set off after her. They caught up with Hare within no time, but as the elephants were about to grab her, she disappeared into a hole. But the elephant managed to catch hold of her tail, at which time the skin from the tail got peeled off. Elephant next grabbed her by the leg. Hare laughed at this loudly, saying: "Oh! You have held a root mistaking it for my leg!" Thereupon Elephant let go of Hare's leg and instead got hold of a root. Hare shrieked from within and said, "Oh father, you have broken my leg!" As Elephant was struggling with the root, Hare manoeuvred her way out and ran as fast as her legs could carry her. Elephant had by this time managed to pull out the root only to realise that it was not Hare's leg. Once more he lifted up his eyes and saw Hare leaping and jumping over bushes in a bid to escape. Elephant ran in pursuit of her once more.

As Hare continued running, she came across some herdsmen and said to them: "Hey you, herdsmen, do you see that elephant from yonder, you had better run away, for he is coming after you." The herdsmen scampered and went their separate ways. When Elephant saw the herdsmen running, he thought they were running after Hare; so he too ran after them. When he caught up with them, he said: "Hey you, herdsmen, have you seen a hare with a skinned tail passing along here?" The herdsmen answered: "You have passed her along the way as she was going in the opposite direction." While Elephant had been chasing the herdsmen, Hare had gained some time to run in the opposite direction.

Next, Hare came upon some women who were sewing outside the homestead and said to them: "Hey, you mothers who are sewing, do you see that elephant from yonder, you had better run away for he is coming after you." On hearing this, the women scampered for the safety of their houses immediately. But soon the elephant caught up with them and asked: "Hey you, respectable ladies, might you have seen a hare with a skinned tail going towards this direction?" The women answered: "There she goes over there."

Hare kept running and this time she came upon antelopes grazing and she said to them: "Hey you, antelopes, you had better run away for that elephant is coming after you." The antelopes were startled and they ran away as fast as their legs could carry them. But soon the elephant was upon them, and he asked them, "Hey you, antelopes, have you seen a hare with a skinned tail going in this direction?" They pointed out the direction that Hare had followed to him.

Still on the run, Hare next came upon a group of other hares, to whom she said: "Hey you, hares, do you see that elephant coming from yonder? You should all skin your tails for he is after those hares with unskinned tails." There upon all the hares quickly skinned their tails. At the same moment the elephant arrived and asked them: "Hey you, hares, have you seen a hare with a skinned tail going towards this direction?" The hares replied: "Don't you see that all our tails are skinned?" As the hares said this, they were displaying their tails confident it would please Elephant. On noticing that all the hares' tails were skinned, Elephant realized that Hare had played a trick on him. Elephant could not find the culprit, for all the hares were alike. And there ends the story.

Review Questions

i) "Brain is superior to brawn". Discuss this statement with reference to this story, the one below and any other appropriate examples in these narratives.

ii) Can you relate a trickster tale from your community?

18. Eng'atuny o Esidai

Netii apa, netii ena ng'atuny o esidai. Neisho nabo kata aairiamaki. Ore toonkuti olong'i nenya nkera eng'atuny ilpepedo. Nelo olng'atuny aikonyaa nkera esidai neitu ninche enya ilpepedo. Nelau esidai enias amu meitieu olng'atuny. Niany inkera eng'atuny, neing'uari mewaita olameyu. Nerik ninye eng'atuny ink era esidai nelo.

Neton esidai aisinanuo. Neton adamisho. Nedumunye ake nelo aishiru nkulie ng'uesi. Naa keriku ake eng'ues nariku nejo ineng'atuny inkuoo. Neruk ing'uesi muj nelau enagol kutuk najo inesidai inkuoo. Ina taa peyie eiposha esidai o meeu atum karbobo.

Neinosaki taa esidai karbobo enetaasa olng'atuny. Ore ake peyie ening' karbobo nejoki esidai, "Shomo peyie iitu metabaiki." Nelo esidai. Nedumunye karbobo alo aing'oru olkiu oodo oota inkutukie are. Ore peyie eitu esidai anaa metabaiki nejoki, "Shomo eneje taleenu olkiu oodo oudo empolos toriku ng'uesi pooki peyie kiponu aiguena."

Ore peyie ebau enkolong' enkiguena neiturrur esidai ing'uesi pooki nerik olapa kiu oodo oota inkumot are: Neiguenae taa. Naa ore eng'ues pooki nainyiototo nejo "ineng'atuny inkuoo," amu keure pooki eng'atuny. Ore peyie ebau enkata e karbobo nedumunye aitashe nejo: "lishutua?" Nejo nkulie, "Ee." Nejo, "Ore taa amu kara dorrop tenaitashe tempolo intae nimining'ining'i enajo, enchooki matakedo ele kiu peyie alo sii nanu aliki ntae inainei." Nejo nkulie ng'uesi, "Ai etisipa, etisipa."

Naa keisho ake eng'atuny peyie einyiototo eng'ues naba anaa enainyiototo neikurrukur ejo peyie eiture ing'uesi peyie mepuku aajo inesidai inkuoo. Neureishoyu naa ng'uesi pooki.

Nejo karbobo: "Ore taa, kegol kuna baa. Amaa, keetae eniopir naiu enepapit?" Nejo olkiu pooki, "A-ah!" "Keetae enepapit naiu eniopir?" Neji. "A-ah'" Neitadoyio karbobo oltau, nejo, "Ore naa, musi indaai amu ine sidai inkuoo!" Nejo ninye nyul! adoiki enaduo kumoto. Nejo sii ninye eng'atuny tiam! ajo aitiamaki karbobo aibung' olgos. Nelo ninye karbobo aipang'u tenaduo nkae kumot nelo. Neton eng'atuny arrip enaduo kumoto ejo keimu karbobo omeewa olameyu. Ore peyie eye nelotu ninye karbobo aitiamie eng'atuny enkuram oloikulu etua apa toonkaun. Neiting' ina atini ai eba neijia. Niaku ina oshi peyie eetae endung'et e rashe najo, "Meitemenayu esidai ilopir lenyenak.

18. The Lioness and the Ostrich Chicks

There once lived a lioness and an ostrich, who gave birth to young ones at the same time. After a few days, the lioness' cubs were attacked by scabies and she decided to go and snatch the ostrich's chicks who were healthy. The latter did not know what to do, for she was afraid of the lioness. Not wishing to exchange her chicks with the cubs, she left them alone, and they died from hunger. The lioness took the chicks and went her way.

The ostrich was troubled. She thought of a plan that would aid her in recovering her young ones. She set off in search of other animals to help her, but whoever she sought support from said: "The chicks belong to the lioness." She went to all the animals, but none was brave enough to say: 'The chicks belong to the ostrich." The ostrich, nonetheless, continued to search and search, until she came across the mongoose.

The ostrich repeated the story of the wrongs done to her by the lioness to the mongoose. When the latter had heard the story, he said to the ostrich: "Go and come back tomorrow." As soon as the ostrich left, the mongoose went in search of a tall anthill with two outlets.

The next day, when the ostrich returned to him, he said to her: "Go to such and such a place and you will find a tall anthill with a hole at the tip and gather all the animals there so that we can hold a meeting."

When the day for the meeting arrived, the ostrich gathered all the animals and took them to the tall anthill with two outlets. The meeting was soon convened. Each animal stood up to speak. And each time an animal arose to speak, the lioness roared so as to scare him and prevent him from saying that the chicks belong to the ostrich. Each of them was scared. Since they were all scared of the lioness, each of them said: 'The chicks belong to the lioness." When all the others had had their turn to speak, Mongoose's turn came. He rose up and said: "Have you finished what you had to say?" The others answered in unision: "Yes, we have." "Now, since I am rather short and if I stand at your midst you will not hear what I have to say, let me climb this anthill so that I too may speak my mind," continued Mongoose. "You have indeed spoken the truth," the others consented.

"These matters are rather difficult," spoke the Mongoose. "Is there a feathered one that begets a hairy one?" The congregation answered, "No." "Is there a hairy one that begets a feathered one?" continued the mongoose. Again the congregation answered in the negative. The mongoose took a deep sigh before his final submission, whereupon he said: "Then you may all disperse for the chicks belong to the ostrich!" As he uttered these final words, he quickly disappeared into the hole on top of the anthill, through the other end, and got away. The lioness tried to pounce on him but she was too late. She sat at the entrance to keep watch for the mongoose until she died of hunger. Whereupon the mongoose went to play the bouncing game on her brisket and the ostrich got her chicks back. From this story there originates the saying: "The ostrich cannot be deprived of her feathers." The end.

Review Questions

i) The mongoose is portrayed as a sage in this narrative. What qualities of his character can you identify to support this remark?

ii) Comment on the narrative style of this story.

iii) What is the moral of this story?

19. Enkltejo o Enkoilii

Netii apa, netii ena kitejo. Ore nabo olong' eloolo tosero nedumu embae. Ore errinyo alo ang' neinepu iltorrobo ooyieng'isho. Nejoki, "Lotorrobo kulo, enchooki enkiring'o peyie aisho ntae entoki natii ene." Nejoki iltorrobo, "Kainyioo ina?" Nejoki enkitejo, "Embae ai naishoo enkai." Neishori naikitejo esunyai neishooyo sii ninye embae aisho iltorrobo. Nenap enkitejo enaduo sunyai nelo.

Ore eloolo neito atum ilmurran oonyaita olmuny nemeeta esunyai napiore. Nejoki, "Lomurran kulo, enchooki esaei peyie aisho ntae esunyai nipiorere." Neisho ilmurran emporroi neisho ninye enaduo sunyai. Ore peyie eidip enkinyiang'a nelo ninye naikitejo. Neito ainepu enkoilii. Nejoki, "Koilii, ing'ura sii iyie ena porroi ai." Nejoki enkoilii, "Kang'ae nikinchoo?" Nejoki enkitejo, "Ilmurran lang' laishoo?" Neikilikuan enkoilii ajoki, "Ilmurran linchoo nyoo?" Nejoki enkitejo, "Esunyai ai aishoo." Neitoki ake enkoilii aikilikuan, "Esunyai nikinchoo nyoo?" Nejoki enkitejo, "Iltorrobo laishoo." Nejoki enkoilii, "Iltorrobo linchoo nyoo?" Nejoki enkitejo, "Embae ai naishoo enkai ai." Neing'or ake enkoilii ena porroi enkitejo nedol ajo keisidai oleng' nejoki, "Nchooki siyie matetemakinoyu." Neisho. Ore ake peyie epika enkoilii emporroi nejoki enkitejo, "Naikitejo kaanare?" Nejoki, "Ee pae kinare oleng'." Ina taa oshi peyie ejo enkoilii pirkash. Nemir enkitejo nelaikino ainepu.

Ore ake peyie elo enkitejo, neinepu iltorrobo. Nejoki, "Lotorrobo kulo, entang'or ena koilii." Neikilikuan iitorrobo, "Enkoilii nataasa aa?" Nejoki enkitejo, "Enkoilii naawa emporroi ai, emporroi ai naishoo ilmurran lang', ilmurran lang' laishoo esunyai ai, esunyai ai naishoo oltorrobo lang', iltorrobo lang' laishoo embae ai, embae ai naishoo enkai ai." Nejoki iitorrobo, "Miking'or."

Neitoki enkitejo alo neinepu enkima nayupuyup. Nejoki, "Nakima, inosa kulo torrobo." Nejoki enkima, "Iltorrobo ootaasa aa?" Nejoki, "Iltorrobo ootanyaita eng'or enkoilii." Nejoki enkima, "Enkoilii nataasa aa?" Nejoki, "Enkoilii naawa emporroi ai, emporroi ai naishoo ilmurra lang', ilmurran lang' laishoo esunyai ai, esunyai ai naishoo iltorrobo lang' iltorrobo lang' laishoo embae ai, embae ai naishoo enkai ai." Nejoki enkima, "Manya."

Neing'ua enkitejo enkima. Neitoki alo ainepu enkare. Nejoki, "Naare, taara ena kima." Neikilikuan enkare ajoki, "Enkima nataasa aa?" Neliki enkitejo inaduo pooki naatiaka enkima. Ore peyie ening' enkima nejoki, "Maar." Negiroo enkitejo. Neito alo ainepu iltomia. Nejoki, "Lotomia kulo, entook ena are." Nejoiki iltomia, "Enkare nataasa aa?" Nejoki enkitejo, "Enkare natanya ear enkima, enkima natanya enya iltorrobo, iltorrobo ootanyaita eng'or enkoilii, enkoilii naawa emporroi ai, emporroi ai naishoo ilmurran lang', ilmurran lang' laishoo esunyai ai, esunyai ai naishoo iltorrobo lang' iltorrobo lang' laishoo embae ai, embae ai naishoo enkai ai." Nejoki iltomia, "Mikiok."

Nelo naikitejo, neitoki ainepu ilkeek, nejoki: "Lokeek kulo, enturokinoto kuldo tomia." Nejoki ilkeek, "Iltomia ootaasa aa?" Nejoki, "Iltomia ootanyaita eok enkare, enkare natanya ear enkima, enkima natanya enya iltorrobo, iltorrobo ootanyaita eng'or enkoilii, enkoilii naawa emporroi ai, emporroi ai naishoo ilmurran lang', ilmurran lang' laishoo esunyai ai, esunyai ai naishoo iltorrobo lang', iltorrobo lang' laishoo embae ai, embae ai naishoo enkai ai." Ore ake peyie ening' ilkeek enejo naikitejo nejoki: "Mikiurokino iltomia." Negiroo naikitejo neitoki alo ainepu oriri. Nejoki, "Loriri kulo, enturoi kulo keek." Neikilikuan oriri aajoki, "Ilkeek ootaasa aa?" Neliki enkitejo inaduo pooki naatolikio inkulie. Neitoki sii ninche oriri aany euroo ilkeek. Negoro enkitejo oleng' kake eitu eiturraa osiligi.

Neitoki ake alo neinepu isirkon. Nejoki, "Losirkon kulo, entunyo kulo riri". Nejoki, "Oriri ootaasa aa?" Neitoki ake enkitejo ainosaki isirkon inaduo pooki nainosaka inkulie. Ore ake peyie ening' isirkon enetaasa araki eneitu eas 'oriri nejo sii ninche "Mikiintuny."

Negoro taa naikitejo oleng' nenaura sii eloolo ade. Neitoki ake alo, neinepu ilng'ojinia. Nejoki, "Long'ojinia kulo, enosa kulo sirkon." Nejoki ilng'ojinia, "Isirkon ootaasa aa?" Nejoki enkitejo, "Isirkon ootanyaita eituny oriri, oriri otanyai enya ilkeek, ilkeek ootanyaita eurokino iltomia, iltomia ootanyaita eok enkare, enkare natanya ear enkima, enkima natanya enya iltorrobo, iltorrobo ootanyaita eng'or enkoilii, enkoilii naawa emporroi ai, emporroi ai naishoo ilmurran lang,' ilmurran lang' laishoo esunyai ai, esunyai naaishoo naaishoo iltorrobo lang', iltorrobo lang' laishoo embae ai, embae ai naishoo enkai ai." Nejoki ilng'ojinia, "Aikinya."

Ore pee edol isirkon ajo etaa kenyae nejo, "Aikiintuny oriri." Nejo oriri, "Aikiuroo ilkeek." Nejo ilkeek, "Aikiurokino iltomia." Nejo iltomia, "Aikiok enkare." Nejo enkare, "Kaar enkima." Nejo enkima, "Kanya iltorrobo." Nejo iltorrobo, "Aiking'or enkoilii." Nejo enkoilii, "Kashuku emporroi e naikitejo." Neishori naiketejo emporroi enye. Neshipayu oleng'. Neiting' enkatini ai eba neijia.

19. Hare and Antelope

There once lived a Hare who, one day, as she was sauntering about in the bush, found an arrow which she picked up. On her way back home, she came upon a group of hunters who were skinning an animal they had killed, and she said to them: "If you give me a fat piece of meat I will give you something nice in exchange." The hunters asked: "And what could that be?" Hare replied: "It is an arrow head given to me by God." Hare was given a fat piece of meat in exchange for the arrowhead. She bid the hunters goodbye and went on her way.

Next, she came upon warriors who were applying ochre on their bodies, and realising they had no fat, she said to them: "Hey you warriors, if you give me a necklace, I will give you a fat piece of meat that you could use as fat." The warriors consented and gave her a necklace in exchange for the fat piece of meat. When the exchange was finalised, Hare took leave of the warriors and continued on her way.

Next, she came upon Antelope to whom she said: "Look at my necklace." On enquiring where she had got it, Hare replied: "It is my friends the warriors who gave it to me, the warriors to whom I gave my meat, the meat that the hunters gave me, the hunters to whom I gave my arrow, my arrow which my god gave me." Antelope looked at Hare's necklace admiringly, and said to her: "May I please try it on?" On wearing the necklace Antelope sought the opinion of her friend by asking: "Does it suit me?" To this Hare innocently replied: "It suits you perfectly well." Thereupon Antelope ran as fast as her legs could carry her, running away with Hare's necklace. After trying to pursue Antelope, Hare soon realised that she would never catch up with her, and so gave up the chase.

Walking away sorrowfully, Hare soon came upon another group of hunters and said to them: "Hey you hunters, please shoot that antelope for me."

To this the hunters asked: "What is she guilty of?" Hare replied: "She took away my necklace, my necklace that the warriors gave me, the warriors to whom I gave my meat, my meat that the hunters gave me, the hunters to whom I gave my arrow, my arrow that my god gave me." After hearing of Hare's complaint, the hunters declined to shoot Antelope.

Taking leave of the hunters, Hare next came across a burning fire, to whom she said: "Hey you fire, could you please eat those hunters?" Fire asked, "What have they done?" Hare replied: "They refused to shoot Antelope, Antelope who took my necklace, my necklace that the warriors gave me, the warriors to whom I gave my arrow, my arrow that my god gave me." Again, on hearing Hare's complaint, Fire too said: "I will not eat the hunters."

Hare next came upon Water and said to it: "Hey you water, could you please put out that fire?" Water asked, "What has Fire done?" Hare repeated to Water all that she had told Fire. Water on listening to Hare's complaint declined to do as she was bid. Hare left Water feeling disappointed. Soon she found a herd of elephants, to whom she spoke thus: "Hey you elephants, could you please drink that water." On enquiring why Water had to be drunk, Hare replied: "Water refused to put out Fire, Fire who refused to eat the hunters, the hunters that declined to shoot Antelope, Antelope who took away my necklace, my necklace that the warriors gave me, the warriors to whom I gave my meat, my meat that the hunters gave me, the hunters to whom I gave my arrow, my arrow that my god gave me." On hearing Hare's story, the elephants, too, declined to carry out Hare's request as all the others had done.

Undaunted by her inability to convince anyone to take action on her behalf so far, Hare moved on, next coming upon trees to whom she spoke, saying: "Hey you trees, could you please fall on those elephants?"

On enquiring the wrong committed by the elephants, Hare replied: "They refused to drink Water, Water that refused to put out Fire, Fire that refused to eat the hunters, the hunters that declined to shoot Antelope, Antelope that took away my necklace, my necklace that the warriors gave me, the warriors to whom I gave my meat,my meat that the hunters gave me, the hunters to whom I gave my arrow, my arrow that my god gave me." When the trees had heard Hare's story, they too said, "We will not fall on the elephants." Hare then left the trees and came upon termites whom she asked to fell the trees. The termites demanded to know the wrong committed by the trees. Hare told termites of how the trees had refused to fall on the elephants and went on enumerating what everyone else had done or refused to do in the same way she had told the others. The termites also declined to carry out Hare's request. The refusal by the termites to fell the trees upset Hare, but she was by no means daunted.

Moving on with persistence, Hare soon came upon some donkeys whom she asked to trample on the termites. On learning what the termites had done, the donkeys too declined to trample on then.

By this time Hare was beginning to feel exasperated and weary, having walked all day with no success. It was not long before she came upon a group of hyenas, to whom she said: "Hey you hyenas, could you please eat those donkeys?" The hyenas asked: "What have the donkeys done?" Hare replied, "They refused to trample on the termites, the termites which refused to fell the trees, the trees that refused to fall on the elephants, the elephants who refused to drink Water, Water who refused to put out Fire, Fire who refused to eat the hunters, the hunters who declined to shoot Antelope, Antelope who took away my necklace, the necklace that the warriors gave me, the warriors to whom I gave my meat, my meat that the hunters gave me, the hunters to whom I gave my arrow, my arrow that God gave me."

Finally agreeing to carry out Hare's request, the hyenas said: "Very well, we will eat the donkeys."

On the realisation that they were about to be eaten, the donkeys said: "We will trample on the termites." The termites said: "We will fell the trees." The trees said: "We will fall on the elephants." The elephants said: "We will drink Water." Water said: "I will put out Fire." Fire said: "I will eat the hunters." The hunters said: "We will shoot Antelope." Antelope said: "I will return Hare's necklace." So Hare was given back her necklace, and she was very happy. My story ends like that.

Review Questions

i) Can you identify instances in which personification is used in this narrative?

ii) Explain how Hare found herself in a predicament.

iii) "Hyena's presence in this story was indispensable for the attainment of justice." Discuss this statement in the light of what you know about Hyena's personality.

20. Entito e Tiyiogo

Netii apa ena tito sidai oleng' niaku keyieu pooki ng'ae neya. Neisho ena tito nelrrlWaa olkilikuai ajo ore pooki ng'ae oyieu neya nelo metishila entito. Negeluni enkolong' napuoi enkesha. Nepuo taa ng'uesi pooki naaing'oru oshi ena tito. Naa naikitejo naituruk. Nekuso ake nelo, paa kerany ajo:

> Natito e Tiyiogo
>
> Tupuku ng'uraki
>
> Enaten orinka
>
> Nemeinepu ilayiok

Ore pee ening' entito nepuku ake ainining' nerany sii ninye ajo:

> "Maayieu nanu iyie
>
> Entito e Tiyiogo
>
> Naikodo enkang' enye
>
> Nepiki imporro nkaik
>
> Nepiki intuyutia
>
> Maayieu x 2"

Neitoki enkopera alotu, nejo sii ninye:

"Natito e Tiyiogo

Tupuku ng'uraki

Enkoilii napera

Terishat ang'itie."

Neitoki ake entito ajoki enkoilii, "Maayieu, Maayieu", tosinkolio. Nelotu oloitiko nerany ajo:

"Natito e Tiyiogo

Tupuku ng'uraki

Oloitiko on kuyiana

Inkuyianat e long'o

Oitiko oyiogiyiog

Nkiyigot olmurran."

Neranyaki entito ajoki maayieu, maayieu. Nelotu olng'atuny.

"Natito e Tiyiogo

Tupuku ng'uraki

Oloipurro telerai

Nedotu ntana enkop

Pooki o nkutiti."

Niany entito olng'atuny. Nelotu olng'ojine etukuse sii ninye nerany ajo:

"Natito e Tiyiogo

Tupuku ng'uraki

Leuu ng'ojine

Nimijo eing'ojine

Ilpisia meidimu

Le Iikae apa otua

Otara torinka

Karurum iloik

Terishat ang'itie

Nimijo esulare

Amu keon eitagol

Olmurrani tenkolong!"

Netoki ake entito aany sii ninye leng'ojin. Neitu emuny eyieu sii ninye netil entito.
Nerany ajo:

"Natito e Tiyiogo

Tupuku ng'uraki

Enkaiserri olmunoti

Namiru ilchekuti

Kilome meitadiak

Oritet olmoruo

Nelo enkumpau enkop

Neipirrar emakat."

Niaraa entito emuny ajoki maayieu. Nerukunye taa ake ing'uesi. Neitu enkiteng', nerany ajo:

Natito e Tiyiogo

Tupuku ng'uraki

Pararang' eibala

Nalepi tosiang'au

Nelo olaburra enkop

Nesaru ilchekuti

Pooki o ng'aturan."

Neing'or ake entito enkiteng' nerany ajo:

"Maayieu nanu iyie

Entito e Tiyiogo

Naikodo enkang' enye

Nepiki intuyutia

Nepiki imporro nkaik

Maayieu x 2"

Nerukunye taa ake ing'uesi eponu ake aakesha niany entito pooki. Ore te siadi tukul nelotu Karbobo. Nerany sii ninye ajo:

Natito e Tiyiogo

Tupuku ng'uraki

Lentore e Topisia

Nemeidimu sirkon

Olopeny ake onap."

Nening' ake entito enetejo Karbobo nerany sii ninye ajoki:

> Kaayieu nanu iyie
>
> Entito e Tiyiogo
>
> Naikodo enkang' enye
>
> Nepiki intuyutia
>
> Nepiki imporro nkaik
>
> Kaayieu, Kaayieu.
>
> Neya Karbobo entito.

20. Daughter of Tiyiogo

There once lived a girl who was so beautiful that everyone admired her. So when she learnt of everyone's admiration, she sent a message that all those who wished to have her should present themselves to her, each giving an account of his or her talents. A date was set for a special parade where all admirers would appear.

Hare was the first to arrive, dressed in the finest attire for the big day. He sang to the girl, and his song went like this:

> *Daughter of Tiyiogo*
>
> *Come out and look at me*
>
> *The one with a swift club*
>
> *So swift that boys cannot catch*

On hearing Hare's song, the girl also replied in song saying:

> *I do not want you*
>
> *I daughter of Tiyiogo*
>
> *Whose family has adorned her*
>
> *Adorned her with brass coils*
>
> *Adorned her with beads*
>
> *I do not want you*
>
> *I do not want you.*

Next came Antelope, singing his own praises, saying:

> *Daughter of Tiyiogo*

Emerge and look at me

I am Antelope the fast runner

And I leap between homesteads.

On listening to Antelope's account of himself, the girl replied in song, telling him that she had no desire for him. Next came Zebra with his beautifully decorated body. He sang to the girl and this is how his song went:

Daughter of Tiyiogo

Come out and look at me

Zebra with fine patterns

Patterns like the shields

Zebra with hiccoughs

The hiccoughs of the warriors.*

The girl once more sang to Zebra, dismissing him as she had done the others. The next to arrive was Lion, who followed suit, singing his own praises:

Daughter of Tiyiogo

Come out and look at me

The one who roared at Elerai

Uprooting roots from the earth

The big and the small.

The girl refused Lion, who was immediately followed by Hyena in his best, ready to present his feats in a praise song:

Daughter of Tiyiogo

Come out and look at me

Hyena the limper

Though none can notice it

He's only overweighed by chains

Chains of the dead one

The one he killed with a club

But think not of it as shameful
For, by munching
The warrior builds up strength.

Turning down the limping one, the girl was next approached by Rhinoceros; he too hoped to win her. He sang:

Daughter of Tiyiogo
Come out and look at me
The horned one of the Laiser clan **
The one who chases shepherds home
And with his horn he never ever misses
The thigh of the old man
When his tobacco falls to the ground
And up flies his soda ash. ***

Rejecting Rhinoceros, the girl sang to him, saying: "I do not want you, I do not want you."

The animals continued tripping along one after the other. Cow also came along singing her praises:

Daughter of Tiyiogo
Come out and observe me
The obviously loud one
The one milked with esiang'au ****
And the milk lather flows down
Rescuing shepherds
As well as infants

The girl, looking at Cow, sang the same song, dismissing her as she had done the others. So the animals continued parading and relating their feats and talents. But the girl did not feel impressed by any of them.

At the very end, there came Mongoose, and he too sang his praises the way the others had done. His song went like this:

Daughter of Tiyiogo
Come out and look at me
The one with a chain belt
One that overweighs donkeys
It is the owner alone who can carry it.

On hearing what Mongoose said the girl responded by singing:

I do want you
I the daughter of Tiyiogo
Whose family has adorned her
Adorned her with brass coils
Adorned her with beads
I want you
I want you.

So Mongoose took the girl.

*Refers to the noises made by the warriors when they are having fits especially during the major rites of passage.

**Refers to one of the Maasai clans. Some animals are said to display characteristics of certain members of the society. Characteristics which are evidently common among clans. The rhinoceros is said to be quick tempered and so are the members of the Laiser clan, and vice versa.

***Tobacco is chewed with soda ash.

****A wide-mouthed gourd.

Review Questions

i) Consider the praises of all the animals and choose one that you think describes the composer most appropriately. Give reasons.

ii) Identify some metaphors in these praises.

iii) How did Mongoose succeed in winning the girl's hand?

iv) Does this story have a moral?

21. Olng'ojine o enkiteng'

Netii apa neimin enkiteng'. Nepuo nkolong'i uni enkop etii ake ang'ata. Ore tenkolong' e uni nelo olkeju aing'oru enkare naok. Neinepu olng'ojine nerany ajoki:

"Aasai Ie uu enkiteng' nalepo

Enkolong' e uni ena eitu aokisho (airraga ang'ata)

Naar enkure olapa Ie ntung'us."

Neranyaki olng'ojine ajoki:

"Meekure ebaiki maimanya Ie munchu

Aang'as amurut aitaar entirbo

Naaitoki aidosu iigisoyia Ie nyewa

Naaitoki aijurum olendia napong'a

Meeta elimoto nemeish eewuo

Eisha kinosa Ole Wuargas onyokie

Obatat oltuala ole polos kimirta

Kimirta, kimirta!

Kainyioo naning'o tenda tim ejo kau!

Murunya nkiyiaa oitalala endaata

Olonapu ndaiki meturua enapita

Nemeng'arie entolut naitaa ng'otonye

Nelotu nerrorro tembata emoyoo

Netukuny tenkutuk entanun natong'ua

Neyieyio nashomo nkang'itie e eiking'a

Nkarra olpaashie intebebek kidamu

Idamu Ole minyi otiooyo tiauluo

Intaa enkikarret embibi natoyio

Naiwuang'ie tolng'ejep naimu oloing'oni

Meraposh leng'ojin enkiteng' nalepo

Enjipati olalae intare tikitam

Pukoret nashirraki olkiteng' loltuaia.

Hoe hoo maimanya Ie munchu!

Ore ake peyie eidip olng'ojine ataranyaki enkiteng, neimanya, nekweniki, nenya. Neiting'.

21. Hyena and Cow

Once upon a time, a certain cow strayed and could not find her way home. Three days passed before she was found. On the third day, she went to the river for a drink of water. At the river, she came upon Hyena to whom she sang:

> *I beg you please Ie uu**
> *I am the cow with a suckling calf*
> *This is my third day without a drink*
> *And the December sun has made me thirsty.*

Hyena answered:

> *It is rather too late (swearing)*
> *First I will suffocate you with my smell*
> *Then I will rip off the roots of your udder*
> *Next I will make you squat like a constipated bitch***

> *There is nothing that does not come to an end*
> *Our feasting on the brown Ole Wuargas*** has ended*
> *The one who is felled by the bell as we chase*
> *As we chase, as we chase!*

What is heard in that bush saying kau!

> *It is the large eater with blade-shaped ears*
> *He that carries food until he is overcome*
> *Yet he does not share it with his poor mother*
> *He came and tripped near the stomach*
> *And with his mouth he pressed against a rotten spleen.*

> *Oh sister**** who has gone visiting other villages*
> *As you fence the homestead, do so but remember me*
> *Remember your brother who is yet to come*
> *For fencing use dry straw*

The ones that I would simply push aside with the tongue
As I, the bull, walk in

A suckling cow satisfies not the limper

Twenty sheep are but a speck between the teeth
An ox with a bell is pure starvation.

Hoe hoo I swear!

When Hyena had sung to the cow, he swore, laughed, and ate her all up. And that is the end.

*Onomatopoeic name for Hyena.

**By eating the hind legs.

***An ox.

****The hyena is supposed to belong to the Ilmolellan clan.

Review Questions

i)   Discuss the imagery in Hyena's song.

ii) In what ways is Hyena's behaviour and attitude in this story consistent with what we have learnt about him so far? (You may quote examples from other stories.)

MAN STORIES

22. Olmoruo oulu o Emintilisi

Netii apa, netii ele moruo. Nelo aparan enkang' enkaputi. Ore peyie ebaya ang' nejing' enkaji enkaputani. Neinepu etii emintilisi enkima o kulie kiri, nemetii entasat aji. Nedumu ake ena mintilisi nepik emootian. Nerikito ena mintilisi enkukuo naishu kake eitu ninye eyiolou olmoruo. Neiken emootian asiokisioki peyie meinepu entasat.

Ore enatonie nejing'u entasat openy enkaji. Netoni aanya lomon leseriani oonkera. Ore peyie eidip aainosa lomon niaku duo enkata narrinyo olpayian. Nedol entasat epuru emootian nejoki olpayian, "Shye, Paker anaijo kepuru emootian?" Nejoki olpayian, "Olakaishirtita lotii ene onana lukunya lolpiron laa teneoshiosh imbaa o onoose nepuru." Negira entasat, neinyiototo aitarioo olaputani.

105

Ore oton eitu epuo eneedo nenya enaduoo mootian enkima ometung'ung'uro. Nejo mbaa tiak!

O enaduo mintilisi! Netii entasat tesiadi. Nejo entasat, "Orrid' Keitu due ake ayioluo'" Nejoki olpayian, "Oi Paker ai minya!" Neipirri entasat arrinyo ang' tenkurruna, nekwet sii ninye olmoruo alo. Neishoro 'Ilkurumi. Nelo sii ninye ilo moruo oulu aikunari neijia.

22. A Greedy Old Man and the Sausage *

Once upon a time, there lived an old man. One day, he paid a visit to his in-laws. On entering the house of his mother-in-law, he found that she had been roasting some meat, among which was a delicious-looking sausage, and she was not in the house. He immediately took the sausage and quickly shoved it into his quiver. And it so happened that a piece of live coal had got stuck on the sausage, but the old man did not know. He quickly shut the quiver.

No sooner had he sat down than the owner of the house came in. They sat down to talk about the children's health. When they had finished, it was time for the old man to return to his home. Just then, the woman noticed smoke issuing from the quiver and asked the old man: "Paker**, how come the quiver is smoking?" The man answered: "Oh it is some naughty firestick *** with a soft head that smokes whenever it comes into contact with soft wood**** and the arrows." The woman kept quiet and got up to escort her guest.

When they had walked only a short distance, the fire made a hole in the quiver and the arrows fell out *tiak*! together with the stolen sausage! The lady, who was walking closely behind, exclaimed: "See, had I not known it!" Then the old man fearing that his sausage might be eaten, shouted: "Oh my Paker, please do not eat it!" So while the lady ran home in shame, the greedy old man continued with his journey in extreme embarrassment. They showed each other their backs, and there ends the story of the greedy old man.

*This is the large intestine. After it has been cleaned it is roasted and eaten.

**Name used by people after exchanging rams.

***This is a thin stick from the 'Olpiron' tree that is rubbed against a soft piece of wood to make fire.

****The flat pieces of soft wood that is rubbed against hard wood to make fire.

Review Question

The old man in this story was so overcome with greed that he disregarded basic rules of proper behaviour. Discuss this in relation to his behaviour towards his mother-in-law.

23. Olmoruo otara keon tiorrondo oyiara

Netii apa, netii ele moruo, nelo nkang'itie. Nelo abaya etadoyie enkolong'. Nejo: "Koree nkajijik olaji lang'? Neutakini.

Nejing' duo enkaji natijing'a. Neinepu emoti natii enkima nayiarare olorrondo oishori enkiteng' naiboo emudong'. Neilep alo erruat aiperipera. Nedol ele orrondo oyiara nejo kenkiri. Kake ore tenkaraki naa olomoni neureyu eyet emoti.

Nelotu entasat aji eetuo nkishu. Nebolu lasho alo alep. Ore peyie eidip atalepo ilkuti asho neng'as alotu aji aisho olomoni endaa. Nejo entasat aisho olomoni kule nejoki: "Elee maok tule amu aimua naaji olpejet loolewa naisuutisho niaku menare naok kule." Ore peyie ening' entasat enetejo olpayian nenyamalu amu meeta ae toki naisho olpayian omoni. Nerrinyo ninye alo alepisho.

Ore kiti nejoki entasat enkerai, "Nakerai, ng'urai siyie oladuo orrondo lenkiteng' tenaa ketaa kemit enkare peyie idotu." Nening' ake olmuro ina neyiolou ajo mme nkiri inaduo naayiara, neidipa duo atanya kule. Nejo, "Oi oi oi atara sii taata keon tiorrondo oyira'" Nejo ang'om nebuak nening' entasat. Nelotu entasat ajoki, "Lopayian, tooko duo nkuti Ie amu meeta enikinko." Memus oladuo payian peyie ejoki entasat nji. Nejo: "Nchooki otiake amu pae sii duo alotu aar keon tiorrondo oyira'" Niaku ilo payian oshi ilo oji 'etara keon tiorrondo oyiara'. Ilo moruo apa oulu oiterua ina dung'et e rashe.

23. The Greedy Man Who Almost Went Hungry

A certain elderly man went to visit a certain village and arrived when the sun was just about to set. He asked the villagers: "Which are the houses of our age-set in this village?"* He was directed to one of the houses.

When he went in, he found a pot that was cooking. Inside the pot was some herb known as **olorrondo**** that was being prepared for a cow whose placenta had not come out. Assuming it was meat, the old man lay down on the bed to rest. Being a visitor, he dared not check the pot since it would be improper.

When the cattle came back from grazing, the woman of the house went to let out some calves from the pen to join their mothers. After she had done some milking, she went back to the house to feed the visitor.

When she handed him a gourd of milk, he said: "I cannot drink milk since I had earlier eaten some meat." *** On hearing this, the lady was at a loss, for she had nothing else to offer the visitor. She left the house to continue with her milking.

After a little while, the woman of the house called out to her daughter and said: "My child, check the pot of **orrondo**, and if it is drying up, take it off the fire." When the old man heard this, he realised that what was in the pot was not meat after all, and he had just turned down the offer of milk for supper. He said: "Oh, how I have destroyed my own self with the cooking **orrondo**!"**** He meant to say this to himself, but he spoke so loudly that the lady of the house heard him. She came inside, and pretending she had not heard anything, she said to the old man: "Oh, please do drink a little milk for it will do you no harm." The old man was overjoyed by her plea and quickly said: "Oh do give it to me, please for today I almost destroyed myself with the cooking **orrondo**!"

This greedy man is the one who originated the saying, "He has destroyed (killed) himself with the cooking **orrondo**."

*Custom requires that a person finds out the houses of his age-mates first before he enters any house. This is where he would by right obtain the necessary hospitality.

**This is an ivy-like plant with slightly broad leaves and plum-like berries (but much smaller) that has medicinal elements. The red berries have a sweet taste.

***The Maasai normally avoid eating meat and drinking milk on the same day due to the belief that the cows will take offence and their teats will get blocked.

****Destroyed his reputation as well as his chances of having supper.

Review Questions

i)   Explain how the old man almost went hungry.

ii) How can the old man be said to have spoilt his reputation?

24. Enkolong' natomonire esipolioi

Netii apa, neiriamari nabo olong' olpayian inkishu o esiankiki enye naa enarikorie, enoshi nesej eji enkaibartani araki esipolioi. Ore eirrita nkishu neponu ilmurran aare, ne toni aashil nkishu. Nejoki olpayian: "Papaai, amaa imonira tenikiya kulo mong'i linono?" Nejoki olpayian: "Oi mamonira nanu ilasho lainei, tenememonira ake ninye enda sipolioi, ewaita." Nening' ake ilmurran enetejo olpayian nejo: "Ijo metapaashari olpayian, amaa tenememonira olee ijo kenkitok namonira? Mawaita ilmong'i."

Neshilu ake ilmong'i aare oisul nkishu neboinaa. Nejoki olpayian esiankiki meshomo ayiolou ajo kaja ilmong'i oowaki naa ke loong'ae oowaita. Neya ilmurran ilmong'i nepuo.

Nelusoo ilarin kumok. Neisho esiankiki neiu olayioni. Neitoki ake aisho neitoki ake aitusuj likae ayioni. Ore eishoi e uni neiu ilmao naa ilayiok. Nebulu kulo ayiok pokira oong'uan. O metumurati, nebarni, niaku ilmurran. Neisho menye olkiteng' oshomo aayieng' tolpul. Ore peyie emut ilo neishori likae. Nenya taa ake iyie ilmong'i looikash nesapuku oleng'. Meeta taa aikata oltung'ani otolikio ilayiok enyamu.

Ore ake peyie edol olpayian ajo etasapukita ilmurran lenyenak oleng' neipot pooki nejoki meterretenata. Nerik enkop natii ilapa murran oowaita ilmong'i. Etaa taa apa ilpayiani, oluati etii aar enkeshui. Neirorokino ake pooki nejoki olpayian, menye taa ilmurran, ilkulikae meshomo olkiu amu eeta enkiti bae nayieu neigwanare.

Ore ake peyie eiturrurro pooki tolkiu neipot olpayian olmurrani obo toolapa oowaita ilmong'i lenyena. Nejoki: "Papa lai, aikiyiolo? Keton kidamu?" Neyiolou olpayian olikae, nejoki, "ee". Nejoki olpayian: "Idamu olapa kekun irara ilmurran peyie iponunu aaya ilmong'i lainei aare najoki apa ntae ewaita tenememonira esipolioi?" Nejo olikae kedamu ina olong'. Nejo olpayian: "Ina sipolioi naa natomonire neyieu ntokitin enyenak. Ilayiok leina sipolioi kulo ooetuo aareu ntokitin enye." Kaaee! Neboinari nkishu artam ooudo tolkiteng' obo neboinari nkulie artam ooudo tolikae amu enyamu apa ina. Niaku enapa natejoki: 'Meyaroyu enenkitok.' Neiting'.

24. The Day a Woman Minded the Loss of her Oxen

Once upon a time, an old man and his newly-wed bride went to graze cattle. As they were doing so, two warriors arrived and started to examine the cattle admiringly. They said to the old man: "Father, would you mind us taking these oxen of yours?" The old man said: "Not at all my calves, if that young bride does not mind it, you may go ahead and take them." On hearing what the old man had said, the warriors were quite surprised and said: "Isn't this old man funny! If a man has no say, how can a mere woman have any say at all! Let us take them." They chose two of the best oxen in the herd and took them aside. The old man instructed his young wife to go and verify the number of oxen that were being taken and who the people were. The warriors took the oxen and left.

Many years passed. The young wife conceived and gave forth a baby boy. She did the same for the second birth. When she gave birth for the third time, she gave forth to twin boys. These four boys grew to be big boys and were circumcised. They became warriors after they were shaved. Their father gave them an ox which they went to slaughter at the meat camp (**olpul**). When they had finished one ox, they were given another, and yet another, until they had eaten quite a few oxen. They grew very big and strong. And all this time no one had told these boys about the theft of the two oxen.

When the old man realised that his warrior boys were strong enough, he called them to him and told them to take up their weapons and come along with him. He took them to the country of the warriors who had taken his oxen. By then, the warriors had become elders and were sitting outside their homesteads playing the pebble game, **enkeshui**. After they had exchanged greetings, the father of the four warriors told the other elders to come together in counsel, for he had something he wanted them to discuss.

When all the men had gathered for the meeting, the old man called one of the men who had taken his oxen and said to him: "My friend, do you know me? Do you remember me?" Recognising the old man, the former warrior replied in the affirmative. The old man continued: "Do you remember the day you took two of my oxen and I told you to take them if the young lady did not mind?" The other man said he remembered the day. "That young bride is the one that turned around and now minds your having taken her property. These boys you see here belong to that young bride and they have come for their property." What else was there to do? Forty-nine cattle were driven away being the fine for forcefully taking one ox, and another forty-nine for the second ox, since the men had committed robbery or force taking.

This confirms the truth of the saying: "That which belongs to a woman cannot be taken away." The end.

* Often used as a respectable and endearment term for the young by older people.

Review Questions

i) What is the moral of this story?

ii) The young bride did not complain when the oxen were being taken, but later she turned around and minded their loss.
Why did she do this?

iii) Compare and contrast the legal system of this community regarding robbery with any other traditional legal system that you know about. You can support your answer with a narrative.

25. Ole Sayialel Olmotonyi Loolmurran

Netii apa, netii kulo murran, nepuo enjore. Neari olmurrani obo oji Ole Sayialel metua. Ore peyie edol ilkulikae ajo etua nedumu osesen aaya entim, nelak ilpapit. Ore peyie eidip aatalak neing'ua tentim. Nepuo ninche ang! are ake pee ebaya ang' nepuo pooki ang'ae anang'are. Ore intasati aashu ilpayiani leitu edol inkera enye tiatua ilkulikae neyiolou aajo etaraki tenjore, imeitoki aaikilikuanisho.

Ore ake peyie elusoo ilkulikae, nelotu olmotonyi loolmurran neinepu oladuo murrani otua. Near toonkopir, near omeijutujuto olmurrani. Neitoki aar near omeibelekenyayu. Neitoki ake aar near, omeinyio aton. Ore ear, neinyototo olmurrani aitashe ometudumu oloonkejek akwet. Nerik olmotonyi olmurrani omeitabai auluo enkang' enye. Ore epuoito nerany ele murrani osinkolio eranyaki ele motonyi ajo:

> "Lomotonyi lido, olotie enkewarie elotie endama
>
> Shomo iroroki intokitin uni nimimen
>
> Iroroki papa lai lolgisoi onyokie
>
> Iroroki yieyio lai nabaiki imporro enkop eitashe
>
> Iroroki sii enkanashiai nabaiki enkuriny enkop eitashe
>
> Niyiolou ajo nkarunot empere ai napukenya eturruo
>
> Iroroki sii mokopit, mokopit ai narridi toonkokirisia
>
> mowuarak pee mebulu ilasho loonkulie ilairakuj eimula
>
> Tiaki tumulang'a ning'oshoshu enkiteng' ai
>
> Pee mikiya ilajung'ok."

Nerany olmurrani ele sinkolio ometabai auluo enkang' enye. Neinepu intare enye edaa tiauluo. Neikilikuanisnore olmurrani inkera natii intare. Neliki inkera olmurrani ilomon pooki liang'. Neliki ajo etalaki apa olmurrani lenkang' Ole Sayialel tenjore neaku keisinanuo enkang' enye. Neliki sii ajo etaapishe enkiteng' naji mokopit eilo murrani otua neaku ong'ata eirrag anaa apa peyie elai olopeny. Neinosu taa inkera ilomon pooki ebaiki ilentito apa nanyor ele murrani. Neliki ajo etanya apa entito ikulie murran pooki anaa apa peyie elai olchore lenye.

Ore apa ena tito naa kenyor apa ele murrani ake duo entorrono. Ore ake peyie ening' ajo etua neaku keisinanuo anaake. Keton ake aishir endama pooki naa penyo nenya endaa. Naa teneishopo duo inkulie toyie enkolong' naatae osirua, neton ninye

111

tiang' aisinanuo. Nemeishop imasaa anaa inkulie toyie, nemenya olkaria. Nedung'u apa osinkolio oranyaki ele murrani onyor ajo:

"Olowuaru lai lenkare e Koikai

Inosa nimut ning'ua enchabar

Ooi enchabar ai Ole Sayialel

Papa Sayialel oisalata apa

Aibung'a enkare

Aibung'a enarok

Aibung'a maok

Ooi enchabar ai Ole Sayialel."

Neaku ele sinkolio erany ninye inkolong'i pooki metadoi enkolong'. Nejoki ilkulikae murran, "Amaa kenya tenetua olmurrani obo eming'oru likae' Nemeyieu ena ito likae tung'ani Ole Sayialel ake.

Neibung' ele murrani olkine lenye opir, neyiang'aki ele motonyi paa kejoki sere. Nesai inkera oontare aajoki peyie meibung' ilo amu oleina ang' natua olmurrani. Neany ening'. Imeiteiki taa ninche inkera aajo ilo murrani apa ele otejoki etua, naa olenye olkine. Neipirri inkera ang' aalikio ena nataasa olmurrani, nejo: "Eewuo olmurrani lemesheta ilpapit, neibung' olkine aying'aki eng'ues narikito." Neinining'isho ake ena tito neyiolou ajo ebaiki naa olchore lenye ilo oimakini.

Neipoti ilmurran, neing'oruni eneikoni peyie elikini menye ong'otonye. Ore ake peyie edol ng'otonye, neiterre. Neitopiuni. Ore ake peyie eitoki adol, neitoki ake aiterre. Neiterre katitin ong'uan. Nelikini sii ninye menye. Ore ake peyie eidip Ole Sayialel airoroki olorere pooki, neitoki arany oladuo sinkolio oranyaki olmotonyi.

Ore ake peyie ening' Mokopit oltoilo lolmurrani, nekwetu enetii, anaa kejo airoroki. Nesupatu, neishoru metalepi. Ore ena tito apa nanyor ele murrani nelo metabarni, neela anya ereko anaa enoshi nalo osinkolio. Neishop imasaa enyena pooki.

Ore peyie edol intasati neng'as aajo tenaa kenoto likae shore, kake etasiokitio aayilou aajo olchore lenye oewuo. Neiting enkatini teine.

25. Ole Sayialel and Eagle

Once upon a time, some warriors went on a cattle raid. One of the warriors, whose name was Ole Sayialel, was killed during the raid. When he died, the other warriors combed his braided hair*, as is the custom, and went home, leaving his body in the bush. When the warriors got home, everyone came out to meet them, and those who did not see their sons among the warriors assumed they had died in the raid, and so did not ask any questions.

Soon after the warriors had returned home, Eagle came and found the dead warrior. He started beating him with his wings until his body started twitching. He continued beating the warrior until he turned over, then he sat up, stood up, and soon started walking. Eagle kept beating the warrior, and when he started running, he led him up to his village. On their way, Ole Sayialel sang to the bird, and the song went like this:

Oh you great bird

A traveller by night and by day

Go pass my greetings to three super beings,

Pass my greetings to my father with a red ring,

Pass my greetings to my mother whose beads sweep the ground,

To my sister too whose fat layers touch the ground as she stands,

To let you know that she lives off the raids of my white spear

Greet also Mokopit, my cow whose horns are tied with bark,

To prevent her from poking wrapped up kidneys

of others' calves

Tell her to grow cold and give but little milk

so that inheritors do not take her.

The warrior went on singing thus until he and Eagle arrived near his village, where they found goats grazing. On questioning the children who were herding the goats, the warrior was briefed on all that had been happening at home. They told him of the death of the warrior of the Sayialel family in a cattle raid, and how his family was still in mourning. They also informed him about a cow known as Mokopit, belonging to the dead warrior, and how it had gone wild since its owner died. They told him all the latest news including that of his girlfriend who had rejected all intimate relationships since the warrior died.

113

As it happened, this girl was very much in love with Ole Sayialel. When she learnt of his death, she became extremely sad. She would cry all day long and would hardly have anything to eat. When the other girls dressed themselves up for dances during big social occasions, she would stay at home and mourn the loss of her lover. She discarded all her ornaments, and would not apply ochre to her body as the other girls did. She composed a song that went like this:

> Oh great lion from Koikai waters
> Eat and finish but leave the beautiful mouth
> Oh that beautiful mouth of Ole Sayialel
> Oh father Sayialel the bereaved one
> I have touched the water
> I have touched clear water
> I have touched it but would not drink it**
> Oh that beautiful mouth of Ole Sayialel.

As she continued singing this song from dawn till dusk, the other warriors, who could not understand this kind of behaviour, asked her: "If one warrior dies, why don't you choose another for a friend?" But she wanted nobody else but Ole Sayialel.

Ole Sayialel then got hold of one of his fat he-goats which he slaughtered for Eagle, and bade him farewell. The children pleaded with him not to kill that particular goat, since it belonged to the bereaved family, but he defied them. The children by then had no inkling that the man was the warrior who had been reported dead, and that the he-goat was his own. They therefore ran home to report the incident and said: "A warrior with unbraided hair came and got hold of a he-goat and killed it for some animal he came with." The warrior's girlfriend listened to what the children were saying intently. She suspected that they might have been talking about her lover.

The warriors had by then been assembled to discuss how to go about breaking the news of the warrior's appearance to his mother and father. When the mother saw her son, she fainted. When she regained consciousness and saw him a second time, she did the same. She fainted the third and fourth time, in a row. When Ole Sayialel had greeted everyone, he sang the song that he had been singing to Eagle once more.

When Mokopit heard the warrior's voice, she was filled with delight and she ran to him excitedly, as though in greeting. She then became calm, and allowed the women to milk her. During this time, the warrior's girlfriend had gone to have her hair shaven, had applied red ochre to her body and worn all her ornaments, like one preparing for a big occasion.

Her appearance took everyone by surprise because they thought she had found a new boyfriend. But this was before they realised that it was her lover who had come back.

* Unlike old people or babies, it is considered most unfortunate for a warrior to die, since he is at the prime of his life. When he does die his hair is unbraided to simulate another stage of life, either that of a younger or older person, so as to make his death more easily acceptable.

**Drinking nice cold water when one needs it is a very comforting feeling. But the bereaved deprive themselves of this comfort during the mourning period. They can only touch water as a ritual.

Review Questions ■

i)   There are various types of relationships that can be identified in this story. What are they? Comment briefly on each.

ii) Comment on the significance of the girl in the story abstaining from drinking water. Can you think of equivalent mourning rituals in your community?

iii) Comment on the role of Eagle in this story.

26. Olmurrani o Enturkulu

Netii apa nepuo ilmuran enjore. Nepuo aalau nkishu. Nerikito apa kulo murran ildiain imiet. Ore eshukunye niaku keya esumash. Neji ekeyieng'i oldia obo aanya. Neyieng'i, nenyae. Neishori pooki nga'e oldung'oti. Neitokini ake aapuo, neji, "Emanyaaki ayieng' Iikae dia." Neyieng'i, neishori pooki ng'ae oldung'oti. Neikoni neija tolkirragarie Ie okuni. Neyieng'i ildiain o metumuti pokira imiet.

Netii apa ele murrani oji Loolmong'i-Wuasin leitu ninye enya nkiri ooldiain. Keishori ake oldung'oti neisudoo. Neishori olikae nemenya. Ore enoshikata peyie emuta ildiain etaa ang' epuoi niaku keimanya ninye ajo, "Aaku olenjore nainosie olaji lang' ildiain." Ore peyie ening' ilkulikae nejo: "Shye, kejaa toi oltung'ani, keitu apa iyie inya?" Nejoki

115

ilkulikae: "Eitu, naa ore peyie iyiolou ajo eitu, entasho maitoduaa ntae." Neitayu ilapa dung'ot loonkiri ooldiain. Ore eitodol ilkulikae ejo: "Ololdia orok ele, oidia oibor ele, ololdia ng'iro ele ... " Neruku pokira imiet.

Ore peyie edol ilkulikae nejo: "Kaji taa kinko ele tung'ani amu kelo alikioo iyiook ajo kinosa ildiain." Nepuoi o metabaikini olchani loolgum oleng'okino olmoti. Nenya ake duo ilgum oobaikinoyu ore peyie elakuanu nejokini Loolmong'i- Wuasin metakedoki iloolakua aitaiki ilkulikae, keji taa peyie esulakini atua olmoti.

Neked ninye olchani neitadoiki ilkulikae ilng'anayio. Neisho kulo murran ootii entonata olchani neiteru aadung' olchani. Ore peyie eikilikuanu lido murrani otii ilng'osil eniasitae nejokini: "Ai meeta." Nedung'i olchani o meitirra nesulakini Loolmongi-Wuasin atua olmoti.

Nelo entanai aibooyo. Niagut ele moti oleng' nejo tupuku nelaikino. Nepuo ilkulikae aaing'uaa ejo peyie eye. Nepuo aabaya ang'. Ore peyie ebaya ang' nelejisho aajo meyiolo eneima. Nianyu apa enkang' enye o metejo etua.

Ore nabo olong' nelotu oloitiko aok enkare tele moti. Ore eton eitu eok nejoki olmurrani: "Lomurrani inchooki enkare peyie aalo alikioo." Nejoki olmurrani, "Ilo ajo aa tenikilo alikioo?" Nejoki oloitiko, "Ekalo ajo, wuo wuo, wuo wuo!" anaa enoshi ake najo oloitlko. Nejoki olmurrani, "Oh! Shomo iyie amu mikiyiolo ashomo atolikioi."

Neitoki embarie alotu. Nejo: "Lomurrani inchooki enkare peyie aalo alikioo." Nejoki olmurrani, "Ilo ajo aa tenikilo alikioo?" Nejoki embarie, "Ekalo ajo, wua, wua!" Nejoki olmurrani, "Oh! Shomo iyie amu mikiyiolo ashomo atolikioi." Neitoki olng'ojine alotu. Nejoki olmurrani, "Lomurrani inchooki enkare peyie aalo alikioo." Neikilikuan sii ninye olmurrani ajoki: "Ilo ajo aa tenikilo alikioo?" Nejo olng'ojine, "Ekalo ajo, uuu' uuu!" Nearaa sii ninye olmurrani anaa peyie etarayie inkulie ng'uesi pooki.

Ore tenkiti kata nelotu sii ninye emuny eyieu enkare. Neomonu enkare ejo peyie elo alikioo olmurrani. Nejo sii ninye enejo oshi imuny. Nedol olmurrani ajo meyiolo ashomo atolikioi. Niaraa sii ninye. Nerukunye taa inkulie ng'uesi eeraa ake olmurrani.

Ore ade te siadi nelotu entukurlu. Nejoki olmurrani: "Lomurrani inchooki enkare peyie aalo alikioo." Neikilikuan olmurrani, "Ilo ajo aa tenikilo alikioo?" Nejoki emotonyi, 'Tang'asa tolikioki enikiji peyie ayiolou enajo tenaalo alikioo." Nejoki olmurrani, "Ekaaji [oolmong'iWuasin." Neitoki ake emotonyi aikilikuan enetii enkang' enye o enetii enkaji e ng'otonye. Neliki olmurrani pooki. Nejoki emotonyi, "Tenabaya nalo ajo:

"Menye Loolmongi-wuasin

Ng'oto Loolmong'i-wuasin

Etii Loolmong'i-wuasin

Olmoti le kerikere

Nkeenda isiet

Iltargeta isiet."

Ore pee ening' olmurrani enejo emotonyi neyiolou ajo keyiolo emotonyi ashomo atolikioi. Nejoki: "Tooko naa duo enkare peyie ilo." Nelo ake emotonyi ometabai enkang' apa natuutakaki. Neinepu ilpayiani ourita enkeshui toloip liauluo. Neitashe ake tolchani paa kejo:

"Menye Loolmong'i-wuasin

Ng'oto Loolmong'i-wuasin

Etii Loolmong'i-wuasin

Olmoti Ie kerikere

Nkeenda isiet x 2"

Iltargeta isiet

Nejo ilpayiani, "Shye! Kejoaa toi emotonyi?" Neitoki ake emotonyi aigil alikioo enetii olmurrani.

"Menye Loolmong'i-wuasin

Ng'oto Loolmong'i-wuasin

Etii Loolmong'i wuasin

Olmoti Ie kerikere

Nkeenda isiet x 2"

Iltargeta isiet

Nejo olpayian obo, "Shye! emataarai emotonyi meitoki aipotoki iyiook ilmeneng'a." Neeraa.

Neitoki ake emotonyi alo aitashe tenkalo enkaji e ng'otonye ele murrani paa kejo enaduo ake. Nening' intasati etii oloip Ie boo aaripisho. Neun inkiyiaa ainining' enejo emotonyi. Ore ake peyie eigil emotonyi nening' ng'-otonye ele murrani eboitare inkulie tasati. Nebuaku aishir, nejo; "Oooi aaeuo emotonyi aipotoki ilmeneng'a lenkiyio ai natua!" Nearari emotonyi, neitoki ake ashukunye. Neitoki ake alikioo enetii olmurrani o metejo entasat nabo; "Aha! emaape toi aasuj emotonyi amaa naa elimu olmoti nejo eyau inkeenda oiltargeta. Emaape ake ntae aing'uraa." Nenyorraa inkulie.

Nepuei aaliki ilpayiani. Nesuji ena motonyi o meshomoe aabaya ele moti otii Loolmong'i-Wuasin. Neishori inkeenda naaenikino. Neyietuni omeitayuni. are ake peyie eidipi aitayu, neipot olmurrani enaduo motonyi nejoki: "Ore amu kitareto maape ang' peyie aalo ayiang'aki olker." Nepuo pooki o metabai ang'. Neibung' olmurrani olker opir ayiang'aki emotonyi. Neeku ilchoreta emotonyi olmurrani. Naa tenelotu emotonyi ang' naa keikiroteti oleng' neitoomoni. Neishunye enkatini teine.

26. The Warrior and Dove

Once upon a time, the warriors went on a cattle raid, but did not get any cattle. They took with them five dogs. On their way back, they were overcome by hunger and they decided to kill one of the dogs for a meal. This they did and every person was given a piece of dog meat. They continued with their journey, and on getting hungry again, it was decided that a second dog would be killed. When this was done, everyone again got a piece. Another dog was killed when they camped for the third night, and then another, until all the dogs had been eaten.

Among this group of warriors was one known as Loolmong'i-wuasin, who had not eaten any of the dog-meat. Whenever he was given a piece he hid it. When he received another he did not eat it. When all the dogs had been eaten and the warriors were heading home, he would swear by his companions who had eaten dogs. When the others heard this they asked: "What is the man saying! Did you not eat them?" He answered: "No, I did not, but if you want me to prove to you that I did not, let me show you." He showed them all the pieces of dog meat that he had hidden, and said: "This is from the black dog, this from the white dog, this is from the brown dog," showing them all five pieces.

On seeing the pieces of meat, the other warriors said among themselves: "What are we going to do with this man, since he is going to tell that we have eaten dogs?" As they went on, they came upon a tall tree whose branches were spread over a well. After eating all the fruit they could reach, they requested Loolmong'i-wuasin to climb up the tree and pluck the fruits that were higher up. They were planning to drown him in the well.

He climbed up the tree and dropped the fruit to the others. When he was up there, the others began to cut the tree, and on enquiring what the others were doing, he was told that nothing important was happening. Soon, the tree was cut and Loolmong'i-wuasin fell into the well.

Fortunately, a root prevented him from drowning. But this well was so deep that he could not climb out. The other warriors went away, leaving him to die. When they reached home, they lied that they did not know what had happened to him. Back home, his family waited for him until they gave him up for dead.

One day, Zebra went to the well to drink some water. He said to the warrior, "Hey warrior, if you let me drink some water, I will go and relate this incident, and you will be rescued." Then the warrior asked, "How would you relate it?" Zebra said, "I will go and say, *Wuo, wuo, wuo!*", making the sound zebra makes. The warrior dismissed him saying, "You get away because you don't know how to relate it."

Then came Jackal, "Hey warrior, if you let me drink some water, I will go and relate this incident and you will be rescued." Then the warrior asked, "How would you relate to it?" Jackal made his barking sound saying, "*Wua, wua!*" The warrior again dismissed Jackal saying, "You get away because you don't know how to relate it." Hyena was next to come to the well for a drink. He said, "Hey warrior, if you let me drink some water from the well, I will go and report what befell you then you will be rescued." The warrior asked, "How would you relate it?" Hyena answered, "I will go and say, "*Uuu, uuu!*" He howled the way hyenas do. The warrior too dismissed Hyena like he did the others.

Rhino was the next to come in search of water. He made grunting sounds as a way of expressing how he would relate the incident to get the warrior rescued.

Like all the others, he too was dismissed for failing to convince the warrior. Several other animals followed, and they were all successively dismissed.

Finally, Dove came along. "Hey warrior," she said, "if you let me drink some water, I will go and relay the accident, then you will be rescued." Then the warrior asked her, "How would you relate it?" Dove said: "Tell me what your name is first, then I will know what to say." "My name is Loolmong'i-wuasin," answered the warrior. Dove went on to enquire where the warrior's village was located, and the position of his mother's house within the village. The warrior gave Dove all the information she needed. Then Dove said: "When I get there I will sing:

Father of Loolmong'i-wuasin,

Mother of Loolmong'i-wuasin,

Loolmong'i-wuasin is at Kerikere well,

> *Eight straps*
> *Eight hooks."*

On hearing this, the warrior was convinced that Dove was able to relay the incident, and have him rescued, so he said to her: "You may drink some water and go." Dove flew to the village where the warrior had directed her. She found the elders at the game of enkeshui in the shade near the village. She sang:

> *Father of Loolmong'i-wuasin,*
> *Mother of loolmong'i-wuasin,*
> *Loolmong'i-wuasin is at Kerikere well,*
> *Eight straps*
> *Eight hooks.*

The elders wondered: "What is this dove saying?" Dove chanted again:

> *Father of Loolmong'i-wuasin,*
> *Mother of Loolmong'i-wuasin,*
> *Loolmong'i-wuasin is at the Kerikere well,*
> *Eight straps*
> *Eight hooks.*

One of the elders said, "Let us chase this bird away to stop it from calling the names of our dead ones." They did so, but Dove then flew over to a tree near the house of the warrior's mother and again sang the same song:

> *Father of Loolmong'i-wuasin.*
> *Mother of Loolmong'i-wuasin,*
> *Loolmong'i-wuasin is at the Kerikere well,*
> *Eight straps*
> *Eight hooks.*

The women who were doing their sewing in the shade heard what Dove said, and listened again as Dove repeated her song. When the mother of Loolmong'i-wuasin heard what the bird was saying, she screamed out loud, and she said, "Why should this bird be so unkind as to talk about my dead son!"* Dove was chased away, but stubbornly came back and repeated the song for the last time. One of the women said: "Gosh! This bird is telling us about a well and asking us to take straps, let us follow her just to see." They went to inform the elders, then they all set off after the bird until they got to the well. They tied straps on to the warrior and got him out.

As soon as the warrior was out of the well, he called Dove to him and said, "Since you rescued me, I will take you home, and slaughter a ram for you." They all went home and a ram was slaughtered for Dove. Dove and Warrior became very good friends. She would visit him whenever she pleased and was welcome. The story ends there.

*In Maasai tradition it is taboo to call a dead man by name.

**Rams are normally slaughtered for highly-respected guests.

Review Questions

i) How did Loolmong'i-wuasin find himself inside the well?

ii) Why and how did Dove succeed in obtaining water from the well when all other animals had failed?

27. Ilmao lo olnoos

Neeti apa, netii ele payian oota nkituaak are. Naa olupi apa enkitok nabo neeta enkae inkera kumok. Nebik tenebo enkata naado.

Naa keisinanuo apa ena kitok olupi tenkaraki meeta nkera nemeeta oltung'ani oretoki esiaai enkaji. Neishori apa metaa ninye nairrita nkishu neok.

Nepuo apa ake ilarin o metaa kenyamal ena kitok olupi oleng'. Nesapuku olom oleng' tenkaraki eisho enkaini. Ore tenena olong'i neitoki enkaini aisho neiu ilmao naa ilayiok. Nesapuku olom oleng'. Neton nabo olong' nejo: "Kaji sa aiko peyie eibaini ena aini ai elatia pooki?"

Neisho nabo olong' tempolos enkewarie eirura enkaini neleliari ake nedung' inkera inkilintani, neyelie ng'otonye enchonito enkutuk osarge, peyie eji keinosa nkera enyenak. Nedumu ake nkera nepik olnoos araki olbene nenang'aki olkeju meewa enkare. Nelo ainosaa te latia nalulung'a ajo einosa enkaini nkera enyena;;' Neiputukuny iltung'ana peyie ening'.

Ore peyie ekenyu netem entomononi ajo alikioo enetaasa nianyi eiruki tenkaraki nadolitae osarge tenkutuk nemeyioloi eneima nkera. Neiruk sii ninye olpayian enetejo enda kitok olupi, niar enda kitok duo nainosa nkera, nejo aparripar, neishir o

121

metalaikinoyu aishira. Neitoki ajoki metamooki airrita sirkon hoo duo naa sinkan oshi o nkera ooirrita. Niaku ina esiaai enye ebaiki ilo kekun, Ore apa ele noos otii inkayiok neya ilopir lenkare o mewaita ae kop. Ore nabo olong' eigwana ilpayiani nedol ele noos tolkekun lolkeju. Nejo obo "Olalai elde noos," Nejo al ikae: "Anaai entoki natii atua." Nesar taa ilpayiani olnoos neitayu ilmao. Neya obo olnoos neya oladuo oitera nkera. Neya ake olpayian inkera ang' neitoti o metubulu aaku ilmurran pooki. Nedung'okini apa enkarna aajo 'ilmao lo olnoos.'

Ore ebulu kulo mao neinosakini eneikunaki apa peyie enotoki tolnoos. Neyieu oleng' neyiolou enkop apa naing'uaa. Nejokino nabo olong': "Maape esotore aaing'oru enkiti toki nikimbung'aa peyie kipuo aing'oru enikintipat apa."

Nedumunye taa ninye aapuo aaing'oru enkop apa naitipat. Ore epuo neinepu enkiti tokode entasat natii isirkon. Neitu aikata ninche edol entasat nairrita isirkon. Neiroroki, nejoki: "Yieyio, anaijo iyie natii isirkon, koree nkera?" Neinosaki entasat ilomon pooki Ie eneikununo paa ninye natii isirkon. Neikilikuan ilmurran entasat aajoki: "Kalo monekie naaji iyiolounyie nena kera ajo ininono?" Nejoki entasat: "Ilkimojik amu kedung'o nkilintani." Neitodol ilmurran entasat inkilintani enye naatudung'o apa enkaini olupi. Neliki ilomon apa oinosakaki tenoshi kop natii. Ore peyie eyiolou aajo ng'otonye ina neshipa naleng'. Neishopoki ilkarash ng'ejuko neing'uaa isirkon tiang'ata.

Neing'asia olorere peyie edolu enoshi shekut oosirkon oishope duo enenking'asia. Neyiataa aajo: "Kenoto toi duo enchekut oosirkon ilapa ayiok ooinosa!"

Neibung'i enkiguana ina kata ake nelimuni aajo ilapa mao ootejoki einosa ng'otonye ninche kulo ayiok. Negoro olpayian oleng', nekurru sii tentaboi apa naitayio aar enkitok enye neitu eas ae neisho meirrita isirkon. Nejo asesekuan enda kitok olupi nejoki ilayiok lenyena meishoo meirrita isirkon. Neishori meirrita isirkon o metaa kenya neye. Nebik ninye olpayian o enkitok enye olmao lenye.

27. The Twins of the Drum

Once upon a time, there lived a man who had two wives. One of the wives was barren and the other one had very many children. The man lived with his wives for many years.

The barren woman was unhappy because she did not have children of her own. She did most of the work in her house, since she had no one to assist her. Compared with her co-wife, she had fewer domestic duties to keep her at home. She was assigned the task of herding and watering the flock by her husband. These are chores which are normally performed by men and barren women.

As time went by, the barren woman felt very bitter, neglected and lonely. She became extremely jealous of the other woman. After a while, the fertile woman gave birth again, this time to twin boys. The barren woman became even greener with jealousy; she worked out a plan to run down the image of her co-wife in the home and in the neighbourhood.

One night, while their mother was heavily asleep, the barren woman took the twins – and cut off their little fingers to let out blood, which she smeared around the mouth of their mother. It was going to seem obvious to everyone that the fertile woman had eaten her own children. The barren woman grabbed the twins, put them in a drum and dumped the drum into the river. She went around the village and told everyone she met about how her co-wife had eaten her children. Everyone was bewildered.

The mother of the twin children tried desperately to explain to the incredulous neighbours what had actually happened, but no one would believe her, especially on seeing the blood on her mouth, and failing to trace the twins. The husband, too, believed the story of his barren wife and his fertile wife was then declared a cannibal. He beat the bereaved woman who cried and cried until she could cry no more. As if this was not enough, he sentenced her to a life-time herding donkeys, a menial job which is normally performed by children and labourers.

Meanwhile, the drum containing the twin brothers remained afloat on the river: season in, season out. It was swept away by a gentle current to another country, until one day, elders who sat under a cool shade by the river deliberating on affairs of the clan, noticed the drum as it was swept adrift to the river bank:

"That drum is mine!" one of them said. "Whatever is inside it is mine!" another one burst out.

The elders scampered to the drum, and holding it by both ends, removed it from the water. They plucked it open and pulled out the frail twin boys. The drum and its contents were shared out equitably amongst the anxious rescuers. The elder who had been given the share of the twin boys quickly brought them to his home, nursed them until they became big strong warriors. They were nick-named "the twins of the drum".

As they grew into big men, the twins became restless. They were told many stories about the way they had been rescued. They grew curious and anxious. They wanted to know their country of origin. Eventually they said to each other: "Look, let us gather some presents and search for our motherland."

They set out on a homebound journey. It was a journey of search, in the course of which they encountered a famished, sickly woman, who was tending healthy and rotund donkeys. They had never seen a woman herding donkeys. They stopped and asked her: "Mother, why are you herding donkeys? Where have the children gone?" They showed her the remains of their fingers which had been chipped short by the cruel barren woman and repeated the story which the people in the strange land had told them. On discovering that she was their mother they were overjoyed. The young men dressed their mother, in new garments and set out for the village. They left the donkeys in the field.

When the villagers saw 'the donkey woman', as she came to be called, all dressed up, they were mesmerised: "Has the donkey woman found the sons she had eaten?" they wondered. A Council of Elders was convened. It was established that the young warriors were the twins who were said to have been eaten by their mother. The old man, their father, raved in shame and pain and humiliation when he remembered the way he had punished his innocent wife. He threatened to kill his barren wife, but his sons advised him to let the barren woman do the donkey job. She was sentenced to herd the donkeys for the remainder of her life. The old man, his wife and the twin sons then lived happily ever after.

Review Questions ■

i)   The barren woman was driven by desperation to discard the twins. Discuss.

ii) What do we learn about sex roles in this story?

iii) An undue amount of significance is attached to fertility in the Maasai community. Find examples in this story, the next one, or from any other oral literature genres in this book that support this view.

28. Nkera olng'aboli

Etii apa ena tasat nemeeta olmoruo nemeeta sii nkera. Ninye ake openy tenkaji enye. Nenya apa eliyio oleng' nelau enias. Nejo nabo olong', "Kadumunye taata alo oloiboni aing'uraa tenaa keeta enaitaas. Nedumunye alo."

Ore peyie ebaya enetii oloiboni nejoki: "Oloiboni kitok, osina laayaua enitii amu kayiolo ajo iyie ake Iikindim atooru ele sina." Neing'or ake oloiboni nejoki, "Tomononi, tolikioki osina Iikitimitua." Neinosaki entasat oloiboni osina oota nejoki, "Ataa kitok neme olmoruo aata neme nkera, naateekua eliyio." Neikilikuan oloiboni ajoki, "Kolmoruo iyieu anaa nkera?" Nejoki entasat, "Mayieu olmoruo nkera naaji ayieu." Nejoki oloiboni: "Shomo ang' ng'oru motioo nisotoki ilng'abolo ning'uaa tiaji nilo iyie arere nkejek tiauluo." Ore peyie errinyo entomononi ang' nias pooki natiaaka oloiboni. Neiput ake ilng'abolo motiook neipang' alo nkang'itie.

Ore peyie elotu ang' teipa nening'oo iltung'ana erany nejo, "Shye, anaijo toi ening'o nkera erany tenkang' ming'ani!" Nejo tabaiki nekwetiki nkutiti kera ejo, "Hooyia nini, hooyia nini!" Nejo nkuna nji ilmurran eduaaya erany tolosinko. Nejo tabaiki aji eisujaki duo pooki toki neori enkaji, neitobiri pooki toki. Nelo osina enelakua. Neshipayu entomononi oleng'. Nebik ilapaitin kumok onkera enyena tenchipai.

Ore nabo olong' neinepu nkera oolasho eimalimal neimina lasho. Ore inaatii ang' niara niaku keishiraa pooki nemias esiaai tenaduo ang'. Negoro ake entasat neisikong' nkera nejoki: "Kainyioo kuna kiyioitin olng'aboli" Neitirring'a nkera. Nianyu ake meshomo ng'otonye nkang'itie neiturrurro pooki nerrinyo olapa shani oing'uaa. Niaku ilng'anayio lolng'aboli anaa apa ake.

Oo naa peyie ejo entomononi tushukunye neinepu enkang' naliyio. Neishir oleng'. Nedumunye nerrinyo olapa oiboni. Nejoki: "Kaji kinkuna, aikinyiaaka aoru nkera naatoorutuo oshi eliyio!" Nejo oloiboni ainining'u ilomon lentasat neyiolou ajo ninye naitarruoyie. Nejoki: "Tomononi meekure eeta enaidim aitaasa." Nejoki entomononi, "Amaa sa tenalo aing'oru tolapa ng'aboli ijo katum?" Nejoki oloiboni: "Shomo tetema amu etejoki apa 'mme nkidimat epuoyieki, nyuaat'."

Neing'ua ake entasat enkang' oloiboni nelo aya inapa motiook nerrinyo olapa ng'aboli. Neked olchani. Nejo ntayu olng'anayioi nepoku ilng'anayio pooki nkonyek aing'or entasat. Neirut entasat oleng'. Nelaikino atadou toladuo shani. Ore peyie emutu neponunui aadol neitadouni. Nepeji olkimojino etoonye duo enkutuk tolkirutoto. Eitu aikata eitoki aing'oru inapa kera naaisikong'a ajo 'nkiyioitin olng'aboli.

125

28. The Children of the Sycamore Tree

There once lived a woman who had neither a husband nor children. She lived all by herself. She felt so lonely that she did not know what to do.

One day, she said to herself: "I shall set off to look for a diviner who will perhaps be able to help me." When she found a diviner, she said to him: "Oh great diviner, I have come to you with my problems, for I am convinced that you alone can help me." The great diviner looked at her and said: "Dear woman, what troubles you?" The woman told the diviner all her problems and said to him: "I have grown old and I have neither husband nor children, and loneliness is wearing me out." The diviner asked her: "Which of the two would you want, a husband or children?" "I do not want a husband," said the woman, "it is children I would love to have." The diviner then said to her: "Go back home and find some cooking pots and fill them up with the fruits of the sycamore tree and then take a stroll out into the fields." When she got home, the woman did as she was bid. She filled the pots with fruits of the sycamore tree and went out to visit another homestead.

When she returned in the evening, she heard the voices of people singing and talking. "What do I hear," she wondered, "like children singing in a usually lonely village!" On reaching the village, she was met in greeting by little children, saying: "There comes mother, there comes mother!" On looking up, the woman's eyes were met by the sight of dancing warriors. When she got to the house, she found all the dishes had been washed, the house had been swept, and everything was spick and span. Her problems had been solved so far, and she was delighted. She lived happily with her children for many months.

One day, when she got home, the woman found the children, who were supposed to be tending the calves, playing about. The calves had wandered away and got lost. At the same time, the children had fought among themselves and were all wailing and crying and no work had been done in the home. She felt very upset and reproached them saying: "Look at these brats of the sycamore!" The children remained silent. They waited until their mother went out visiting, then they all gathered together and returned to the same sycamore tree and turned into fruit again.

How great was the woman's sorrow when she found a deserted homestead! She wept very bitterly. She then set off for the home of the diviner, to whom she said: "What have you done to me, you have snatched back the children who had driven away my loneliness!" On listening to the woman's story intently, the diviner realised that she was at fault. He said to her: "Dear lady, there is nothing else I can do for you."

"Do you think I could find them if I went back to the sycamore tree?" proposed the woman. The diviner said to her: "Go and try, for as the saying goes, 'we do not go by abilities but by determination.'"

On leaving the diviner's home, the woman took her cooking pots to the same sycamore tree. She climbed up the tree and when she tried to pluck the first fruit, all the other fruits opened their eyes wide and stared at her. The woman was so startled that she was unable to descend from the tree. She was discovered late that evening and was helped down from the tree, still unable to utter a word due to fright. She never again ventured to search for the children that she had referred to as "the brats of the sycamore".

Review Questions

i)   In a short paragraph state what happens in this story,

ii) What do we learn in this story about the role played by the diviner (medicine-man)?

29. Olmurrani oshomo enkop Enkal

Netii apa, nepuo ilmurran enjore, nedung'o olmurrani enamuke nejo: "Lomurran entaanyuaki." Nejoki ilkulikae: "Nchoo kianyu olesiadi." Naa kejoki ake ilkulikae metaanyu nejokini: "Nchoo kianyu olesiadi." Neikoni neijia ometabau olesiadi, Nejoki olikae: "Loinurrani taanyuaki." Nejoki olikae: "Inepu iyiook amu kapik embeneyio enkoitoi nikiima teneoro nkoitoi," Nejoki olikae, "Ayia."

Nelo ake oladuo murrani Ie siadi ore ake peyie eoro nkoitoi nedung'u embeneyio nepik enkoitoi naima, Nepuo ninche, Nelotu ake osiwuo sapuk teina kata neya embeneyio ae oitoi, Ore peyie ebau oladuo murrani otudung'e enamuke neinepu embeneyio, neibung' ina oitoi ajo ainepu ilkulikae.

Nelo ake, nelo o meshomo ainepu olapa edaa. Negira aing'or. Nejoki olapa: "Lomurrani, kaji ing'uaa naa kaji ilo tene?' Nejoki olmurrani: "Ang' aing'uaa naa enjore kipuo paa kaing'ataitie duo ilmurran aitobirita enamuke natudung'e," Nejoki olapa; "Amaa iyie

127

tenikidol ijo kaji aikununo?" Nejoki olmurrani: "Meeta, ira ake sidai." Nejoki olapa: "Shomo taa mbung'a ena oitoi naa teninepu entoki ninepua mijoki ake eneikununo, tiaaki ake kaisidai, nimiya toki tenitum, naa tenikinkilikuani tenaa kentoki sidai iyieu tenaa kentorrono, nijo entorrono." Nejoki olmurrani, ayia, nelo.

Nelo ake olmurrani neinepu olkeju lenkare oruko. Nejo alang' nejoki olkeju: "Lomurrani tookoki peyie kitum atalang'a." Nejoki olmurrani: "Ntasho maatang'asa alang' peyie aalo aok telido kekun." Nelang' ake nelo. Neitoki atum olkeju Ie kule. Ore enoshi kata ejo aitadoiki enkeju peyie elang' nejoki olkeju enetiaaka oladuo lenkare. Neitoki ake olmurrani ajoki enatiaka oladuo keju. Ore ake peyie eidip atalang'a nelotie. Ore peyie eitoki atum olkeju lo sarge nejoki metooko, neitoki olmurrani aiko eneikuna ilkulikae, nelang' ilkejek pokira okuni eitu eok.

Nelo ake olmurrani neitoki atum ilalema aare ooii ate. Nejoki ilalema: "Lomurrani iiyio iyiook peyie iya olopi." Nejoki olmurrani: "Ntasho matabai ende peyie alotu aii ntae." Negiroo ake olmurrani ilalema nelo.

Neitoki ake olmurrani alo o menoto' ironkena sidan naayier ate. Nejoki ironkena olmurrani: "Lomurrani (tukurto) teyiara iyiook peyie iya enao." Nelej ake olmurrani neing'uaa.

Nelo olmurrani neitoki ainepu ntoluo naara. Nejoki ntoluo olmurrani: "Lomurrani tirisha iyiook peyie iya nabo ayaki ng'utunyi meiperrie ilkeek." Nejoki olmurrani: "Ntasho taa penyo maeu." Nelotie. Nelo taa ake olmurrani naa ketum ake ae toki nelej, negiroo eitu eitaas ae. Netum ae nelej, neing'ua. Neing'uaa pooki toki.

Ore ade neitoki atum oltung'ani otii nkishu Enkai. Neeta ele tung'ani ilukuny are, neeta nkishu ilkidong'o maare. Neirorokino ake nejoki olpayian olmurrani: "'Amaa iyie tenikidol ijo kaji aikununo?" Neing'or ake nejoki olmurrani: "'Meeta, itiu ake anaa iltung'ana pooki." Neitoki olpayian ajoki: "'Naa kaji eikununo kuna kishu?" Nejoki olmurrani, "'Etiu ake anaa nkishu pooki." Neutaa ake olpayian olmurrani, neoro.

Nelo ake olmurrani ore peyie ejo abaiki enkang' Enkai neing'ataa enkang'. Nelo maakutiti o menyaaki abaiki. Nejo tijing'a aji neing'ataa enkaji. Neitoki alo o meinepu. Nejo atonie olorika neing'ataa sii ilo. Nesuj o meinepu. Netonie. Netii duo entasat Enkai ena aji. Neirorokino ake, nenya ilomon, nejoki entasat olmurrani: "'Ke kule naarropil iyieu tenaa inaaisamis?" Nejoki olmurrani: "'Kaji aiko kule naarropil etii inaaisamis!" Neisho entasat inaarropil. Netoni ake ore tara neitoki entasat ajoki olmurrani: "Ke kule naaoto iyieu tenaa inaairowua?" Nejoki olmurrani. "Inaairowua." Neishori inaaoto. Ore peyie eaku enoshi kata nadung'o nkejek olorere nejoki entasat olmurrani: "Ke erruat nakurro iyieu tenaa enemekurro?" Nejoki olmurrani: "Enemekurro." Neishori enakurro. Nepuoi aairura.

Ore tolakira nelotu entasat ajoki olmurrani: "Totona taa tiaji naa tenining' entoki naikurrukurr miro ake nimimpang'." Neitirring'a olmurrani tiatua aji. Ore tenkiti kata

128

nening' eikurrukur o metaa keikirikira enkaji. Neitirring'a, o metaa ade nelotu entasat ajoki meipang'a. Ore peyie eipang' neinepu olaram loonkishu o ntare o sirkon. Nejoki entasat: "Ininono taa kuna masaa pooki, terewa nilo sere." Nereu olmurrani nkishu aimie ae oitoi neme enapa naimua nelo enkop enye.

Ore peyie eeku kebaiki ang' neduari enterit. Etaanyutua taa apa ilkulie murran nelau nejo ebaiki neinosa ng'wesi. Neishir enkang' enye o metigirata.

Nebau entoros ereuta nkishu nemeba toki. Neikilikuani enenotie nkishu neinosaki ilkulikae pooki toki. Eshomo taa apa ilapa murran nepuo aalau nkishu.

Neinining'isho ake olmurrani ong'arie kina olikae nejo kedumunye sii ninye alo enkop Enkai peyie epuoi aaisho nkishu. Nejoki olalashe: "Milo amu mindim ataasa inataasa nanu." Nejoki: "'Meeta duo nchere keitu alo."

Nedumunye, neilo, nelo neim enkoitoi natuutaka olalashe o meshomo ainepu olapa edaa.

Neikilikuanishore olapa anaa apa olalashe. Nejoki: "Kaji aikununo?" Nejoki olmurrani: "'Eitu aikata nanu adol entoki nijo iyie." Neitanap olapa anaa enapa naitanapa olalashe, neutaa aliki eneim. Nelo.

Ore ake peyie einepu olkeju lenkare nejoki olkeju metooko eton eitu elang'. Negil kung' aok. Ore peyie eidip nelang'. Neok sii olekule o olosarge, nelang' pooki eidipa atooko. Neinepu ilalema ooii ate, ore peyie ejoki meeiyio peya olopi, neii neya olopi. Neinepu ironkena, nekurt emoti nenya inaaoto. Neinepu ntoluo naara; nerish neya nabo, anaa enatiaakitia ntoluo. Nias pooki neitu eas olikae.

Ore peyie einepu olpayian oota ilukuny are otii nkishu naata ilkidong'o maare neirorie ake olpayian nejoki: "'Ijo iyie kaji aikununo?" Nejoki, "Iyata ilukuny are." Neitoki olpayian ajoki: "'Kaji eikununo kuna kishu?" Nejoki: "Eeta pooki ilkidong'o maare." Neutaa olpayian olmurrani aliki enetii enkang' e Nkai, nerrinyo ninye airrita nkishu.

Nelo ake olmurrani ore etaa keim kishomi neing'ataa enkang'. Nenang' torinka. Neitashe enkang'. Ore peyie ejo ajing' enkaji neigut enkaji neosh torinka, neitashe enkaji. Nejo aton tolorika neing'ataa, neosh torinka neiper, neton te nkop.

Ore peyie eikilikuan entasat tenaa ke kule naairowua eyieu tenaa ke naaisomis nejo: "Kaji aiko kule naaisamis etii inaairowua!" Neishori inaaisamis. Ore tara nejo meyieu inaairowua inaaoto eyieu, neishori inaairowua. Nejo erruat nakurro eyieu neishori enatii nkuruon. Neishori pooki toki torrono teneomonu esidai.

Ore tolakira nelotu entasat ajoki peyie eitirring'a nemeiro, nemeipang' tenening' enkikurrukur. Neisho ake peyie eiteru aikurrukur neitiamu, neipang' alo aing'uraa entoki naikurrukur. Nejoki entasat metorrinyoyu aji. Neton ake ore peyie eitoki aikurrukur neilo, neipang' boo. O metiaki ade entasat, "Shomo iyie amu miyieu imasaa." Nerrinyo' enkop enye toonkaik naarook enapita entolu, olalem, onkulie areta. Neishunye.

129

29. The Warrior Who Went to God's Country

Once upon a time, a group of warriors set off on a cattle raid, and on the way, one of the warriors' sandals broke and he had to sit down to repair it. As he did so, he said to the others: "Comrades, please wait for me." The others said: "Let the last one wait for you." He said the same to another group of warriors, who also told him the same thing: "Let the last one wait for you." This went on until the last warrior came by. "Please wait for me comrade," said the warrior with the broken sandal." "I will place a branch on the path that we will take when I get to the fork on the path, then you can follow that path and catch up with us," said the last warrior, as he hurried to catch up with the others. The other warrior agreed with him and continued mending his sandal.

The last warrior went on, and when he got to the fork he cut a branch and placed it on the path that the warriors had followed. As the warriors went on, a strong wind came and blew off the branch to the other path.

When the warrior with the broken sandal got to the spot after repairing his sandal, he found the branch and he followed the path on which it lay hurriedly, in a bid to catch up with his friends.

As he went along, he came upon the moon grazing. He stopped to stare at him. The moon asked him: "Hey you warrior, where do you come from and where are you going to in these parts?" The warrior answered: "I am from home and we are off on a cattle raid but the other warriors left me as I was repairing a broken sandal." The moon further questioned him: "When you look at me, what do you say I look like?" "Oh, you look very fine to me," answered the warrior. The moon further said to the warrior: "You may proceed and when you come across anybody, do not tell them what they look like, just tell them they look just fine, and do not take anything along the way, and when you are given a choice between a good and bad thing choose the bad thing." With these instructions accepted, the warrior continued with his journey.

Soon, he came upon a river with flowing water. As he was about to cross it, the river said to him: "Hey you warrior, have a drink before you cross me." The warrior answered: "Let me first cross you, then I will drink you from the other bank." He crossed the river and went on without drinking the water. He next came upon a river of milk, and as he was about to step into it, the river requested him to drink from it before he crossed over to the other side. The warrior spoke to the second river in the same way as he had spoken to the first, whereby he crossed and continued on his way. When he next came upon a river of blood, the same thing happened. He crossed all the three rivers without drinking from any of them.

As the warrior continued on his journey, he came upon two swords that were sharpening themselves. They said to the warrior: "Hey warrior, sharpen us then you can take the sharper of the two."

The warrior said to them: "Let me walk a little, then I will come and sharpen you." He went past them and continued on his journey. He next came upon delicious-looking pieces of meat that were frying on their own. The meat said to him: "Hey warrior, stir us, then you can eat the cooked one." The warrior again managed to trick the meat as he had done with the other things, and left it.

As he went along, the warrior found two axes that were fighting each other. They said to him: "Hey warrior, please separate us, then you can take one of us to your mother to hew wood with." The warrior said: "Hold on a little while, I'll be right back." He went on with his journey. The warrior continued on his journey, and whenever he came upon something he played tricks with it, and left without doing anything with it. He left everything behind.

Eventually, he came upon a man who was herding God's cattle. This man had two heads, and all the cattle had two tails. After exchanging greetings, the older man asked the warrior: "Hey, how do you find me?" "Oh, you look just like everybody else," answered the warrior. "And how do you find these cows?" the old man further asked the warrior. The warrior answered: "They are like all other cattle." The old man then gave the younger man directions, and they parted.

The warrior went on. When he was about to reach God's homestead, the homestead moved further away. He walked on with patience until he reached it. When he was about to enter the house, it also moved away. He went on until he got near it and entered inside it. As he tried to sit down, the stool also moved away from him but he followed it and managed to sit on it. And it so happened that there was a lady of God* in this house. After greetings and exchange of news, the old lady asked the warrior:

"Would you like fresh or stale milk?" The warrior answered: "What use do I have for fresh milk when stale milk is in plenty!" He was given fresh milk. Later on, just before bedtime, the old lady again asked the warrior: "Would you want curdled or fresh milk?" The warrior said he wanted fresh milk. He was given curdled.** When the time for people to retire for the night came, the old lady asked the warrior whether he wanted a bed that had been cleared of dust or one that was not. The warrior chose the latter, and was offered the former, whereupon he retired and was soon sound asleep.

At the earliest flickers of dawn, the lady went to wake the warrior up and said to him: "I want you to stay inside and when you hear the sound of thunder you should not utter a sound or come outside." The warrior did as he was instructed. In a few minutes, he heard the sound of thunder and the house vibrated. The warrior remained still until the old lady invited him outside, whereupon he found a large herd of cattle together with sheep, goats and donkeys. The lady said to him: "All this is your property, drive it and go in peace." The warrior took the cattle through a different route from the one he had followed before, and returned to his country.

As he was nearing his village, some clouds of dust were seen a distance away. After waiting for a long time, the other warriors had given up on their companion with the broken sandal. They assumed he had been eaten by wild beasts. His family had mourned until they had become sober. Then the warrior arrived with an enormous herd. When asked how he had obtained the cattle, he related his whole experience in God's country. His companions had returned empty handed.

Meanwhile, when the brother of the fortunate warrior heard his story, he made up his mind to go to God's country, so that he may be granted cattle. His brother forbade him to go, saying: "Please do not go, for you are not able to do the things I did." But he insisted. He said: "I must go."

The warrior's brother went on and on until he came upon the moon as he was grazing. The moon talked to him in the same way he had talked to his brother, and asked him: "What do you think of me?" "I have never ever seen anything like you!" answered the warrior in astonishment. The moon gave him directions, and he proceeded on the same path as his brother.

132

On coming upon the river of water the river, requested him to have a drink before crossing. He knelt down and drank to his fill before crossing. He also drank from the river of milk and that of blood, crossing them all after doing so. He next came upon swords that were sharpening themselves. When the swords asked him to sharpen them and take the sharpest, he did so, leaving with the sharpest. He found meat that was frying itself. He sat down, cooked it and ate the cooked bits. When he found the fighting axes, he separated them, and took one along as they had asked him to. He did everything that his brother had not done.

He next came upon the two-headed man as he was grazing two-tailed cattle. They talked together for a little while, and the old man posed the same question he had put to his brother: "How do you find me?" The warrior boldly answered: "You have two heads." "And how do you find these cattle?" continued the old man. "They each have two tails," added the warrior. The old man, nonetheless, directed the warrior to God's village and returned to tend his cattle.

He walked on. When he was about to go through the gate, the village moved further away. He swung his club and threw it at the village, which then stopped. When the house moved as he was about to enter it, he hit it with his club and it stopped.

When he tried to sit on the stool as it moved off, he took his club and hit it, splitting it into two, then he sat on the floor. When the old lady asked him to choose between fresh and stale milk he said: "Why should I choose stale milk when there is fresh milk!" He was given stale milk. At bedtime, he said he did not want fresh milk; he wanted curdled milk. He was given fresh milk. He chose a fine clean bed and he was given one with ashes. He was given all the bad things when he expressed preference for good ones.

Very early the next morning, the old lady went and gave him instructions to remain still and not to utter a sound nor leave the house when he heard the sound of thunder. But no sooner had he heard the sound of thunder than he shot up and went outside to check on what was making the sound. The lady once more asked him to go back to the house. But once again, as soon as he heard the sound of thunder, he rushed outside.

He did this over and over again, and eventually the lady said to him: "You go, you do not want property." He returned to his country empty handed, but for the axe, the sword and the other weapons. The end.

*Some versions of this story state that this lady was God "herself". The Maasai term for God always carries the feminine gender form 'en'.

**Curdled milk is more substantial in terms of food and is customarily offered to guests except when there is none available.

Review Questions

i) Summarize this story in 3 short paragraphs.

ii) Compare and contrast the characters of the two brothers as portrayed in this story.

30. Enkoipapaai ai e nanu

Netii apa, netii kuna ayiok are naang'ar menye. Naa kenyorra apa kuna ayiok imeor toki. Neye ng'otonye enkayioni nabo neeku enkaini e ng'otonye naing'orita. Naa keisho apa ena tasat, naa keiba ena ayioni neme enenye. Ore kuna ayiok naa ninche pokira oopuo inkishu anaake. Neeta apa kuna ayiok inkishu naadas dama tenetir esumash. Naa keisho ake obo peyie eidip atadasa, neipotoki olikae menyaaki sii ninye adas nerrinyo olikae inkishu. Naa kejoro apa kuna ayiok "enkoipapaai" tenkaraki nang'ar menye.

Neton apa ake ena tasat adamu eneiko kuna ayiok peyie meitoki aanyorra, nelaikino. Nejo toltau lenye, "ekaing'oru enaiko peyie aar ena ayioni metua." Neisho nabo olong', nejoki ena ayioni enye meshomo shoo ore teneipir enkolong' neshukunye ang' metabarno. Nelo enkayioni shoo ore peyie eipir enkolong' neshuko ang' metabarni, neok kule, paa kerrinyo inkishu. Ore ekenyu anaa taisere, neitoki entasat ajoki ena ae ayioni pee elo sii ninye metabarni teneipir enkolong'. Neisho ake etioyo enkayioni, netur enkumoto nagut oleng' tedukuya erruat. Ore peyie elotu enkayioni nejoki, "Shomo sii iyie dukuya iyau olmurunya maatabarno." Nejo enkayioni airrapirrapu olmurunya nedoiki enaduo kumoto. Neiteleiki entasat enkumoto osoit sapuk nelo aing'uaa. Neenyu enkayioni olikae te shoo ejo ake kelotu, o memuto. Nereu ninye inkishu ang' ejo ebaiki neeta esiai naibookoki olikae.

Ore peyie ereu enkayioni inkishµ ang' teipa nelo aing'oru olikae. Ore peyie elau nelo aikilikuan ng'otonye. Nejoki ng'otonye, "Oi atabarno ake ninye nanu nelo shoo." Neing'oruni apa ena ayioni, ore peyie elai neji ebaiki neinosa ng'uesi tiang'ata. Nepalari olorere.

Nebiki apa omeidurri tenapa ang' nepeji olmuate. Ore peyie esha, nelengu ene wueji apa netii ele muate oleng'. Ore nabo olong' nereu enkayioni inkishu ele muate. Eishira taa apa ometigirayu tenkaraki nataIa olalashe. Ore edaa inkishu nelo ninye atonie ele soit apa opising'are ena kumoto natii olalashe. Neeta apa kuna ayiok osinkolio orany teshoo teneaku kedas inkishu. Neton ake ena ayioni tele soit, nedamu olalashe. Neiteru arany ilo sinkolio:

"Enkoipapaai ai e nanu

Eituyupuyupakitia nsampin e papa

Enkoipapaai ai e nanu

Nemadas ilki linono

Enkoipapaai ai e nanu."

Ore ake peyie ening' idia ayioni natii enkumoto olikae erany, neirukoo sii ninye ajo:

"Enkoipapaai ai e nanu

Tadasa sere sere mikintotio

Enkoipapaai ai e nanu

Tadasa sere mikintotio

Amu ng'utunyi apa naatipika enkumoto."

Ore peyie ening' enkayioni neng'as ajo kentim nairukoo. Neitoki ake arany. Nejo inining'o 'nening' ajo ekeeta eneing'ua ilo toilo. Nejo aitoki ainining' nening' ajo abori osoit otonita ening'ore ilo toilo. Nejo aiwuang'ie osoit nedol olalashe. Neitayu. Einosa apa inkulukuok nemuta ilkarash, naa penyo nedolisho meitieu aing'ura enkolong'. Neisho enkayioni olikae olkarasha obo, nelepoki inkishu. Neisho metang'asa alopu inkulukuok paa keisho kule metooko. Nerik ang' teipa.

Ore epuo inkayiok ang' teipa, neinosaki ena ayioni apa natii enkumoto olikae eneikunaka ng'otonye enkumoto.

Negoro olalashe oleng' amu meitanyaanyukie apa ele alashe Iikae tung'ani. Neisho ake peyie edol ajo etaa kebaya ang' neii eremet metipija. Neisho ake peyie ebaya ang' neng'as aing'oru ng'otonye. Neng'or ake neye teine. Nelo aing'oru menye aliki enataasa. Neipoti ilpayiani aaliki. Neji akaae. Nebik inkayiok pokira meeta inoong'otonye.

30. Two Step-Brothers Who Were Friends

There once lived two step-brothers who were such close friends that no one could separate them. One of the boys lost his mother at an early age, so the surviving woman was charged with the responsibility of taking care of both boys. And this woman, who was the boy's step-mother, had no liking for her step-son. And the boy's duty was to look after cattle, among which was one gentle cow that the boys used to milk each day whenever they became hungry. Each of the boys drew from two of the cow's four teats, and this became a rule which they always observed. The boys referred to each other as "son of my father" because they were the sons of one man.

Their mother, as the surviving woman came to be called by both boys, did not like the idea of the two boys being such good friends, and so tried unsuccessfully to separate them. She said to herself, "I must find a way of killing this boy." So, the next day, as the boys took the cattle out grazing, she told her son to return home in the middle of the day to have a hair cut. The boy did as he was bid, and at around midday he went back home, had a haircut and a drink of milk and returned to the cattle. The next day it was the turn of the other boy to have his hair cut. But before the boy went home, the woman dug a deep hole at the head of the bed. On arrival, the boy was sent to fetch a razor at the head of the bed. But as he tried to rummage for the blade, he fell into the hole which the woman quickly covered with a big stone. The other boy waited expectantly for his friend until evening when he drove the cattle back home, assuming that his friend may have been assigned some other duty at home.

As soon as he got home, the boy looked for his step-brother, but not finding him, he asked his mother where he was. She categorically denied having any knowledge of his whereabouts, saying: "I gave him a hair cut and he went back to the cattle." The people looked for the boy everywhere, and when they could not find him, they assumed he had been eaten by wild animals.

After some time, the villagers moved home and burnt up the old village. When the rains fell, some long grass grew at the old settlement. One day, the surviving boy, who had cried until he could cry no more for his brother, took the cattle there to graze. While the cattle grazed, he went and sat down at the big stone that covered the hole inside which was his step-brother. And it so happened that the boys had a song they used to sing when they were milking their cow. As he sat on the stone, the boy remembered his step-brother and he started singing the song:

Son of my father

The udder of the dapple grey is bursting with milk

But I will not draw from your teats

Son of my father.

When the boy in the hole heard the other one singing, he responded to him in song:

Son of my father

You may draw and let it nurture you

Son of my father

You may draw and let it nurture you

For it was your mother who put me into the hole.

When the boy on the top of the stone first heard the reply, he thought his voice was simply being echoed by the forest. He sang one more time, and again his brother sang in response, and he realised that the singing was coming from underneath the stone. On rolling the stone away, he was astonished to see his brother whom he helped out of the hole. He had eaten soil and his clothes were all tattered. He could barely see, for his eyes had grown sensitive to light. The boy gave his brother one of his sheets to put on, and he milked one of the cows for him to drink fresh milk. He first made him vomit all the soil he had been eating, and then fed him with some fresh milk. When evening came, he took him home with him.

On their way home, the boy who had been rescued related to his step-brother how their mother had put him inside the hole. His step-brother became furious because he loved his brother more than any other person. When they were about to reach home, he sharpened his spear till it was razor sharp. On arrival, he headed straight for his mother, whom he instantly speared to death. He next sought his father to inform him of what he had done. The men were then assembled, and when the story was told, the people simply listened without comment. Nothing could be done. So the two boys lived happily without a mother.

Review Questions

i)   Stories of cruel step-mothers are common all over the world. Think
     of one from your own community and write it down.

ii) In the end, when the boy killed his mother, we are told that none of
     the villagers made any comment. Why do you think this was so?

31. Ori enkine ai – enkayioni oo ntare

Netii apa ena ayioni naa ninye olchekut loontare. Naa ore tiatua kuna tare netii enkine
naiba olkuo lenye. Neeku keisij ena ayioni ena kine aisijoki olkuo tadekenya o teipa. Naa
ore eisij naa inji ejo:

> "Ori ori, ori enkine ai
>
> Tonyorra enkuo ino, ori enkine ai
>
> Maayieng' ake, ori enkine ai
>
> Tenoshi alem, ori enkine ai
>
> Natumutie nkulie, ori enkine ai
>
> Iyie o enkuo ino, ori enkine ai
>
> Ori ori, ori enkine ai ..."

Ore nabo olong' neitushuli intare onkishu neishori ena ayioni meshomo airrita. Ore
ake peyie eipir enkolong' neponu ilmurran liae kop aaya kuna kishu o ntare, niaraa sii
ena ayioni. Neya pookin enkop enye. Nerikokini ena ayioni olpayian oitaa menye oentasat
naipot ajo ng'otonye. Naa kenyor ele payian ena ayioni oleng' kake keiba entasat. Neitoki
ake ena ayioni aaku ninye olchekut loontare. Ore tenapa kop naing'ua, neing'oruni apa
ena ayioni onkishu eshula ontare nelai. Kake eitu sii epalari olorere.

Ore nabo olong' etii ena ayioni intare neponu ilmurran lenkop enye. Neing'asia ena
ayioni pee edol kulo murran neshipa sii oleng' amu mejo apa ketumi aikata. Netii kulo
murran olong'arie kina ena ayioni, netii sii olong'arie menye olenkapu lenye. Eewuo sii
olmurrani oyamita entito nang'arie ena ayioni kina. Neponu taa aipang'aki ena ayioni te
shoo.

Ore enyae ilomon naa keureisho ena ayioni ejo keinepu ilpayiani teneponu aa leenoo
inchoo dama. Neeku ilkuti omon ake eidima ainosa. Nejoki enkayioni meshomo. Neutaki
taa eneim ade tenepuo enkang', neliki sii enetii ninye enkayioni peyie etum ainosaki
ilkulie omon. Nejoki enkayioni ilalashera peyie tenening' ade eisijoki enkine olkuo
neinining' amu ina kata einosaki ilomon pooki. Nemeyiolo sii tenaa ketii ilmurran ang'
kake keyiolou tenelo ang' teipa. Neing'ua taa enkayioni ilalashera meisudori omemuto
peyie etumoki aashom ang'.

Ore ake peyie eidipi eramatare, nelo enkayioni aisijoki enkine olkuo. Etang'asa taa aleenisho tenaa ketii ilmurran enkang' nedol ajo metii. Nepik ake osiang'au sapuk kule, neshum te kioni peyie eok ade ilalashera teneponu. are eisij enkine nening' entasat ajo ijo keinosu ilomon kumok. Nejo, "Shye! kejo aa toi enkayioni teneisij enkine?" Nejoki enkayioni, "Neijia oshi iyiook kijo tenkop ang'." Nejoki olpayian entasat, "Tapala inchoo ejo eneji oshi tenkop enye."

Neinosu taa enkayioni ilomon eitaakuno kenkine eisij. Naa inji ejo:

"Ori ori ori enkine ai
Tonyorra enkuo ina, ori erikine ai
Maayieng' ake, ori enkine ai
Tenoshi alem, ori enkine ai
Natumutie inkulie, ori enkine ai
Iyie o enkuo ino, ori enkine ai

Teniponunu ade, ori enkine ai
Enteryioli ake, ori enkine ai
Ara olole Sinyai, ori enkine ai
Olotarayioki ori, enkine ai
Atii ilapa mong'i, ori enkine ai
Inkishu ontare, ori enkine ai

Ng'ole adol intae, ori enkine ai
Temisigiyioi ori, enkine ai
Netii ole yieyio, ori enkine ai
Netii ole papa, ori enkine ai
Netii olenkapu, ori enkine ai
Netii enkaputi, ori enkine ai

Eteyiang' aki apa, ori enkine ai
Parpusi lino, ori enkine ai
Naa olikae ilo, ori enkine ai
Oning'o entuala, ori enkine ai
Teidie tolosinko, ori enkine ai

Teniponunu, ori enkine ai

Leilo osiang'au, ori enkine ai

Oshuma tende, ori enkine ai

Entang'as engatai, ori enkine ai

Emiureishosho ake, ori enkine ai

Amu ilayiok lelo, ori enkine ai

Ooikoroj enkang', ori enkine ai

Metii ilomperria, ori enkine ai

Oomut intae, ori enkine ai

Entayioloki ake, ori enkine ai

Amu abayie tene, ori enkine ai

Naishopito ake, ori enkine ai

Emekiti onkerra, ori enkine ai

Neina yieyio, ori enkine ai

Entang'as engolai, ori enkine ai

Amu kaiba, ori enkine ai

Leilo papa, ori enkine ai

Emiar ake, ori enkine ai

Amu kaanyor, ori enkine ai

Ori ori ori enkine ai.

Ore ake peyie eidip enkayioni aisijo enkine teilo sinkolio neidu ilmurran enkang·. Neer olorere pooki intasati ake etung'ayioki. Neer ng'otonye ena ayioni, neing'ua menye. Nearaa intoyie, neya inkishu pooki, inkuti ake etung'ayioki aing'ueki ele payian apa onyor ena ayioni. Neiting' enkatini teine.

31. The Shepherd Boy

There once lived a shepherd boy who herded a large flock of sheep and goats. Among his flock was a goat that did not like its kid, and so the boy used to soothe the goat every morning and evening. He composed a song that he sang to the goat and the song went like this:

Calm down my goat
You better like your kid
Or else I shall slaughter you
With the usual knife
That has finished the others
You and your kid
Calm down my goat.

One day, when there was no one to look after the cattle, the boy was instructed to combine them with the sheep and goats and take charge of them all. But in the middle of the day, warriors from another country came on a raid and took all of them all along with the boy to their country. And in this new country, the boy found a foster mother and father, but while the man developed a great liking for the boy, the woman disliked him a great deal. The boy was again assigned the duty of herding sheep and goats. Meanwhile, back home, the people had been searching everywhere for the boy, together with the livestock, and although they had not found any of them, they had not given up.

One day, as the boy was out grazing, some warriors from his country appeared to him. The boy was astonished to see them, but he was also delighted, since he never expected his whereabouts to be discovered. Among these warriors, one was the boy's brother. His step-brother was also there and so was his cousin as well as his brother-in-law. As they were exchanging news, the boy felt uneasy, fearing that the old men might find them for they conducted surprise visits to the flock; so he quickly dismissed his brothers. He directed them to the village, explained the location of their house, and instructed them to return for more news. He told them to wait until evening when he would be soothing the notorious goat, at which time he would convey to them all the relevant information. It so happened that the boy needed to find out whether or not the warriors of his adopted village were home before he could get back to his brothers. After making this plan, the boy left his brothers in hiding, until evening time, when they would be able to go to the village.

That evening, when the milking and other domestic duties had been completed, the boy went to soothe the notorious goat as usual. He had by this time checked on the warriors and realised that they were out that night. He filled a big gourd with milk, and stood it against the gate post for his brothers to drink when they arrived. As he was soothing the goat, the woman whom he had come to regard as his mother realised that the boy was giving away some very suspicious information, and she exclaimed, "Goodness me! How is the boy soothing the goat?" The boy replied that that was what they did back home. On hearing the lady's complaint, her husband intervened and told her to let the boy soothe the goat the way he was accustomed to in his country. So the boy continued giving his brothers information on the pretext of soothing the goat. This is what he said:

Calm down my goat
You had better like your kid
Or else I shall slaughter you
With the usual knife
That has finished the others
You and your kid
So calm down my goat.

When you come tonight
Do recognise me
I am ole Sinyai
The one who was abducted
As I was tending those oxen
The cattle and the sheep

Yesterday was when I saw you
At Emisigiyioi
The son of my mother was there
The one of my father too

So was my cousin
As well as my brother-in-law

Your fine blue ox
Was slaughtered
But there is the other one
Whose bell is heard
Jingling at the village centre

When you later come
There is the gourd
Leaning against the gate post
You may gulp it down

Do not be afraid
For those you hear over there
Are only boys acting up
The spear owners are away
Those who would wipe you out

Do recognise me
For I am at the very end
And I am wearing
An untanned sheep's hide
Over there is my mother
First finish her
For she hates me
Over there is my father
Do not kill him
For he loves me
Calm down now my goat*

When the boy had finished soothing the goat with that song, the warriors jumped over the gate and killed all the people of that village except the women. They also killed the boy's foster mother, but not his father, and took with them all the girls, the cattle and the sheep, except a few they left for the old man who loved the boy. The story ends there.

* The chorus 'my goat' is repeated at the end of each line of the song.

Review Question ▄

What method did the shepherd boy use to convey information to his brothers and how effective was this method?

32. Ntoyle enkung'u

Netii apa, netii ele payian. Ore nabo olong' nenutayu enkitok enye. Ore ele payian, anaa empukunoto enye, naa keiba tenedol enkitok enye eton ayengiyeng'a. Keisho ake peyie eidip entasat ae siai nejoki menyaaki aas ae. Erisio eidipa ina eishooki enkae. Niaku neijia eiko anaake o meitorito enkewarie eitu eyeng'iyeng'a enaduo tua.

Nelusoo taa ilapaitin kumok enyok ake entasat aasisho meisho olpayian eyeng'iyeng'a. Kedumunye anaake eton eitu emanaa enanyokie alepisho, ore peyie eidip elepore neirriki ilasho ilaleta. Nelo aoku enkare tolkeju, neitoki alo ilkeek, nemur enkaji. Niaku ore esiaai enaduo ang' pooki naa ninye eing'orita, netashala.

Eya ninye nejoki olpayian meshomo aok nkishu peyie eton ninye tiang' aperno. Neton taa apa ake ele moruo aisilisil entomononi enye o meeu kenya ae. Neye eeta ilapaitin oopishiana.

Ore ake peyie elaiy entasat anaa taata neyoki akenyu eteijia olpayian enkung'u oleng'. Neng'as ajo koltudutai oimua kake aisapuk sii. Nejarari taa ake enkung'u ajeyu o metaa penyo neidimari oladuo moruo. Nelusoo taa enkata naado etiu nji ake enkung'u olpayian. Nianyu apa meo oltudutai peyie edany o metisia. Ore nabo olong' nedumu enkalem nejo: "Ore amu meekure apa eoku ele tudutai ekadany taata peyie etiu enatiu." Oo naa peyie edany olmoruo entusui neipurjukunye nkutiti mao are! Neiputukuny oladuo payian kake etishipe sii peyie etum inkera. Nedung'oki nkarn, nejo nabo Nasira nejo enkae Noltau.

Neitubulu taa olpayian nkera enyena tenyamali sapuk. Tenelo enkare, anaa ilkeek nenap inkera. Ore elepisho nenap enkerai nabo tenkoshoke nenap enkae tenkoriong'. Ore elo shoo o tenemur enkaji o tenias pooki toki naas nias enapita ake imao enyena. Nenyamalu taa olpayian enimimba. Kake nenyok aing'or inaduo kera enyena o metubulu aaku ntoyie botorok. Ore peyie ebulu nkera aaku noshi naing'uaroyu oopeny niaku keikenoo papaai lenye tiaji eiguran o metaa neshukunye ninye teipa. Ore peyie eshukunye

144

olpayian neeta osinkolio orany peyie eyiolou nkera aajo ninye oewuo. Nejo:

"Eijiija nemedanya

Ntoyie ainei e nkung'u

Nasira, Noltau lanyor

Taboluoki."

Naa tenening' nkera ele sinkolio nesioki aabolu papaai lenye. Niaku neijia eiko anaake. Ore nabo olong' neponu ilmag'ati oing'ua ae kop. Neirrib ena ang' olmoruo. Nening' nkera eiro tiatua aji. Neisudori tentim aaleenu ilopeny inkera. Ore peyie edoyio enkolong' nebau olpayian, nerany oloshi ake sinkolio:

"Eijiija nemedanya

Ntoyie ainei e nkung'u

Nasira, Noltau lanyor

Taboluoki."

Nening' taa ilmang'ati osinkolio lolpayian. Neirrag ina kop. Ore peyie eyoki akenyu neitayok olmoruo nkishu daa neikenoo nkera tiaji. Neisho ake kulo mangati peyie eyiolou aajo etaa enashukunye olpayian nepuo aarany oloshi sinkolio aajoki nkera metabolu. Nening' ake nkera osinkolio nekwet aabol enkaji ejo ke papaai lenye otushukunye. Ina taa peyie eya ilmang'ati nkera enkop enye.

Nebau olpayian ina kata ake. Nejo taranya oloshi sinkolio meeta entoki natang'amayie. Ore peyie einepu enkaji eisiu neyiolou ajo ewaki nkera enyena. Nelo alilita aing'oru. Neing'oru, nelilita toonkadoru, nelau tukul. Ina taa oshi peyie elotu olmoruo aaku olotala enkitok, neitoki sii alau nkera tenkaraki enkarruisho enye. Neiting' enkatini ai teine.

32. The Girls of the Knee

Once upon a time, there lived a cruel old man. His wife conceived at one time. And as was his habit, the old man disliked seeing his wife taking a rest. As soon as she had completed one task, she was told to take on another. And no sooner had she completed a second, than she was commanded to take up yet another. This routine was repeated every day, from morning till night, so that the poor old pregnant woman was kept on her feet each day until the early hours of the morning.

And so, many months went by. The woman persevered and kept on working, since her husband would never permit her to rest. She would wake up every morning before dawn to do the milking, after which she would lock up the calves in their pens. Having done this, she would scamper to the river to fetch water for the household. Then firewood. It was also her duty to plaster the house. Every single job in the home was supposed to be her responsibility. And as though that was not enough, she was often called upon to water the cattle while her husband stayed idle at home. And so the old man kept pestering his wife thus, until one day, overwhelmed with fatigue she collapsed and died. She was seven months pregnant.

The morning after his wife died, the old man woke up with one large swelling on one knee. At first he thought it was a boil, but the swelling grew bigger and heavier by the day, until the old man could barely walk. After what seemed like months, the old man's patience wore out. He took a knife and said to himself: "Since this boil is never coming to a head, I am going to lance it, come what may." And as he lanced the boil, alas, there emerged two adorable little girls. Amazed as he was at this strange occurrence, the old man was, nevertheless, delighted at the arrival of his twin daughters. He named one of his daughters Nasira and the other Noltaulanyor.

The old man brought up his daughters with a certain amount of difficulty. Whenever he went to fetch water or firewood he strapped one child on his stomach and the other on his back. He also carried the children while he was out grazing cattle, when he plastered the house, and while he did everything else. He went through many difficulties but he, nevertheless, succeeded in bringing up his daughters until they were big girls. When they were big enough to be left on their own, the old man locked up the girls in the house whenever he had to go out. They remained there until his return. When he came back, he would sing a song he had composed to alert his daughters, thus:

> It had grown tender
> But would not burst
> My daughters of the knee
> Nasira, Noltaulanyor, my beloved ones
> Let me in.

On hearing the song, the children would immediately know it was their father and they would open the door for him. This went on for a long time.

Then, one day, some people from an enemy country came into the old man's village. They heard the voices of the two girls talking inside the house. They hid away in the nearby bushes to await the parents of the children whose voices they had heard. In the evening, the old man returned and sang his usual song:

> It had grown tender
> But would not burst
> My daughters of the knee
> Nasira, Noltaulanyor, my beloved ones
> Let me in.

The enemies listened to the old man's song. They spent the night in that country. Early next morning, the old man took his cattle out grazing, leaving the children locked up in the house. The enemies timed the old man, and on realising that he was about to return home, they went to the door and sang his song, asking the girls to open the door for them. The girls did so thinking it was their father who had returned. Thereupon the enemies abducted the twin girls to their country.

The old man arrived soon after, but when he sang his usual song, he received no response. Finding the door ajar, he entered the house only to find no one in the house. He realised that his children had been stolen. He conducted a search for them far and wide, but to no avail. The old man had lost a wife and then his children because of his cruelty. And there ends my story.

Review Questions

i)   Explain how the old man became "pregnant"?

ii) What is the moral of this story?

iii) Did the old man deserve what he got?

CHAPTER FOUR

Riddles: Iloyietia and Ilang'eni

Riddles are posed at the opening of each oral literature session to alert the audience, usually children, and to prepare them for the evening's entertainment. The Maasai distinguish two types of riddles which have here been labelled simple and complex types, owing to their character. The simple types of riddles are what the Maasai call **Iloyietia** on account of their opening formula **oyiote**, which precedes riddles of this type. **Ilang'eni** (literally means "those for the clever") constitute the complex-type riddles and are also named on account of the formula that introduces them: **Ira ng'en?** (are you clever?). Each type has its distinct characteristics.

An obvious feature of the simple type of riddles is that they are commonly stated in the form of declarative sentences rather than questions. In riddle **3**, for instance, we have a statement which is also an implied, not a stated question. But while it is understood that one is expected to guess the identity of the two "people" crossing the wilderness "without talking to each other", it is not as simple as that in other cases. In riddle **51** the question has been tagged to the statement for the purposes of clarity. Notice that the question part is missing in Maa because the riddle is well understood without it. For contrast, compare this with the way the two riddles of the complex type have been stated. The question is asked in a careful and systematic manner. But as every rule has an exception, riddles **74** and **75** are two examples of exceptions to this rule.

Another feature that differentiates the two types of riddles is theme. While complex riddles always have reasonably logical images that are easily visualised, the majority of simple riddles tend to have predetermined and often nonsensical images and answers. Most of the answers cannot be guessed even by Maa speakers unless they are familiar with them. Compare for example riddles **29, 40, 41, 105, 109** and **110**, on the one hand, with the two complex riddles.

An even more obscure case is seen in riddle **4**, which is nothing but an exclamation "mm-hm!". The reason for this difference probably lies in the fact that, while complex riddles for the most part function to sharpen a child's wits and reasoning ability, the simple riddles serve this function only to a lesser degree, their main function being to test the child's memory and thinking speed.

Simple riddles are also posed in a funny and light-hearted mood, while complex riddles are told in a straightforward and rather serious manner. This light-heartedness is achieved in different ways in simple riddles. In riddle **57** we find the fire being personified as a girl with "long strands of beads", and even being given a girl's name, "Nanyokie" in **59**. This personification has the effect of obscuring the otherwise ferocious image of a fire in flames. On his part, the fly is named **Kavirondo (97)** and **Karanja**, thus portraying him at least as an acceptable "being" rather than as a distasteful pest.

This light-heartedness is also achieved through associating images that are far removed and rather bizarre. There is also teasing and poking fun at ordinary situations. This has the effect of inducing laughter and mirth into a riddle session and making riddles sound like jokes. Thus an initiate, with his fat greasy black look is likened to a buffalo (**5**); pack saddles are said to resemble a thin old man with veins; and what fun to visualise the limping gluttonous hyena performing a domestic duty, showing goats their kids! (**108**); or a rhinoceros sewing a boyfriend's garment (**110**).

There is also a frequent use of exaggerated images. In reference to the structure of poles and rafters of a house, the image is drawn of "your father strangling your mother" (**4**); the stone for sharpening knives is likened to a grave condition of barrenness (**32**); imagery with sexual overtones is used when referring to the simple act of pushing a sword inside the scabbard (**36**). These images tend to manipulate one's emotions in the way a serious topic is alluded to, in each case, and then immediately dispelled by a response with which there seems to be no apparent association. It is interesting to note how embarrassment caused by the allusion to sex in riddle **36** is relieved in the end by the knowledge that after all it is one's mind that is dirty and not the riddle. In contrast, complex riddles are direct and to the point.

Another aspect that is worthy of note is the way the simple type of riddle makes liberal use of otherwise forbidden linguistic terms. In Maa, for instance, use of the terms "your mother" and "your father", **ng'utunyi** and **minyi** respectively, is restricted to impolite conversations. In fact they constitute abuses even in isolation. Yet in riddle **10** we are told that "something is issuing out of your mother's body?" Owing to the use of the word **ng'utunyi**, the audience gets psychologically prepared for some vulgar reference, only to learn that she is only carrying a baby whose feet protrude out of the garment. "Your mother's" abusive behaviour is further referred to in riddles **11** and **44**, but again we are immediately told that she is only chewing gum and mouthing tobacco leaves, respectively.

The same pejorative remarks are made with reference to father (**minyi**) in quite a few riddles. In riddle **46** his gown is likened to a dunghill, to which there seems no resemblance at all. When a hide is pegged down to dry, it is compared with "your father" struggling as he is being shaved (**51**), a sight which would be extremely embarrassing, at least for the girls. Again, the patterns that are made by foam along the river bank are not likened simply to ribs but to "your father's ribs" (**60**). The whole list is interspersed by apparent grossness and vulgarity which is not found in complex-type riddles.

Despite this apparent light-heartedness, simple riddles, in their own unique way, teach lessons and impart knowledge in the same way as other oral literature genres, such as stories, proverbs, songs, poems etc., do. Riddles are essentially metaphors that are created from the processes of association, comparison, and the perception of likeness and difference. Riddles prod children into thinking and perceiving rather than simply seeing. Other riddles are based on puns, and these cannot be answered without a knowledge of the language. This is particularly true of some complex riddles that have been avoided due to the difficulty they pose in translation.

Riddles have been categorized according to the theme of their answer, except in a few cases where the image seems prominent. This arrangement was simply to facilitate easy handling, and does not in any way reflect on the manner in which they are relayed in the traditional setting.

A brief analysis of some of the riddles in their categories is necessary.

The first category of riddles pertains to people in different situations or playing various roles. Riddle **1**, aptly opens a riddling session and alerts the audience/participants in a rather interesting manner, for it plays on the formulaic opening of riddles. When the propounder says *oyiote*, "are you ready?", the audience normally replies **e-ewuo**, "it has come", without paying any attention to the literal meaning of the words. When suddenly confronted with the question, "why do you say it has come?", those who do not know the answer find themselves at a loss. They will start analysing the actual meaning of their utterance in a bid to figure out what has come. Further reasoning soon reveals that it is merely the formulaic opening of riddles that is being referred to, thus forming a riddle within a riddle, and that the expected answer: "a discussion between you and me", is a witty way of saying: "we have commenced a riddling session and everyone's participation is expected."

Riddle **2** compares a tree with many branches with a man who has many sons. The falling of the tree signifies either the ageing or the dying of the old man. And as with any plant, withering is followed by the sprouting of numerous offshoots that are products of the main. These siblings are said to wander far (**Kinopop** symbolises distance), or to head in one direction, the way siblings keep together. Note the precision of the imagery.

Riddle **5** makes fun of the initiate by comparing him with the buffalo. The comparison can be viewed in three ways. Both are black, one from a natural colour, and the other from applying charcoal on his body and being prohibited from taking a wash, as well as wearing black togas; they both have a smooth shiny look, the buffalo's being natural while the initiate's comes from applying grease to his body; and they are both heavy and stocky, the former from his natural size and the latter from feeding on special foods while convalescing from circumcision. The comparison may seem far-fetched, but it is by no means inaccurate.

Still on people, riddles **7** and **8** ridicule the Dorobo, both for their appearance and occupation. From his hunting adventures and escapades in rocky country the Dorobo is bound to incur scratches and bruises (**8**).

From carrying a quiver over his shoulder, the originator of this riddle thought the Dorobo and his quiver were preparing for a fight.

Many ideas are transmitted in this group of riddles. We learn for instance, of the collective spirit observed in a session where riddles are posed (**1**); that numeracy in children is viewed with admiration (**2**); that hospitality is assumed by visitors (**4**); that this community observes initiation as a rite with its accompanying social taboos and dietary habits (**5**); that raiding of stock is not uncommon (**6**); that hunting as an occupation is not viewed positively (**7** and **8**); that their sense of beauty lies not in brown gums and teeth but probably on very different features (**9**); and that women carry children strapped on their backs (**10**) and frequently chew gum (**11**). In the same way, all riddles, when analysed from a wider perspective, reveal values, attitudes, biases, habits and customs that may not obviously stand out.

The second category of riddles calls for a closer look at the housing and settlement pattern of a Maasai homestead. We learn that the doors of houses face the gateway to the village (**12**) appearing as though they are all gazing at people as they enter; that from the doorway, only two of the poles supporting the house are visible (**13**) giving the impression that they alone, of all other "warriors", have the pastoral flair for watching and tending cattle; that when erecting a house rafters are placed on top of forked poles, appearing as though the latter is strangling the former in the same way a physically stronger man may strangle a weak woman (**14**). We learn that the strips of bark used for fastening poles and rafters together are so long that, if used as belts, they would be too loose even on the widest of persons. Verbs of everyday usage, like "tending", "strangling" and "spinning", are employed to create rather bizarre associations.

From the third category of riddles, we see that waste products are portrayed in a positive light and that some fairly hidden information is imparted. We are taught how to distinguish between good and bad herdsmanship by examining the texture of the dung (**18**); that fresh dung coming into contact with a cold atmosphere appears as though it is steaming (**19**); and that people sometimes spit as they walk and the patterns formed by their spittle could be likened to cowries (**20**).

With a little stretch of the imagination, one could also associate sheep with their droppings (**22** and **23**) and goats, or any caravan of animals, with the dust they raise (**21**).

Riddles tend to assume a knowledge of the institutions, customs, mannerisms, artefacts and other aspects that are typical of a particular community. The fourth category, more than any other, portrays life in a pastoral community. Here, we are told of various items and their utilization. The collective use of shopping bags (**24**); tobacco containers (**27, 51**); the existence of special poles for boring holes when erecting houses (**28**); uses of razor blades for shaving heads clean (**30**); the use of stones in place of files for sharpening knives (**32**); swords (**36**); cow hide beds (**38**) gourds (**39, 40, 41**); pots (**42**); firestones (**43**); garments that are decorated with beads (**48**); and toothbrushes (**49**) are but a few of these. Images are drawn and rotated around a pastoral environment. The colour, shape and character of a sisal plant is said to resemble cattle (**66**) and an army (**68**). It is significant that the white spot on the donkey's forehead is associated with a clearing on the landscape that could be suitable for settlement. In the last category of riddles, we observe that figures are drawn from colours, patterns, sizes, habits and movements of various types of insects.

For the purposes of comparison, two complex riddles (**ilang'eni**) have been listed at the end of this chapter.

Review Questions

i) List characteristics of the two types of Maasai riddles.

ii) Select ten riddles from your community, translate and explain them so as to enable a person from another culture to fully understand them.

iii) "Riddles are essentially metaphors that are created from the processes of association, comparison and the perception of likeness and difference." Discuss this statement using examples from riddles in this collection.

iv) Explain how light-heartedness is achieved in riddles.

RIDDLES ON PEOPLE

The propounder says **Oyiote**, are you ready?

The audience replies, **E-euo**, it has come, (we are ready).

1. *A naa ijo eewuo?*
   Enkiroroto ai o enino.

   Why do you say it has come (you are ready?)

   Because it is a discussion between you and me.

   This riddle alerts the audience and makes them appreciate their role in replying and propounding riddles.

2. *Eturori olchani nepuo ilng'osil Kinopop,*
   (neing'or ilng'osil nabo alo.) Olmoruo obore ayiok.

   The tree has fallen and its branches went up to Kinopop (or the branches faced one direction).

   A man with many sons.

3. *Kidung' ang'ata kira aare nimiking'amaro.*
   Iyie oloip lino.

   The two of us cross the wilderness without talking to each other. You and your shadow.

4. *Mmm-hm! (or siisi).*
   Ilomon latala endaa naisho

   Mmm-hm!

   Visitors have arrived and I have no food to give them.

   This is a common exclamation when one is in a "fix". Hospitality in the form of supplying food to visitors is usually assumed, making it difficult for one to refuse it.

5. *Arro onyil*
   Olaibartani.

   Who looks like a greasy buffalo? The initiate.

   The initiates wear black togas and put grease on their bodies.

6. *Ejo tirkash nejo hio!*
   Ilainyiamok.

   They approach hesitantly yet bravely.

The raiders.
Depending on the confrontation, raiders may either steal or take by force.

7.   *Eidikirrokino nampois o nang'iyo.*
     Oltorroboni o emootian.
     They are ready to fight.
     The bluish one and the brown one are ready to fight.
     The Dorobo and the sheath.

8.   *Esika kejek.*
     Oltorroboni oked esoit.
     His legs are bruised.
     A Dorobo who has climbed a rock (cliff).

9.   *Edoku te supalera.*
     Nyirta oolkokoyo.
     They rise from over the acacias.
     The gums of the Kikuyus.
     The Maasai know the Kikuyu to have slightly swollen brown gums, yellowish brown teeth and heavy lips, leading to a general indistinctness as to which is which, making the beholder wonder which of the three they see.
     The lera trees have a brownish yellow colour.

10. *Edung' ng'utunyi olosinko erumisho enebanji.*
     Enkeju enkerai.
     Your mother walks across the village with something issuing out of her (body).
     The leg of a baby.
     When the baby is fastened on the back and strapped with a garment, a little leg is seen issuing from its mother's side while the rest of the body is hidden.

11. *Edung' ng'utunyi olosinko emorisho.*
     Entasat nanyaal enaing'urre.
     Your mother walks across the village using abusive language.
     A woman chewing gum.

There are various clicks and sounds made by sucking in air, which children are prohibited from making because of their likeness to the noises made during sexual intercourse. But children are merely told to stop being abusive. The same kind of sound is made by chewing gum, obtained from various plants chewed often by women.

RIDDLES ON HOME AND HOUSE STRUCTURE

12. *Anaa kajo aimu kishomi naing'or pooki?*
    Nkutukie oonkajijik.
    As I walk through the gate, they all gaze at me.
    The doors of houses.
    All doors of houses face inwards towards the village centre.

13. *Murran lainei kumok naa aare ake oipang'aki nkishu.*
    Mbokishie kutuk-aji.
    I have many warriors but it is only two who appear to be looking after cattle.
    The poles of a house.
    The construction of a Maasai house allows two poles to stand upright at the entrance. These are the only poles that are seen from the outside.

14. *Egor minyi ng'utunyi.*
    Eng'ape o erishina.
    Your father strangles your mother.
    The pole and the raft.
    The poles of a house stand upright with a little fork at the top where the rafter is placed. The two are bound with a string appearing as though the pole is strangling the rafter, the former, being bigger, is the more masculine of the two, personifies the father; and the other is feminine.

15. *Anaa ira sapuk nimikijing' entore ole partololong'?*
    Olkirine Ie nkaji.
    You are so big, yet the belt of ole Partololong' is still loose on you.

The strips that are used to tie the rafters of the house together are usually very long so that around anyone's waist is still loose.

16. *Ampurlulu?*
    Elusie e shumata.
    What is unfathomable?
    The hollow in the sky (or roof).

17. *Toosho shartula metamanai.*
    Osinkolio; olkirine Ie nkaji.
    Strike it and let us see it spin.
    The dance (or song); the rafter of a house.

RIDDLES ON WASTE PRODUCTS

18. *Shipishipi kayoi.*
    Enkorotik enkiteng' sas.
    Name some loose substance.
    The bowels of an emaciated cow.
    The elders normally tell whether or not the cattle have been well grazed by the texture of their dung.

19. *Epuru nemeishu.*
    Emodiei enkiteng!
    It steams but it is not lit.
    Fresh cowdung.

20. *Sikira tioitoi?*
    Nkamulak.
    What resembles cowrie shells on the path?
    Spittle.

21. *Anaa keidurraki neshukunye olkine ng'iro ang'?*
    Enterit.
    Why have they moved home and the brown he-goat has returned?
    Because it is the dust.

22. *Eidurraki neing'uari ntare inyi ebore boo.*
     Ilkileleng'.

     They have moved home and left all your sheep behind.

     The sheep's droppings.

23. *Anaa ketooshoki inkuti neing'uari inkumok eirrag?*
     Ilkileleng'

     Why have they taken a few for grazing and left so many
     resting?

     Because they are the sheep's droppings.

RIDDLES ON MATERIAL CULTURE OBJECTS

24. *Elopi tiauluo idia ang'?*
     Olbene.

     Who is being made to vomit outside that village? A bag.

     It is common for a few people to do shopping for the whole village.
     When they arrive, people gather around them and everyone takes
     whatever he/she had ordered, until the bag is left empty.

25. *Eng'udi ai nadoku tentorror aata.*
     Enkidong'.

     My staff which I have had ever since I came up from Entorror.

     The tobacco container.

     Sometime in the mid 18th century (C. 1760) the Maasai,
     Samburu, Iltiamus, etc., separated at Entorror, which is
     now somewhere in Samburu country.

26. *Moruo sas loong'onyo.*
     Ildireta.

     What resembles an old thin man with numerous veins?

     Pack-saddles.

     These saddles are oval shaped and are made by crossing thin
     strips of leather and encasing them in a wooden frame. They are
     used to load stuff on donkeys. The thin leather strips resemble
     veins.

158

27. *Murran lainei kumok nemeetae olobayie.*
    Ncheito.
    I have many warriors but there is none at the end.
    Pegs.
    Hides are normally spread out and pegged to dry.

28. *Kilikuai oshe kop.*
    Enkoitoi; enauner.
    There is a message that stretches across the world (land) surveying it.
    The path; the pole that is used to make holes when a house is being built.

29. *Eiperipera toltiren.*
    Eminyor naya nkonyek.
    It is fidgeting beside the fire.
    A stomach with sickly eyes.

30. *Barnoti ai nasulu ntare te ndoinyio.*
    Olmurunya.
    What is the young man like when he is driving the sheep down from the hill?
    Like a razor blade.

31. *Nelido nele.*
    Oloijililiai Ie kule.
    That over there, this right here.
    A drop of milk.
    A drop of milk is seen at the bottom of the gourd, over there, and when the gourd is tipped up to the mouth, the drop is seen at the mouth of the gourd, right here. (Note the punning of the alliterative sounds.)

32. *Pus Olupi?*
    Enkii.
    What is blue in colour and barren?
    The stone used to sharpen swords, spears and knives.

This stone is usually blue in colour, and since it is a stone it does not procreate.

33. *Eru mukumper toldoinyio?*
Entolu naiper ilkeek.

What do we hear braying up on the hill? An axe hewing wood.

34. *Anaa ipi nabaa o nabaa nimintieu atakedo enkashe e kirkoris enkoriong?*

Eremet.

Why are you so brave yet you cannot sit on the back of the heifer from Kilgoris?

Because it is the spear.

There may have been some blacksmiths who lived at Kilgoris in the olden days, so the spear may have been made and brought from there.

35. *Mugie ai naten ilasho.*
Enkawuo o mbaa.

My brown one with speedy calves.

The bow and arrows.

36. *Ting'iria maaishaki.*
Olalem opiki enchashur.

Will you persevere while I put it all inside you?

The sword that is being put inside a sheath.

37. *Tilida maampeu.*
Embae nang'or esoit.

What bounces violently?

An arrow when it hits a rock.

38. *Or namutareki.*
Endapash.

What is the bare spot where people die in millions?

The bed.

Maasai beds are made from piling branches and leaves and covering them with cowhides.

39. *Ejo rrokirrok eito idia alo nejo mukumuk eitu ena.*
Ilkukurto le nkare.

What makes a loud noise when going in one direction, but none as it returns?

The gourds without and, later, with water.

40. *Epong'a toltiren.*
Olmosori.

It is constipated by the fireside.

The gourd for brewing beer.

These are very large in size and are left by the fireside for the beer to brew. The fermentation process is here likened with constipation.

41. *Eigirigiro te rishat ildoinyio.*
Emala oolkidotu natanya epukuri.

Something is heard quivering in between mountains.

It is the big gourd of the Ilkidotu age-set, that has refused to be closed.

42. *Anaa ipi nabaa a nabaa nimitonie enetonie entito nayok?*
Emoti.

How come you are so brave yet you cannot sit at the place where the little black girl sits.

Because it is the fire.

The little girl is the pot which has turned black with soot.

43. *Bitiro tiaji.*
Soito le nkima

What resembles warthogs in the house? The firestones.

The Maasai use three stones for the fireplace, like many other African groups.

44. *Edung' ng'utunyi olosinko emukita enapiak.*
Eng'amurai olkumpau.

Your mother walks across the village mouthing distaste.

Tobacco leaves.

Normally these are chewed by older men and women.

161

45. *Anaa keidurraki neing'ueri menye nkishu?*
Oltim.

They have moved home and left the father of cattle behind, what is it?

It is the tree branch that is used to close the cattle gate.

46. *Anaa keidurraki neing'uari esumpat e minyi te ming'ani?*
Olchala.

They have moved home and left behind your father's gown, what is it?

The dunghill.

47. *Anaa keidurraki neing'uari menye ntare.*
Olchala.

Why have they moved home and left the father of sheep behind?

Because "he" is the dunghill.

48. *Sampurumpuri santetua.*
Olkila loo saen.

What resembles a butterfly with multicolours?

A garment that has been decorated with beads.

Women's sheep-skin garments usually have elaborate patterns of beadwork.

49. *Kiteng' ai naibor-kutuk nang'ar oreren.*
Enkike.

My white-mouthed cow that is shared by all.

The toothbrush.

This is a stick toothbrush that has been peeled on one end so that the white inside is seen. All toothbrushes therefore look the same, and it is not rare to see them being shared.

50. *Asuria tiaji.*
Nkeenda.

What resembles snakes inside the house?

The straps.

Leather straps are put to many uses in a household, and are bound to be numerous.

51. *Eikirnyianya minyi ebarni.*
    Olchoni oshei.
    Your father struggles as he is being shaved.
    What is he like?
    A hide that is being pegged to the ground.

RIDDLES ON NATURE AND NATURAL PHENOMENA

52. *Ndapan ainei naarisio.*
    Enkewarie o endama.
    Shumata o enkop.
    I have two hides that are of equal size.
    Night and day.
    The sky and the earth.

53. *Parkinyeyie oinyeyie iloreren.*
    Enkakenya.
    What acts as an alarm to awaken all people?
    The morning.

54. *Emanaa entoki pus aman enkang' ang'.*
    En koileelio.
    There is some blueish substance that is surrounding our village.
    Dew.

55. *Einosa enkop enkima neing'uari Naikoro.*
    Olpura.
    The whole world has been burnt to ashes leaving Naikoro standing on her own.
    The bare spot.
    It is not infrequent to find bare spots that are inhabited only by ants. Since no grass grows on such spots, fire does not burn there.

56. *Eimariri nankoid ilkeek.*
    Empuruo.
    She looks up at the trees above.
    Smoke rising.

57. *Tito e tale naado mporro.*
    Enkima.
    The beautiful girl with long strands of beads.
    The fire. (When it is in flames)

58. *Eman enkeeya pus enkang!*
    Injo; Eman ake. Empuruo.
    What is the deadly disease that surrounds the village?
    Sleep; smoke.
    When all people are fast asleep it seems as if all are dead.
    Then when fires burn, the whole settlement is engulfed with smoke.

59. *Anaa keidurraki neini nanyokie?*
    Enkima.
    They moved homes and the red one was born. The fire.
    The Maasai often burn up the old village when they move.

60. *Mayopa ele reyiet maing'oru ilaras Ie minyi.*
    Ilabur Ie nkare.
    Let us walk along this river and look for your father's ribs.
    The foam from the water.
    When the water runs furiously, it forms patterns (Jines) of foam. These are being likened to the ribs.

61. *Eitalang'akino ilperesian imbaa.*
    Ilkekuno Ie nkare.
    They point arrows at each other.
    The reeds growing on the banks of the river.

    Reeds and other river vegetation normally grow facing the stream, making it seem like they are deliberately facing each other.

62. *Bornoti ai nashal kutuk.*
    Enkoitoi nalo enkare.

    What is a strip of leather like when the end is wet? It is like a path leading to the water source.

    There is a play on meaning of the word mouth (enkutuk), which in this case applies to the end of the leather strip and the beginriing of the path.

63. *Anaijo eedo ena anashe ng'utunyi nemebaiki enyewa enker?*
    Enkoitoi.

    Why is your mother's sister so tall (long) but cannot reach up to a sheep's udder?

    The path.

    The adjective for long and tall is the same in Maasai and is only distinguished by its context.

64. *Tamanai teidia alo oldoinyio matamanu tena nimikitumo aikata.*
    Nkiyiaa.

    Go round one side of the mountain while I go round the other side, but we will never meet.

    The ears.

    Ears do not move.

65. *Or nememanyi, ore pee emanyi neishiri.*
    Enkong'u.

    There is a bare place where no one ever settles, and if one did so, there would be crying. What is it?

    The eye.

    When a speck gets into the eye tears flow out of it.

RIDDLES ON PLANTS

66. *Anaa ipi nabaa o nabaa nimintieu enkanasa oonkishu sampin.*
   Ildupa.
   How come you are so brave yet you dare not approach the army of dapple-grey cattle?
   Because they are the sisal plants.

67. *Kalo shani oshi oota olkikuei obo?*
   Oldupai.
   What tree has only one thorn?
   The sisal plant.

68. *Anaa ipi nabaa nimintieu atijing'a enkanasa olmakele?*
   Ildupa.
   Why are you so brave yet you cannot join the army?
   Because it is the sisal plant.

69. *Sarng'ab enkinanash.*
   Entonata olpopong'i.
   What is muddy-like?
   The foot of the candelabra tree.

70. *Edoku tionyoi.*
   Kule oolpopong.
   What rises from the green ones?
   The sap of the candelabra tree.

71. *Murran lainei kumok naa enkeju nabo eitasheyie.*
   Olpopong'i.
   I have many warriors all of whom stand on one leg.
   The candelabra tree.
   Maasai warriors are often seen standing on one leg. The candelabra tree has a long stem with branches growing only at the upper part.

72. *Mirrimir nimitum.*
    Ilng'anayio limibaiki.
    There you are but you will not get it.
    The fruit that you cannot reach.

73. *Tamano teidia alo oldoinyio matamano tena nikitumo,*
    etodoro yiook inkaik.
    llama.
    Go round one side of the mountain, while I go round the other, and we will meet when our hands are red.
    Going round a bush eating red berries.

74. *Kalo shani oshi otolo oiba ilkulikae?*
    Olpiron.
    Which tree is cruel and hates all the others?
    The tree which they use to make firesticks.
    It burns the others.

75. *Kaja oshi ilkeek ootii ena kop?*
    Aare, olotoyio oloshal.
    How many types of trees are there in this country?
    Two types, the dry one and the green one.

76. *Anaa keidurraki duo neiborru pooki ilukuny?*
    Ndung'ot oo nkeek.
    They have moved home and all their beads have turned white?
    The bushes when their tops have been cut.

77. *Murrani ai naipiru oltaika te nkop.*
    Oloiropiji.
    What is my young man like when he generates his pig tails from the earth? Like a turnip.
    This is not quite a turnip but it is very much like it, and is eaten by children. Its leaves are here likened with hair while the root is compared with pigtails.

RIDDLES ON DOMESTIC ANIMALS

78.   *Or nememanyi.*
      Entibili osikiria.
      There is a clearing in which no one settles; what is it?
      The donkey's spot.

79.   *Tiinka narikito tiinka.*
      Emuny narikito enkuo.
      Something that is leading something.
      Rhinoceros leading a calf.

OR

      Tiinka nadung'o tiinka narikito tiinka nadung'o tiinka.
      Esikiria nadung'o enkidong'oe (enkiok).
      Narikito enkurrarru nadung'o enkidong'oe (enkiok).
      Something with a cut something leading.
      Something with a cut something.
      A donkey with a cut tail leading an ass with a cut tail.

80.   *Adung' ang'ata pus naturu iloiropij aare.*
      Ilki Ie sikiria.
      I walk across a bare wilderness and I uproot two turnips (turnip-like roots).
      The teats of a female donkey.

81.   *Ejo rrokirrok edoyio te parsilale.*
      Isirkon oiroto.
      They are heard clamouring downhill.
      The donkeys who are carrying loads.
      Various items in a donkey pack knock against each other and make such a noise that the donkeys cannot pass quietly and unnoticed.

82.   *Tilida ting'ami.*
      Emurt oloing'oni.
      What is knotted all over?

The neck of a bullock.

83. *Eipirri eng'obu.*
Olashe ong'ar nkishu.
He sips (gulps) as he runs.
The calf who shares two cows.
When a calf is suckled by two cows, he tends to feed from both cows whenever he gets a chance.

84. *Tirrida ndapan maape kinopop.*
Nkidong'o oondiain.
Let us fold and tuck in the hides on our way to Kinopop.
The tails of bitches.
Bitches are often seen with their tails tucked in as though they are prepared for a long journey.

85. *Medoli ti oreren.*
Enker sampu.
What is it that can never be found in the whole world.
A dapple-grey sheep.

86. *Ene manturlugum.*
Eilata olmeregesh.
What smells like the droppings of sheep?
The fat of an uncastrated male sheep.

87. *Olkiteng' lai otii erishata oolmang'ati.*
Olng'ejep.
I have an ox who lives in the midst of enemies.
The tongue.

88. *Ebobolae te lang'ata.*
Osikiria eboe.
Ebobolae ake.
Embitir epiki olkataar.
Why is there such a struggle in the valley?
It is a donkey's incisors that are being removed.

OR

A warthog is being fitted with a bracelet.

Two rather formidable tasks.

RIDDLES ON INSECTS AND OTHER ANIMALS

89.   *Eidurraki nepaashiki nkasho sopiain enkang'.*
      Ilpidila.

      They have moved home but the brown calves have settled in.

      The fleas.

90.   *Ekur enchani eibelekeny.*
      Olpidilai oudi enkiok.

      It beats the bush as it turns it over.

      A flea whose ears are being pierced.

91.   *Eimugumugu tosinyai.*
      Lemunchu (Lekonkor) oidulie olalem.

      What is seen clambering over the sand?

      A beetle that is weighed down by the sword.

92.   *Kiti ena anashe ng'utunyi neyiolo atushumu kule.*
      Olotoroki.

      Your mother's sister is very small but knows how to store milk well.

      The bee.

93.   *Mugie ai naaru entim.*
      Olotoroki.

      I have my little brown one that forces itself through the wilderness.

      The bee.

94.   *Edung' pose melioo orregie?*
      Osampurumpuri.

      What moves across the world but leaves no trace? The butterfly.

95. *Timini nkuuni.*
Enkume enkalaoni.
What is so very tiny?
The nose of an ant.
(Not possible to arrive at a literal translation.)

96. *Murram lainei kumok naa emua nabo eeta.*
Emuyoo.
I have many warriors all of whom are one colour.
The red ants.
(Also other social insects)

97. *Anaa iten nabaa o nabaa niminepu kapironto etagore?*
Olojong'ani.
Why are you such a fast runner but you cannot catch up with the Kavirondo when he is annoyed?
Because he is the fly.

98. *Anaa iten nabaa o nabaa niming'asie Nekarancha kutuk – aji?*
Olojong'ani.
Why are you such a fast runner yet you are unable to get to the door before Karanja?
Because he is the fly.

99. *Anaa keishiri tedukuya nekua kishu nemeishiri oshi ake?*
Olojong'ani loontorosi otigile.
Why is there wailing at the front of that herd of cattle when it usually doesn't happen?
It is the tsetse fly that has attacked.

OR

A naa keishiri ake x 2
Olmoruo otalaikine atabolo olkidong';
Nkisulat.
Another reason? x 2

It is the old man who has been unable to open the tobacco container;
It is the whistling (from the herdsmen).

100. *Anaa kepuru idia soil nemepuru oshi ake?*
Ilmokuain eudi nkiyiaa.

Why is smoke coming out of that rock over there when it usually does not do so?

It is the lizard's ears that are being pierced.

Red-hot metal rods are normally used to pierce ears. Since it is lizards that dwell in rocks, it is appropriate to assume that lizards are undergoing an ear-piercing ceremony if smoke rises from rocks.

101. *Anaa aidorrop enkanashe ino nemeeta olng'anayioi oing'ataa?*
En taritiki.

Why is your sister so very short yet there is no fruit that is beyond her reach?

A bird.

102. *Eman enkiu te siare.*
Emotonyi naitaapa ilayiok.

It goes round a bush with a club.

A bird that has been impregnated by boys.

103. *Elutoo ntarama oonkishu.*
Entaritiki.

What walks on the stomachs of cattle?

The bird.

104. *Barnoti ai e karteyia nayiolo olosek.*
Olwuapishoi.

What is the young man like when he uses his tricks?

Like the snatcher (i.e., Vulture).

Vultures are notorious for snatching meat from people's hands.

They are tricky in the sense that they always manage to take people by surprise by swooping down unexpectedly.

105. *Eparana tiauluo.*
Ndero naatupurro oloiboni.
Why have they all gathered outside the homestead?
Because they are rats that have stolen from the diviner.
(Considered quite daring, but it creates a stir.)

106. *Ejo rraa nemesha.*
Nkejek oontarakueti; mbenek olng'aboli.
It is droning as though the rain is falling, yet it is not raining.
It is the noise made by the feet of the impala as they run; the leaves of the sycamore tree.

107. *Eluaa te kitet.*
Oloitiko omishira.
One cannot arrive at a literal translation, but the riddle refers to the stripes at the back side of a zebra that are lined differently from the rest of the body.

108. *Elang' elang'u.*
Olng'ojine oliki ntare ilkuoo.
What goes across here and there in a hectic manner?
A hyena (the limper) showing goats' kids their mothers.

There is here a play on the meaning of hyena's name, the one who limps. The work of directing goats' kids to their mothers is done by shepherds and it is such a hectic exercise that one is seen bustling about.

109. *Ene mankumukum ene matirrintir.*
Olowuaru kedianye.
It moves with a funny gait.
A left-handed beast/lion.

110.	*Eik enkeju te ng'osua.*
	Emuny narip olkila lo lang'ata.
	Who is seen hanging the leg up on the tree?
	A rhinoceros that is sewing her boyfriend's garment.

111.	*Soit e sikile naudo isiet.*
	Endukuya olenkaina.
	What is rocky and has eight holes.
	The head of an elephant.
	The skeleton of an elephant has little pores and the depressions for the eyes, ears, etc., could number eight.

112.	*Barbal te nkusero.*
	Emudong' olenkaina.

	Barbal ake?

	Enkong'u enkitejo.
	What is so big and obviously seen on a plain?
	The afterbirth of an elephant and the eye of a rabbit.

113.	*Edoiki ilmotonyi enkaldaupe.*
	Empopong' olenkaina.
	The vultures descend on it in drones.
	The carcase of an elephant.
	(Because of its massive size.)

COMPLEX TYPE RIDDLES (ilang'eni)

114.	*Amaa naaya, o naayieu o naaipieu, kainyioo?*
	Answer: enkaya, enkiyieu o ilkipieu.
	This riddle consists of puns; when translated, it loses its meaning. See if you can get it. Riddle: What is it that takes me (**aya**), that which wants me (**ayieu**), and that which smears me (**apio**)?
	Answer: It is **enkaya**, **enkiyieu** and **ilkipieu**, all parts of a cow.
	Note the punning on similar sounds. The trick is in the sounds, not in the meaning.

115. *Amaa naaji teniyieu niyieng' enkiteng' nimiaata enkeene nireyie, nimiata enkalem niyieng'ie, nimiaata enkare niyierie naa entim itii, kaji nko?*
Answer: Ekajoki enkeene-e-nkai metaa enkeene, najoki ologilalem metaa enkalem, najoki oloitiko ntiko shomo enkare.

Supposing you want to slaughter a cow and you need a strap to lead it with, you need a knife to slaughter it with, and you need water to cook it with, and you are in the middle of the forest, what would you do?

Answer: I would ask the worm (**enkeene-e-nkai**) to act as the strap (**en keene**); I would ask the **ologil-alem** (type of lizard), to act as the knife (**enkalem**); and I would ask the zebra (**oloitiko**) to run (**ntiko**) and fetch some water.

CHAPTER FIVE

Proverbs: Ndung'eta-e-rashe

Proverbs form a very important part of Maasai oral literature, since they summarize the wisdom of sages. The Maa word for proverbs means, "the cutters of fine, thin leather". This refers to the precision and brevity of the proverbs. When quoted in the right context, a proverb summarises an idea that would otherwise need explaining in very many words.

A proverb is usually stated in the form of a maxim, epigram or aphorism. It can also be in the form of a poetic statement.

The basic difference between the proverb and other forms of oral literature is that while some of them, like riddles, can be posed or listed in succession at a specific time and in a specific context, and songs are sang during various functions, and occasions proverbs cannot. They in fact sound odd when read out in succession. This is because proverbs enter into all forms of communication. They comment on behaviour, whether in commendation or criticism, in the household, in a public place, or in determining cases in traditional law courts. It is indeed a mark of admirable elegance in speech to be able to use the apt aphorism skilfully. Proverb **179,** for instance, discourages revenge. They can also be used to sum up cases just as lawyers cite precedents, or to point up the moral of a story or tale. In fact, in the last sense, it is not infrequent for a narrator to cite an appropriate proverb in the course of relating a story, as is done in narratives **9, 26** and **27**. More interesting is the fact that a character in a story or drama can be seen quoting the apt proverb for its philosophical implications in the course of a dialogue. An example of this is seen in story **31**.

From proverbs we gain insight into behavioural patterns of a people. They give commentaries on happenings that reveal the system of values under which the culture functions. Proverb **71,** for example, not only stresses the importance of hope, as opposed to despair, but also reveals the existence of polygamy and the varying levels of affection that exist between marriage partners. It also sheds light on the domestic residential pattern.

Proverbs could be generally summed up as the core of a people's culture, since they phrase their philosophy as well as poetry. This is of special significance in cultures whose literature is oral. From the images contained in these proverbs, we learn a great deal about the values and attitudes of a people within a pastoral setting.

One important thing that must be mentioned about Maasai proverbs is that they are usually cited by the senior members of the society when they are addressing the junior people, but never the other way round. And although the proverb goes: "Wisdom does not have a white head (grey hair)" (**157**), it is indeed an accepted fact among the Maasai that wisdom is enshrined in the older members of a community. Seniority is a mark of wisdom.

Proverbs in this collection have been categorized according to theme. This is merely to facilitate easy reading and layout. But as with the stories, riddles, songs and poetry, there is a certain amount of overlapping between these themes. This categorization should, hence, not be taken rigidly. As a matter of fact, this arrangement has led to a large number of proverbs being included in a vague category entitled "On life in general". This could obviously have been avoided were there a better way of categorizing proverbs, if categorization is necessary in the first place.

Another shortcoming of this form of categorization is the fact that it tends to limit the application of proverbs, and by so doing reduces their flexibility and value. For this reason, it is important to note that the use of a particular proverb in the context that has been quoted here is but an example of its common usage. A proverb is often used in such unique circumstances that one can never exhaust its resourcefulness.

Proverbs come in different forms. Most of the commonly used proverbs are metaphors drawn from daily life; "Poverty cannot be hit with saplings" (**61**), or "You cannot patch together a piece of gourd with that of a pot" (**192**); others are mere statements: "He who allocates behaviours" (**6**), while others are metaphors applied to situations: "Do not climb rocks with the shoes on" (**252**), and "Truth does not fill the palm of the hand" (**255**). There are also quotation proverbs such as

(216): "The cow said, 'do not lend me out, give me away,'" or the popular, conventional phrase, sounding like a formula, as in **288** and **296.**

Proverbs are often created taking already existing types as models. For instance, an old and widely known proverb: "The zebra cannot shed its stripes" **(190)** seems to have occasioned the invention of: 'The Meru will never stop growing large jaws' **(187)**. The Meru are in Kenya and in Tanzania but have no relationship.

Proverbs use simple stylistic features such as contrast: "a string could do while you wait for the rope" **(64)**, "hope and despair are not equal" **(65)**; alliteration: *Iyiolo ening'ua nimiyiolo enilo* **(82** and **(83)**. They also use rhyme, repetition and allegory, but most of these features can only be appreciated in the original language, not in the translation. Another characteristic feature of proverbs is the existence of many variations of equal authority: for example, proverb **200** has two opposite variations, each of which is used adequately, depending on the context. It is not at all uncommon to find proverbs that contradict each other.

Review Exercises ■

i) Collect as many proverbs as you can from your community, translate and analyse them.

ii) Explain fully the circumstances in which they are used.

iii) Comment on the stylistic features used in some of the proverbs.

PROVERBS ON RELIGION AND THE PARAMOUNCY OF GOD

1. *Erisio Ilmaasai o Enkai.*
   Equal are the Maasai and God.

   If you maintain good relations with the Maasai you are as safe as you are with God.

2. *Menya Enkai enanya tung'ani.*
   God does not eat what man eats.

   This is in terms of thoughts and ideas. God does not base his/ her decisions according to what man wants. Often uttered in a rhetorical form.

3. *Erisio olporror o Enkai.*
   The age-group is equal with God.

   One's age-group is held in very high esteem, and there are rules and regulations as to what one may or may not do to and for the group. If a person commits a very grave error, he could easily have himself ostracised, which amounts to being cursed to death. Comparing the abilities of the two simply goes to show the importance of the age-group in the life of the Maasai. *

* The ritual head of the age-group keeps a string of beads, each one representing an individual member. When one commits an unpardonable sin, the leader removes one of the beads and throws it away saying: "I have thrown you like that bead." And the person is supposed to die.

4. *Menyanyuk otoputo tung'ani, o lotuputo Enkai.*
   The one chosen by God is not equal to the one chosen by people; the one chosen by God is greater.

5. *Meetae arriyia anaa enopeny.*
   There is none as accurate (precise) as the owner.

   Stresses the importance of individual tastes, likes or preferences. Sometimes said when a person meddles too much in the affairs of somebody else, but more often used as a justification to leave things as they are, especially natural creations, because God, the Creator and the owner, willed it that way.

6. *Naorioriki irregiei.*
   He who allocates behaviours.

   (This is in reference to God).

7. *Mening' Enkai olaisimani.*
   God does not listen to the robber.

8. *Meitore tung'ani Enkai.*
   Man cannot rule over God.

   God determines people's destinies.

9. *Metii kirotet te tung'ani.*
   There is none who is man's favourite.

   In other words, no matter how much a person loves you, he can neither give you everything, nor can he prevent evil from befalling you. These are things God alone can do.

10. *Eret Enkai ilooret ate.*
God helps those who help themselves.

11. *Eipern Enkai emonkoi.*
God does not let lies pass unnoticed.

PROVERBS ON KINSHIP RELATIONS

12. *Enkoshoke naata osotua.*
It is the stomach that holds the umbilical cord.

    This proverb has both a literal as well as a figurative meaning:

    i)   The abdomen literally holds the umbilical cord when a child is born and people from the same family/clan are said to be related because of this cord that once held them or their ancestors together. This is the literal meaning.

    ii) Food is essential for the maintenance of life and, therefore, if one provides this essential commodity, he will have established a relationship with the receiver. In this regard, it is the essential step towards friendship and closeness.

13. *Jurro naaboita.*
It is those who are familiar to each other who can live/stay together (strangers cannot).

14. *Etudung'e sotua te kina.*
The relation was severed from the breast.

    Said when close relations do not treat each other as such. Their relationship is said to have ceased from the time they were weaned.

15. *Ore enemeshula enkikuei nemeshula enkigwana.*
Those who do not share thorn bushes, i.e., the same village enclosure, do not also share ideas in a meeting.

    Emphasises the significance of neighbourliness.

16. *Telejai sotua.*
Send away relatives in a discreet manner.

In other words, if you are not able to provide them with what they ask for, do not be forthright about it, but employ a little diplomacy.

17. *Metumoyu osotua.*
Relationship (blood) cannot be sought.
It is either there or not.

18. *Eeri olkuti ilkulenye o metung'uari eitashe.*
He that has few relatives is beaten until he is left standing.
(For he has few to defend him).

19. *Eya ilamito osotua.*
Distance takes away friendship (or a relationship).
Out of sight, out of mind.

20. *Meeta eoro temat.*
Separation has no trial; you cannot attempt to separate.
Anything can happen to friendship when friends are separated.

21. *Mamoda amu mashulolenkaputi.*
I am not a fool because I do not live in the same homestead as my in-laws. Living with somebody is a way of giving them a chance to observe your character.

The in-laws are the worst type of people to open yourself to, since your weak points can be detected and exposed, to your detriment. Opposite of '*Mejurro mang'ati*', enemies cannot observe each other.

22. *Eshomo osotua ndoyiorot enkolong' niaku olenkaputi otaashua.*
A relation has gone to the setting of the sun and was hooked out by the in-law.

A blood relation may live far away and cease to be of much help to a person, but an in-law could prove to be helpful.

23. *Menyanyuk olinyi likimba oleiking'a likinyor.*
It is not the same when your relative hates you, but a stranger loves you.

In an emergency, blood ties prove to be most important,
fora relative would show more concern. (Blood is thicker than water.)

24. *Meitobirayu oloriyia ilalashera ng'otonye.*
He that has been cursed by his mother's brother cannot be cleansed.

A mother's brother is regarded as very important in kinship relations, so important that he has to be present in every rite of passage. Wronging him is regarded as an unpardonable sin, one that cannot be cleansed or pacified by an outsider. The person wronged would have to plead for mercy directly.

25. *Meetae tonyorraki maibai.*
There is no one-way friendship.

Unless relations are mutual, friendships will not last.

26. *Medolunoyu osotua lenkaji nabo.*
The relation of one family creeps in unnoticed.

When people are united, it is easy for them to re-establish relations and friendship by themselves without outside help. There is advantage in unity.

27. *Migil enkaputi te nkupes.*
Do not break in-law-ship at the thigh.

Do not break a relationship without good cause.

28. *Taara oinoti nireu ong'ata niar oyati nirrinyu.*
Beat up the legitimate son and take him to the wilderness but beat up the foster son and return him home.

The legitimate son would return for lack of elsewhere to go, while the foster son would not.

29. *Aanyor kake maitudutie keon.*
I love you, but not more than I love myself.

30. *Metumi naishoro oishuaa.*
One will never find those who give each other stomachs.

There are limits to what one can give to another person.

PROVERBS OF 'UNITY'

31. *Miaru inkishu ilking'arana.*
They do not procure cows, those who are not at peace (not united) among themselves.

Unity is essential for victory to be achieved.

32. *Meramat inkishu oowuesha.*
They do not tend cattle, those who are not in complete agreement.

33. *Medany olkimojino obo elashei.*
One finger does not kill a louse.

Emphasises the importance of unity.

34. *Eiba itmang'ati enkang' nabayie.*
The enemy dislikes a village that is positioned at the end.

They would attack it frequently.

35. *Meidim olenkaina enking'arra.*
An elephant cannot withstand mob attack, despite its size.

36. *Mirisirasaa anaa inkiyioitin e nkurlee.*
Do not go dropping them like the chicks of the guinea fowl.

The story goes that the family of the guinea-fowl and that of the turkey once set off separately from dry country in search of greener pasture. The turkey organised his people, who had been emaciated by famine, and they all walked slowly together until they got to their destination. The guinea-fowl, on the other hand, asked all his people to fly behind him but did not check who could be able to go and who couldn't. On arrival in the new country, he discovered that only three in his group had managed to complete the journey; the others had dropped off on the way. This is why the guinea-fowls move in groups of threes or fours, while the turkeys move in larger groups. The former regretted not organizing his group better. The proverb advises that to be successful as a group you have to keep together.

37. *Meborayu enamuke tenkalo nabo.*
A sandal cannot be cut out on one side.

You would have to cut around the piece of leather in order to get a sandal. Often quoted, in reference to a discussion, to imply that one person (or one side) cannot sustain a discussion; there has to be an opposition.

38. *Etejoki orori namirta oing'ok.*
It is said that separation is what is chasing the bulls/ stronger members of the community.

Stronger bulls/persons separate themselves from the masses.

39. *Meidip oltung'ani endapana enkiteng' enye.*
A person is not sufficed by the hide of his own cow.

This proverb justifies the need to acquire property and to work together in order to increase wealth.

PROVERBS ON GOOD FORTUNE AND FATE

40. *Miari ayiani.*
You do not beat or kill that which has come your way.

It is not possible to dodge or evade good fortune.

41. *Meoshoyu enkishon lukunya.*
Good fortune cannot be hit on the head.

One hits a snake on the head as it approaches, but you cannot repulse good fortune, for it is invisible and too good to be turned down.

42. *Merrumoroyu ene Nkai tentakule.*
That of the deity cannot be pushed away with the forearm (wrist).

43. *Eng'or emuny otonyorrikiaki.*
He could shoot a rhinoceros, he that has been willed.

There is no task that is insurmountable, for there is always a person who has been willed to do it by the Almighty.

44. *Meipurru enkishon.*
Good fortune does not roar as it approaches.

In other words, do not wait to hear it for you may probably just see it, if at all you ever notice it. The idea being, you may probably already have it, but you do not know it.

45. *Memanikinoyu enkishon nang'u.*
You cannot lose temper over good fortune.

In other words, whether you lose your temper or not will not affect timing of good fortune. Therefore, do not be impatient over things you cannot change or affect.

46. *Epir dukuya nepir siadi.*
The head (front) is fat and so is the bottom (back or behind).

In other words, do not despair or fidget unnecessarily, for whatever you obtain, early or late in life, will be equally good.

47. *Melang'i inkirragat.*
You cannot jump over what was destined for you – even a "sleeping place at death".

PROVERBS ON INITIATIVE, DETERMINATION vs WEAKNESS

48. *Menang' silig kewan.*
Even a simple act of looking back does not perform itself.

A simple act such as turning one's head behind has to be performed. This proverb emphasises the importance of initiative and that of corporate action.

Everyone has a part to play however small it might be, and therefore people do not ignore a small act, for it is just as essential as a big one.

49. *Meibung'akinoyu osuuji enkawuo.*
You cannot hold a bow for a coward.

One can only go a short way to assist another person. You can take a donkey to the river but you cannot force him to drink the water. This is said to a person who puts no or little effort into doing something.

50. *Mme tumoto nagol, barata.*
It is not acquisition that is difficult, it is retention.

If a person is not astute enough to tend property, it is futile to strive to acquire it, since he is bound to lose it anyway.

51. *Mesuja asayiak.*
Beggars do not follow one another (or walk together).

52. *Meitayu enashal enkae.*
The weak one does not help another who is equally weak.

53. *Meikooyu olkuret olasulani.*
You can advise neither a coward nor a person with no shame.

For a coward would be too scared to heed advice, through no fault of his own, while the shameless person would embarrass you without realising what he is doing.

54. *Meitobirayu enkaji naarita enopeny.*
A house that is being destroyed by the owner cannot be repaired.

The owner has to participate in rectifying a wrong, not the opposite.

55. *Meiputayu embene naudo siadi.*
A bag that has a hole can never be filled.

56. *Metii esas naret enkae.*
An emaciated person cannot help another.

57. *Merisio nyuaat o nkidimat.*
Efforts and capabilities are not the same, efforts are greater.

In other words, unless a person is prepared to put a lot of effort into whatever he does, he is not likely to accomplish much, because capability is limited.

58. *Etejo olng'ojine, mme kamunyak keju maitagol.*
The hyena said, it is not that I am lucky, it is that I do not hesitate to use my legs to walk any distance.

59. *Mitum kinyil aik.*
You do not obtain it with greasy or smooth hands.

Smooth greasy hands in this case are associated with luxury.

Unless a person is prepared to work hard and dirty his hands, he will not acquire the desirable things in life.

60. *Meosh osina masilig.*
Poverty cannot be hit with saplings. (You have to struggle to get rid of it.)

61. *Inooloogol intokitin.*
Things (property) are for the strong.

(Survival for the fittest.)

PROVERBS ON HOPE AND DESPAIR

62. *Meetae naimutie kiret.*
There is no help that is late arriving, for as long as it comes, it is still welcome.

(Therefore do not despair.)

63. *Enya enkop enkima neing'uari erashe.*
The whole world might burn but a little patch could survive.

There can still be hope after an apparent annihilation, so do not despair in the face of difficulty.

64. *Kintaanyu enkopito enkeene.*
A string could do while you wait for the rope.

Do not reject help even if it appears insignificant.

65. *Menyaanyuk siligi o pala.*
Hope is not equal to despair.

It is better to hope since despair cannot help you out of difficulty.

66. *Eshe encheitoi nabo olchoni.*
One peg could spread out a hide.

Opposite of "one finger does not kill a louse" (33), depending on how it is utilised.

67. *Osina likiya eniaado.*
It is troubles that take you far.

Living through problems teaches one perseverance and a sense of determination.

68. *Melakua ang' inchu.*
    Home is not far as long as you are alive.

    A story is told of a man who was away from home for many months, and on returning, he found a flooded river just before reaching home. Since he had missed his family considerably, he decided that he could not wait for the flood to subside despite pleas from his companions to be patient in trying to cross. He was carried off by the waves and he drowned, thus making his home so far away. If only he had been patient, his home would not have been that far. Hence the proverb came to warn against impatience.

69. *Mme otirrishaki olopeny keeya.*
    It is not the extreme case that owns death.

    A person does not have to die when he gets close to death, he could recover to the surprise of others.

    Often quoted when an unexpected thing happens.

70. *Edoorie enker modooni nkuta.*
    A blind sheep might chance rain water.

    This proverb warns that good fortune is not restricted only to the affluent members of the society, but to all, irrespective of their status.

71. *Tinki kisikini tenkang' oontare nikiikini olayioni.*
    You unfavoured woman, you will one day get a boy.

    Told to a woman who is not loved, and whom the husband does not often visit. As a way of making her not lose hope, for, one day he will have no one else to sleep with when he visits the sheep's village, and will have to visit her. From that visit, she might conceive and beget a boy who would end her problems.

PROVERBS ON CAUTION

72. *Taleenoi olgisoi lenchashur.*
    Check the ring on the sheath.

    Maasai men normally wear their swords strapped on their waists.

On the tip of the sheath that contains the sword, there is a metal coin or ring. If one checks on this ring, he will also be checking behind and about, in case there is impending danger.

73. *Meeta eneitong'or enkong'u edama.*
The eye for the day does not miss any place.

At daytime, eyes do not miss any happening.

Be discreet in whatever you do, for you are probably being watched.

74. *Ng'en enkong'u enkuoo ai.*
My ram's eye is clever.

Often said by one adult to another to alert him that children might be listening to their conversation, and they know more than adults think.

75. *Ening' siriri king'a.*
Do not talk in his presence for he might hear you.

Often said in the company of outsiders about whom one is unsure, for fear that by talking, you might impart some valuable information to one who might be an enemy.

76. *Eeta entim nkiyiaa.*
The forest has ears.

This is similar to proverb (75).

OR

Epolos enkiook enaimin.
The ear tears through darkness.

77. *Eeta enkewarie nkiyiaa.*
The night has ears.

Be cautious when you speak, for someone might be listening.

78. *Memira mbenek eshal.*
Leaves have not been beaten as long as they are still green.

They will have to display signs of withering before they can be declared dry and no longer useful.

In other words, you have to wait for the end before you can be sure.

79. *Minturrarrie olee enturet eitu iduaki enkirragata.*
Do not take away a man's digging stick until you have seen where he lies (i.e. confirmed his death).

Never believe people's stories, for they could be based on hearsay.

80. *Eyiara kurji.*
An unknown thing is cooking.

Said by a person when he suspects something fishy or suspicious is going on, which others may not be aware of.

81. *Turia esaa e boo.*
Be fearful of talking secrets outside.

In other words, be careful when you discuss secrets with people who live in the same village with you because they might let them out.

82. *Iyiolo ening'uaa nimiyiolo enilo.*
You know where you are coming from, but not where you are going.

83. *Iyiolo enijo nimiyiolo enikijokini.*
You know what to say, but not what you will be told.

84. *Tigila enker amu etii enkiu oonkonyek.*
Break (fold, reduce) the sheep because there is an anthill that has eyes.

Cautions the speaker to be careful, for there is someone listening, usually a child, who could also be a spy.

PROVERBS ON SELF-ESTEEM, BOASTING AND CAPABILITY

85. *Meeta empur nemejo nanu eedo kidong'oe.*
There is no gecko that does not claim to possess the longest tail.

86. *Melam olampu olee.*
Boasting and a male cannot be separated.

Boasting never moves away from a male (man). Men have a

tendency to boast or try to perform impossible feats simply because they are men, not because they are in any way capable.

87. *Meeta emotonyi nemeiro ekenyua.*
There is no bird that does not talk at the break of day.

Often said when a person speaks, but says nothing important. The intention is to discourage idle talk, or restrict talking to valuable discussion.

88. *Meeta olmoruo lemejo suguro lainei oopi.*
There is no elder who does not say my brewing fruit is better.

This fruit is used for brewing honey beer.

Even if the fruit was not good, an elder would never admit it.

89. *Mejoyu maata ang'.*
One can never admit having no home.

It is rather difficult to admit weaknesses or failures, even though one is obviously aware of them. Often said to a person when he boasts.

90. *Meetae entalata natal kewan.*
There is no clearing that looks at itself.

In other words, even if something is as clearly laid out as a plain hillside, it would not be able to examine itself and detect faults. Human beings are not capable of judging themselves, so they should appreciate other people's assessments of them. Often said to a person who is unaware of his shortcomings.

91. *Midol kimanya.*
You do not see when it is residing in you.

It is not easy to examine a situation in which you are a part, it is afterwards that you are able to examine it objectively.

92. *Meetae arriyia le pase.*
There is no designer of nothingness.

There is no use in having grand designs if you have no means of accomplishing them, or, there is no use building castles in the air, usually for someone else. So, there is no use willing something for someone if you do not possess it.

93. *Ekueniyie olchata otii oltiren olotii enkima.*
The firewood on the hearth laughs at the one in the fire.
(Unaware that the same fate will soon befall it.)

94. *Ekueniyie nkuk nkuruon.*
The coals laugh at the ashes.

PROVERBS ON EQUALITY AND DISCRIMINATION

95. *Meoki oinoti nkipa, otisinyunye ake otii.*
The birth fluid of one's child is not drunk.

What matters is the one who emerges in a good way.

Pure breeds are not necessarily special, it is the performance that matters.

There is no significance in the birth fluid itself, so even an illegitimate child could prove better than one's own.

96. *Eikoki ole nkirotet nening' olentinki.*
The son of the beloved wife could be advised but that of the unloved wife may heed the advice.

This proverb originates from the story of Mbatiany's sons: Senteu was advised, but Olonana, after eavesdropping, did according to the instructions given to his step-brother, thus receiving his father's blessings and the ability to foretell the future. This is a true story which took place around 1890, and has not at all been influenced by the Biblical story of Jacob and Esau.

97. *Enyaanyuk oipotoki oloewuo openy.*
He that had been invited is the same as he that came on his own.

During the various Maasai festivities, formal invitations are few; all guests are accorded the same treatment.

98. *Eyop osikiria nkishu.*
The donkey exists alongside cattle.

He benefits from the cattle; when they are grazed he too gets grazed, when they are watered, he too gets a drink of water.

Often said when a person wishes to obtain benefits from another person who seems reluctant to comply.

99. *Etudung'oyie osinka olchekut.*
The labourer has substituted for the shepherd.

The wrong person or thing may show up at a time when you need him, or it, and prove to be very useful.

PROVERBS ON FORESIGHT AND PREPARATION

100. *Medung'unoyu eng'udi tioitoi*
You cannot make a walking stick on the way.

If you have not made proper arrangements for a trip before you set out, do not hope to accomplish much as you go along.

Emphasizes the importance of proper arrangements before one sets out to do a major task.

101. *Ming'asu olkesen etioyo enkerai.*
Do not cut out a cloak before the baby arrives. (Anything can happen.)

102. *Miar enalubalub likae osho.*
That which is weak (floppy) does not triumph in another country.

Refers to war time when warriors are expected to have been well-fed to be physically fit for the battle.
The pre-war preparation should, first and foremost, include feeding properly.

103. *Meruk ong'ata isaen.*
The wilderness does not thread beads.

The wilderness is no place to thread beads.

Sewing and making ornaments is often done during times of plenty, when rainwater and pasture is abundant and women are not occupied during much of the day. It is, therefore, associated with luxury and relaxation. Hence the saying that one does not relax in the wilderness; you need the comfort of home to do so.

104. *Menyaanyuk ooiguanate oleitu.*
Those who have had council are not the same as those who have not.

105. *Melo murrano olemeeta irrapi toonkaik pokira.*
One without arm-bands on both arms does not go through warriorhood. (Preparation is necessary.)

106. *Mimany meleeno.*
Do not inhabit it before you have inspected it. (For you may never know what is hiding within.)

107. *Meetae enamusunoyu.*
There is nothing that can be guessed.

108. *Meituruk enkume.*
The nose does not go before.

One cannot guess what happens before it happens, otherwise evil would be prevented.

PROVERBS WARNING AGAINST BELITTLING OTHERS

109. *Meetae menye alashe.*
There is nothing like father-cum-brother.

Often said by a younger man to his elder brother if the former detects that the latter is out to undermine him or oppress him in some way.

110. *Memurata olayioni oota menye.*
He who has a father is not circumcised. (He still receives orders from his father.)

111. *Melej enamurata enkae.*
One who is circumcised (initiated) cannot (lie to) trick (cheat) another just like him. (Their knowledge is the same.)

112. *Edol enkerai ilainyiamok eitu edol menye.*
The child may see thieves before the father does. (Warns against belittling the ability of a young person.)

113. *Meeta olamal olng'iro.*
There is no delegation that deserves to be viewed in diminutive terms. (They all have important functions to perform.)

114. *Memurut emurt elukunya.*
The neck does not go before the head.

115. *Meishaa ilmoruak aare kishomi.*
A cattle gate is not large enough for two elders to go through.

Both in the literal as well as the figurative sense, the neck is viewed as the lesser of the two, hence it should never strive to get to the top of the head.

Each elder deserves his own gate and the attempt to have them use one amounts to belittling them, apart from the possible friction that may result. In a physical sense, Maasai villages are structured in such a way that there are as many cattle gates in a village as there are elders.

116. *Ntadooi enkong'u tooloshon nimintadooyo too layiok loolmoruak.*
You may look over and beyond the hills but do not overlook the boys who have fathers.

117. *Ng'en enkong'u olainyiamoni kake melang'u enolopeny nkishu.*
The eye of the thief is clever, but not as clever as that of the owner of the cattle.

(You may think you are clever but someone else could be cleverer.)

118. *Meeta olee loldia.*
There is no gentleman who has a doggish behaviour.

Once a person has lost respectability, he ceases to be regarded as a gentleman.

119. *Enya enkurto enkop o metumuta.*
The armyworm can eat the world (land vegetation) until it finishes it.

120. *Edol enkong'u enedol enkae.*
The eye sees where the other one sees.

Emphasis here is on equality of abilities.

121.   *Epi oljipet inkaloli pokira.*
       Both ends of a skewer are sharp.

       Ojipet is a stick sharpened on both ends, used to roast meat or turn it while it is cooking. The proverb says that this stick is sharp at both ends. Whichever way you approach it from, you are bound to meet with danger. Often used in reference to the young and old as a warning that neither of the two should be tampered with, for the consequences could be grave. But while the might of the old could be visible, that of the young is latent; nonetheless it could be equally lethal.

122.   *Ng'en olayioni oinepua menye.*
       A boy who has caught up with his father is clever.

       A boy is clever if he finds his father alive and was raised by him. He learns from him.

       Boys learn from their fathers and it is unfortunate for a boy to lose a father before he has acquired his knowledge and skills.

PROVERBS ON CHANGES IN TIMES AND SEASONS

123.   *Miany enkutuk nainosa nkik enya eilata nemiany enainosa eilata enya kik.*
       A mouth that has eaten fat does not resist eating excrement, and that which has eaten excrement, does not resist eating fat. One may be rich today but poor tomorrow and vice versa, therefore do not boast.

124.   *Melama iltuli o enkop.*
       The buttocks and the ground are not far apart.

       (One may be standing at one minute and the next minute they would be sitting or lying down or even dead.)

125.   *Oata taata oota taisere.*
       It is one who has today and it is another who may have tomorrow.
       Same as:

       Merisio moyok e olong'i.
       The waste products (offal) are not the same amount every day.

126. *Meng'ar inkakeny ilomon.*
Mornings do not share news.

One may wake up one morning having made a decision to do
something but the next morning he may reverse the decision
depending on what transpires within those two days.
This uncertainty has a double meaning.

i) Uncertainty of each day.

ii) Tendency of the mind to change.

127. *Miany olotara enkitung'at eaku osuuji.*
The one who has beaten an army does not resist becoming
a coward.

128. *Miany oledukuya eaku olesiadi nemiany olesiadi eaku
oledukuya.*
The first may be last and the last may be first.

129. *Bitir akenya.*
The morning is like a warthog. (It is unpredictable.)

130. *Emir ilomon lenteipa ilentadekenya.*
The news of the evening may triumph over that of the morning.

131. *Eeku nameni eriroi.*
Even that which is despised could triumph.

Eriroi is a plant that is used for various functions in the home.
The proverb discourages people from despising others due to
their physical appearance, for times change and they too may get
to the top.

132. *Oota taata oota taisere.*
One has it today, but another might have it tomorrow.

Give unto others today what you have, for tomorrow you
will not have it and it will be their turn to give to you. This
saying is frequently quoted by someone who needs
something from a person who seems reluctant to
part with it.

133. *Tenilo olosho onya nkik, inosa.*
If you go to a country where they eat excrement, eat it.
(Do not be too picky.)

134. *Eshomo olmotonyi enkai nedou metari tenkop.*
The bird has flown to the sky then descended to be killed
on earth.

A person could be so successful as to be above everyone else, but
it is possible for his powers to wane, so that he becomes lower
than the lowest.

The sky in this respect is viewed as the highest limit of power, the
earth its lowest ebb.

135. *Inosa (olkar) nijut enkutuk.*
Feed well by feeding on the brisket but remember to wipe your
mouth.

Discourages the affiuent from parading or boasting about
their property.

136. *Meetae oidipa, oitumurrua ake otii.*
There is no one who has finished, there is only he who is
still at it.

Life is so unpredictable that no one should be overconfident in
having completed anything.

137. *Nailoikino motioo kima.*
Pots take turns to sit on the fire.

One may have something today, but have nothing tomorrow, and
vice versa. This is the same as the proverb No.132 '*Oota taata
oota taisere*', one person has today, another one tomorrow.

138. *Murua irraga mimanya.*
Stay uninhabited (to the landscape).

Refers to a situation that used to be, but has since ceased to exist.
When one beholds such a situation, he ponders over it, quoting
this proverb often coupled with a sense of surprise, as wishful
thinking.

This proverb is very often quoted by the Maasai when they
reminiscence on the days when they used to be "Lords of East
Africa", when they see themselves trampled under foot by people
they once perceived as below them in status.

139. *Tenelo neshalu enjore nenya nkopit.*
When an army gets weak, it eats bark.

Habits and actions change according to the circumstances, therefore no one can set limits.

140. *Sasin ebari.*
It is the thin ones that survive.

The healthy cows often die first, leaving behind the thin statured ones.

141. *Meeta embae nalo aa nabo.*
There is no arrow (or issue) that goes singly.

Warns a person not to forget that times may change and he might be in need.

PROVERBS WARNING AGAINST PRETENCE

142. *Meiturujunoyu metii enkiyio.*
You cannot bulge it, if there is no baby.

Do not feign pregnancy, for the truth will soon be known. Feigning pregnancy is not an uncommon practice among Maasai women, and is often done to obtain the delicacies that are normally reserved for women in that state. For instance, a big ox will be slaughtered if a hump is what the pregnancy "demands" or "desires".

This proverb is very literal and warns against a not too uncommon practice. *

*There is a strong belief that when a pregnant woman asks for anything one should never refuse her, for the baby may otherwise be born prematurely: uncouth women take advantage of this.

143. *Menya enkoshoke enyamu.*
The stomach cannot steal.

(It would show.) The stealing refered to is livestock that is raided and slaughtered in bush camps.

144. *Meitemoo olowuaru olkujita.*
Grass does not hide a carnivore/lion. (It will grow and be detected.)

145. *Meetae osher emena.*
There is no one who belches when he is hungry.

To the Maasai, belching is quite acceptable; it is usually seen as a sign of satisfaction with the food. This proverb is often said when a person is trying to conceal something.

146. *Meramatayu engogong'i aras.*
It cannot be cared for, if it has evil ribs.

You cannot cover up evil because it would be detected. Ribs normally bulge out despite the cover provided by meat or flesh.

147. *Mimulumulaki osoit emodiei.*
Do not cover a stone with cow-dung. (Do not trick somebody using softly-wrapped methods.)

148. *Eyopu olasurai eng'udi.*
A snake can follow a staff. (Evil creeps in innocently.)

149. *Pooki olashe oirrusha emaal olonak nkishu are.*
The calf that has a thick dewlap is one that feeds from two cows. (When a person feeds well it shows.)

150. *Eiu barie ng'atuny neiu ng'atuny barie.*
The jackal begets a lion and a lion begets a jackal. (Good produces evil and vice versa.)

PROVERBS ON WISDOM AND FOOLISHNESS

151. *Memut elukunya nabo eng'eno.*
One head does not consume all knowledge. (There are limits to one person's knowledge.)

152. *Ear emodai olopeny*
Foolishness kills (attacks) he who owns it.

A foolish person gets himself into trouble through his own foolishness.

153. *King'as Olemaayi nikintoki oleng'eno.*
We begin by being foolish, but we later become knowledgeable.

154. *Metii ng'en eleji.*
There is no one who is clever when he is cheated.

A man may think he is clever, but someone else could be a better trickster.

155. *Enkong'u naipang'a eng'en.*
The eye which has travelled is clever.

People are known to gain experience and knowledge when they travel outside their own home areas.

156. *Ererei olamuratani.*
Even the circumciser is directed.

Even a specialist, like the circumciser, could go wrong and needs to be directed.

157. *Meibor ng'eno lukunya.*
Wisdom does not have a white head (grey hair).

This proverb has two meanings:

i)   Wisdom does not age;

ii) Wisdom is not restricted to the aged.

158. *Ng'eni ootoni neijia etiu ooponu.*
The ones who are staying at home are clever and so are the ones arriving/visitors. (Same as the proverb above, but refers to different cadres of people).

159. *Meiguen olaigwenani keon.*
An adviser does not advise himself. (Even a clever person may require assistance from others.)

One of the criteria for selecting leaders is intelligence.

PROVERBS ON PATIENCE, IMPATIENCE AND PERSEVERANCE

160. *Mianyu enkoshoke emoti nayiara.*
The stomach does not wait for a pot that is cooking. (Some issues need urgent attention.)

161. *Miput enkaya ejon.*
Do not pick the stomach before it is ready/fully cooked.
(When it is still cooking.)

Do not be impatient, but wait until an issue has taken place. Often said when a person acts or speaks on an issue before it is even mentioned.

162. *Keme baare neretisho.*
Undergoing treatment hurts, but it also helps.

You have to go through difficulty in order to achieve the positive things in life.

163. *Mme kwetita toki, barakinoto.*
It is not the rushing that matters, it is doing it properly.
(Slow but sure; or in Swahili: *Haraka haraka haina baraka.*)

164. *Meokoyu enkare edou.*
Water cannot be drunk while it is flowing.

You have to wait until you have observed the direction issues are taking before you react, in the case of deliberations.

PROVERBS ON FAIRNESS

165. *Taaraki nikiyau monyit ang'.*
Kill me but bring my intestines back home.

If you must perform a good or bad deed, remember to observe the proper rites and behaviour; do not over-react in the heat of the moment.

166. *Mikielie ilkereu lenaisho neitu anya.*
Do not smear me with the "dirt" from the honey that I did not eat.
(Do not draw in innocent people, if you get into trouble.)

167. *Meiger esayiet enkupes.*
Poison does not write on the thigh.

Reference here is made to poisonous plants and their definite effects on the skin. It is not uncommon to see children as well as adult men* drawing figures on their thighs using dry twigs. The proverb means that what a person has not done does not affect him in any way. A person need not worry when he is accused of having done something which he did not do, because no harm would come to him. Fairness prevails.

*Women are usually discreet in their way of dressing and make sure that their thighs are properly covered.

168. *Mikipejie oljipet Ie likae.*
Do not burn me with someone else's skewer.

(Do not direct your anger at the wrong person.)

169. *Teneya nikimbayu mikinor.*
If you get to hating me do not smear me.

(Be fair at all times irrespective of the circumstances.)

170. *Mikiar eitu kirorie.*
Do not beat (kill) me before you have talked to me.

This is because there might be a chance that I did not deserve the beating (killing), full details of which you may not yet have.

PROVERBS OF PUNCTUALITY AND SEQUENCE

171. *Mebaayu etii iloik.**
It cannot be treated when the bones are still there.

In a literal sense "it" refers to a wound. When a bone is broken, there is not much you can do to treat the open sore on the surface, for unless the broken bone inside has been treated the ailment persists.

In a figurative sense "it" refers to the fine that has to be paid whenever a person hits another and breaks a bone. The culprit would have to pay 49 head of cattle in order to appease the patient, otherwise if he dies before this was done, he would be assumed to have been killed by the offender. People are often eager to pay the "fine of the bones" rather than wait to be dubbed a "murderer", which happens even if the culprit dies of natural causes, in which case the offender is said to be "**oloikopani**", or "a man who murdered his own kind".

*During the 19th century Maasai wars, some sections were determined to have closer affiliations with one group than another. When a man kills a member of one of these groups he is dubbed a murderer, and he pays the fine, but if he murders one from the "enemy" camp, he pays no fine and is not termed a murderer.

172.   *Meyietunoyu enkiring'o e atua etii enioriong!*
You cannot pull out the meat from the inside when the outside one is still there.

173.   *Esuj erashe ng'ejuk emusana.*
A new idea (custom) follows an old one.

(If an idea is good it is copied and followed.)

174.   *Eilanya kitojo orinka.*
The hare has gone before the club.

In other words, you acted later than you should have, therefore, you had better time your actions properly if you wish to attain a certain goal.

175.   *Menya enkolong' ilomon.*
The day (sun) does not eat news.

You can't turn back the clock while you are doing something, for the day (time) passes. Said when one is slow or slack or when he has many other things to do in the day.

176.   *Medung'oki oshomoyie.*
One who has left (on a journey) does not make concrete plans. (Because he may never know what may happen.)

PROVERBS DISCOURAGING WAR

177.   *Memira eishoro ilukuny.*
Those who give each other heads are not beaten.

As long as two people face each other in a fight none is defeated, i.e. the fight continues. One has to give up the fight.

178. *Merrinyo olokirikiri eitu eduaa olikae.*
Shaking caused by bad temper does not subside until it has met another like it.

When someone seeks a fight with another person and starts shaking or having a fit because of it, if the opponent starts doing the same, or after they have fought, the shaking ceases.

179. *Mesuji nkiporo.*
People do not follow scars.

(Discourages revenge.)

180. *Misujaki imirat entim.*
Do not follow the vanquished into the bush.
Once a fight has been completed it is unwise for the victor
to continue it.

181. *Elelek ayia (ayia amu ayia nalelek).*
It is easy to say "very well". Often said to a person who has been offended by another to prevent him from fighting, beseeching him instead to ignore the offender. "*Ayia amu ayia nalelek*" is often said by the offended as a warning that he is giving the last warning.

182. *Nchoo meitaa are.*
Let him make it two.

If a person makes a mistake, do not inflict punishment for the first time, but wait until he does it for the second time.

183. *Megel empere kishu.*
A spear does not separate or sort cattle.
Do not use a spear indiscriminately, but wait until the occasion warrants it.

184. *Meorroi nkurrat.*
People do not fight over a rumour.

185. *Eikedienye olarrabal.*
A fight makes people appear left-handed.
It bothers the person who is not prepared for it in the sense that he cannot fight effectively.

186. *Ampu yima ilkeek, Kiguana lotona.*
May boastfulness disappear and good judgement settle in. (Good judgement is better than boastfulness.)

PROVERBS ON PECULIARITY AND INDIVIDUALITY

187. *Mepa ilmero ntikan.*
The Meru will never stop growing large jaws.

The Meru as well as other Bantu peoples are known by the Maasai to have some predominant physical features, the bulging bottom jaws being one of them. There must have been a serious joking and teasing relationship between the Maa community and Bantu neighbours.

188. *Sipat ake eng'ari meng'ari mpukunot.*
It is only truth that is shared, characters are not.

This proverb acknowledges the existence of individuality despite unanimity in decisions arrived at through concensus.

189. *Mepuo otimi tenkop enye.*
Baboons do not leave their usual habitat.

190. *Mepal oloitiko isirat.*
The zebra cannot shed its stripes. (Custom or habit is not easily discarded.)

191. *Mepal olowuaru enetadaare.*
The carnivore does not stop frequenting a place where it has fed.

192. *Meitutumoyu oleleo lemala olemoti.*
You cannot patch together a piece of gourd with that of a pot.

193. *Sidai enepuru neisul enitamoo.*
A smoky place is good, especially one that you are used to.

This proverb has an extended meaning: the significance of smokiness is that it is proof that the place is inhabited, as opposed to a wilderness; yet there is a special type of comfort derived from living in one's own habitat as opposed to someone else's.

PROVERBS WARNING AGAINST DOUBLE-DEALING

194. *Meibung'ayu esiare o embulati.*
It is not possible to hold a walking staff as well as the stomach.

While a walking staff signifies the tending of stock, the stomach signifies greedy and wolfish behaviour. They are not compatible, and mixing them suggests that one is bound to be neglected.

195. *Meibungayu are.*
Two things cannot be held at the same time.

196. *Meisulu oloing'oni murua are.*
A bull does not triumph in two homesteads.

197. *Menyor ilmurran inkimaitie are.*
The warriors are not suited by two camps (fires). It is either   one or the other.

OR

Mebuak oidia too murua are.

A dog does not bark in two homesteads.

OR

Merrip oidia nkang'itie are.

A dog does not guard two homesteads.

198. *Meetae enabik elo.*
There is none that settles as it leaves.

PROVERBS ON STUBBORNNESS

199. *Ore peyie einosa oidia nkik mme oliki etala kiok ming'ani einosa.*
The reason why the dog ate excrement is not because he missed a relative to advise him, it is because he ate the deaf ear.

See the story on how the dog lost favour with God (**7**).

This proverb is often mistaken for the reverse: the reason why the dog ate excrement is because he lacked a relative to advise him.

200. *Mening'isho nkiri nememe.*
The flesh that has not been hurt remains stubborn.

(Spare the rod and spoil the child).

Often said as a warning that a beating might be necessary soon if everything else fails.

201. *Mme oliki etala olikini.*
It is not the adviser who is lacking, it is the advised.

When a person does not show any signs of heeding the sound advice that is being given to him this proverb is quoted.

202. *Irorie amu miany eye.*
Talk to him for he will not stop dying.

Advice does not fend off an eventuality. Often said of a lost cause.

203. *Miingil iloorasha aare.*
Do not repeat two blemished ones.

(Do not repeat the same mistake.)

204. *Meshukunoyu oloomi otashe.*
The stiff rafter cannot be bent.

Often said when children tend to disregard authority. The children are compared to dry rafters that cannot be bent, having gone too far on their undisciplined way. Sounded as a cue to parents that their child needs some disciplining.

205. *Meikooyu olelipong'.*
You cannot advise a man who is after a woman.

Once a man wants a woman, his desire becomes so strong that advising him against his choice would prove ineffective.

PROVERBS ON CATTLE

206. *Reto o reto olashe lenkiteng' ai.*
It is mutual help, the calf of my cow.

Helping is a reciprocal affair. The Maasai take a lot of pains tending their livestock. This proverb stresses the principle of give and take.

207. *Tudumu entasat enkiteng' nimidumu enoltung'ani.*
Help up a cow that is aged but not a human being. (He is bound to be ungrateful and turn against you.)

208. *Erisiore enkiteng' nabo elukunya olee!*
One cow is equal to a man's head.

A cow may appear insignificant compared to a man, but could achieve as much as him. Cows are exchanged in marriage contracts which usually result in the production of children, who later become adults.

209. *Eleji mejing' ang' aajoki nji eba ku/e enkiteng' ino.*
He that does not enter the home is cheated about the amount of milk that his cow has produced.

210. *Meeta enkiteng' olopeny.*
The cow has no owner.

Cattle are normally exchanged so often that the idea of individual ownership ceases to make much sense.

211. *Meye olororita modiok.*
He that steps on cow-dung does not die.

(It is an obvious sign that he has cattle.)

212. *Meidim imparbali oloperriper.*
The cows cannot handle problems.

213. *Merik enkarrueisho nkishu.*
Crookedness does not lead cattle (people).

(Choice of a good leader is very important.)

214. *Etejo enkiteng'; "mikintaaya, nchooyioki"!*
The cow said: "Do not lend me out, give me away."

(The owner treats his property in a better way.)

215. *Enkawuo nabar kishu.*
It is the bow that tends cattle.

216. *Minosie entawuo moyok. (Menya) Entawuo moyok.*
Do not exchange a heifer with offal.

You cannot buy a heifer with offal.

You have to sacrifice something precious in order to obtain a heifer.

PROVERBS ON THE IMPORTANCE OF CHILDREN

217. *Aimenye marmali anaa menye maata?*
Menye marmali.

Which of the two would you rather be, the father of the mischievous one or the father of no one?
The father of the mischievous one.

When it comes to such a choice the Maasai will choose the trials and tribulations of having children rather than have none at all. Often said to a parent when a child gets into mischief, thus dishonouring the family, mainly to console them with the logic that the misery of having no children would be more unbearable than what is at hand.

218. *Olapa oibor inkera.*
The children are the bright moon.

(They bring pleasure into the home.)

219. *Meirrag ten tim otoishe.*
He does not lie in the wilderness he that has given forth.

(He would have children who would take care of him.)

220. *Elelek osina tenkaji natii olayioni.*
The problems of a family that has a boy are easy to overcome.

The boy would grow into a man and relieve his family of the problems.

221. *Toisho mime.*
Give forth without feeling the pain.

(Be tolerant of your children.)

222. *Meetae enkerai enkoshoke o enenkoriong'.*
There is no child who is of the stomach and one who is of the back.

(All children are equal, or should be treated equally.)

PROVERBS ON OWNERSHIP VERSUS DEPENDENCE

223. *Meitemenayu esidai ilopir lenyena*
      You cannot deprive the ostrich of its feathers.

      It would not be fair and would be noticed. See the story of
      the ostrich chicks (**20**).

224. *Meruti lotorok Ie likae.*
      Someone else's honey is not collected.

      (That which was destined to be yours will always remain yours.)

225. *Meyaroyu enenkitok.*
      That which belongs to a woman cannot be taken away.

      (For she might have sons who will reclaim it.) (See story
      No. **24**)

226. *Meyaroyu ene obulu.*
      That of the growing one cannot be taken away.

      (For soon he will be old enough to reclaim it.)

227. *Meiteeng'ayu enjore nitii.*
      It is not possible to reject (ignore) an army of which you are a
      member.

      (If you do, it may be to your own disadvantage.)

228. *Meishu enolikae okiyo.*
      That of another person's does not exhaust desire.

      Do not depend on, or admire, someone else's things for they are
      not satisfying; learn to appreciate your own.

229. *Nayeyu dama enkiteng' e likae.*
      Someone else's cow dries up in the middle of the day.

      Do not depend on other people's things, for they might
      decide to take them back before you are prepared to part
      with them.

230. *Inosa olmejokua lenkiteng' e likae.*
      Eat plenty from another's cow.

      (Said when a person squanders someone else's property.)

231. *Meyek olenkaina ilala lenyena.*
The elephant does not get tired of its tusks. (One carries his burden without flinching.)

232. *Tenenya ilkimojik enkima nisaru ilinono.*
If the fingers get burnt, rescue your own.
(You must remember to take care of your own interests first.)

233. *Mikinyorri miata toki ino.*
You are not loved if you do not have your own thing.

234. *Meitang'e oltung'ani olkikuei leme olenye.*
A person does not itch from a thorn that is not his.
(It is the wearer who knows where the shoe pinches, or as they say in Swahili *Pilipili usioila yakuwashani?*)

235. *Mitum errap etii enkuo intare.*
You cannot obtain an arm band while the ram is with the flock.
The arm band referred to is made of buffalo horn and is made by the hunters (Dorobo) and sold to the Maasai in exchange for a ram. Thus if a man wants the band, he must part with the ram.

236. *Kintirrish likae tung'ani anaa kintololong'.*
Another person either tightens or loosens you.
(It is better to depend on yourself, for you know what you want best.)

237. *Mitemakino anaa masaa eiking'a.*
Do not try it on like someone else's beads (property).
(Strive to get your own.)

PROVERBS ADVISING AGAINST SEEKING TROUBLE

238. *Milo aiseyie empon'.*
Do not tap danger (evil).
(You would be looking for trouble.)

239. *Mioj ilpepedo meng'e.*
Do not scratch scabies when it does not itch.

240. *Mintodol embitir enkawuo.*
Do not show a warthog a bow.

(It will run away.)

241. *Mintodolunyie nkishu ilmurran.*
Do not tempt warriors with cows.

(They will raid them.)

242. *Moti nayier esayiet enkutuk.*
The mouth is a pot that cooks poison.

Do not talk of bad things, so that they may not happen.

243. *Meibung'ayu enapiak olkidong'oe.*
You cannot get hold of the tail of evil.

Once evil has left, you cannot go chasing it or cling to it by the tail. This proverb applies to all unpleasant things and confirms a human desire to forget them and let them pass quietly.

244. *Kurro milau eninang.*
If you look for trouble, you will not miss it.

245. *Minang'u olenkaina toontulele.*
Do not beckon the elephant with adam's apples.

This fruit is commonly used by children in their various games.This proverb warns against seeking, or inventing trouble.

246. *Mikurru enkukuo naishu.*
Do not fish out a live piece of coal.

(You would be courting trouble.)

PROVERBS ON BAD INFLUENCES

247. *Eitaduar ololodo – kulak boo.*
He that has red urine may spread it all over the village.

This is viewed in both a literal and figurative sense. A contagious disease easily spreads through the entire village; a person of bad character can easily influence good people.

248. *Eitong'u olojong'ani obo kule.*
One fly can make the milk go stale.

249. *Shore lai kishoriki enapiak.*
My friend, you bring me evil.

Often said when a person keeps bad company, or when he gets into trouble because of it.

PROVERBS WARNING AGAINST PRIDE

250. *Mikedie namuka soito.*
Do not climb rocks with shoes on.

The Maasai shoes are made of cow-hide and are slippery on smooth surfaces. Often told to a person who is getting conceited or proud, and tries to attempt impossible deeds, especially if by doing so he steps on others' toes.

251. *Mbung'a olorita esuguroi nimimbung' olorita eng'anayioi.*
Hold the one who is suffering from having had too much drink, but not the one who is drunk with affluence.

PROVERBS ON TRUTH AND LIES

252. *Miaku monko enkanyit.*
Lies cannot amount to respect.

253. *Meiput isipat endap.*
Truth does not fill the palm of the hand.

254. *Meitadoyio isipat enkolong' monko naaitadoyio.*
Truth does not make the sun set, it is lies that do.

255. *Menyaanyuk aateleja o aatishirraka.*
It is not the same if I lie to you and if I tell you plain truth.

It hurts less if you tell a lie to someone you respect.

PROVERBS ON DANGER

256. *Meetae kinturiate kiserian.*
Once we have been scared, we cannot be safe.

(There must be imminent danger looming.)

257. *Maor eliyio o bata*
I cannot distinguish silence from danger.

When all is quiet, it could be either from danger or because of loneliness. Do not make assumptions before you have proven something, especially in cases where two opposing issues are closely allied. When all is quiet, there may be danger.

258. *Meikarri olpaashie meimuno.*
A fence is not erected, or raised, if all is well.

A person cannot predict what will happen before it happens, when he learns to deal with it.

259. *Eima aras e kimojik.*
It has slipped between the fingers.

This is a saying that implies that a person has escaped narrowly.

PROVERBS ON PARTS OF THE BODY

260. *Enkiok napolos enaimin mme enkong'u.*
It is the ear that penetrates through darkness, not the eye.
(Use the appropriate object at the right time.)

261. *Ilkipieu eitainyieki nkang'ilie, me oltau.*
It is the lungs from which homes are built, not the heart. In order of importance, the heart is believed to perform the major function in the body, before the lungs, but the heart is at the same time said to be the source of emotional instability as well as the cause for irrationality. In order to attain great things in life, like building up a home, one would be advised to depend on the more stable lungs. Often said to a person when he loses his temper.

262. *Meitayu enkong'u enabara.*
The eye does not choose the best.

Unless a person employs some other means of judgement that does not rely on outward appearances, as does the eye, he should not hope to obtain the best.

263. *Nkamulak enyena eiba.*
It is his own spittle that he does not like.

If all that a person lives on is his own spittle, it amounts to eating nothing, since it is not substantial enough. Since spittle does not satisfy hunger, it would kill the owner.

264. *Medol ilala osina.*
Teeth do not see misery.

People still smile despite problems.

Often said in difficult situations when people still manage to entertain each other and have fun.

265. *Meeta olng'ejep rubata.*
The tongue has no joint.

(It utters unbecoming remarks.)

266. *Tarrush olng'ejep, ejo pooki toki.*
The tongue is clumsy, it says everything.

267. *Ong'u naitasur tung'ani.*
It is the eye that lands man in trouble.

268. *Emen oloing'oni enkoshoke.*
A brave man disregards the stomach.

(Other matters are more important.)

PROVERBS ON FINALITY

269. *Meisimakinoyu enkiteng' erruk.*
You cannot force a hump on a cow.

No matter how desirable a thing is, and no matter how hard you try to change it, there are things in life that are predetermined, and hence remain as they are.

270. *Miarakinoyu enkare oloipang'i.*
Water cannot be forced up a ridge.

(Attempting to do the impossible is futile.)

271. *Melonyayu embae meng'oruno.*
It is not possible to dodge the arrow (an issue) before it has been thrown (released).

Wait until you know what is expected of you before you take action.

272.   *Meituku olkine ng'iro.*
It cannot be cleansed with a brown he-goat.

Brown he-goats are customarily slaughtered during cleansing rituals, since the colour brown in the case of goats is associated with purity. If a person commits an "unpardonable sin", normally one which has never been committed before, this proverb is quoted to indicate the magnitude of the misdeed.

273.   *Meibooroyu ootiyi.*
He cannot be advised while there is a streak of a curse.
(A bad person cannot be advised.)

274.   *Mesarunoyu oltau oipurupure.*
Once a heart has fallen down, it cannot be retrieved.

Explains the necessity of accepting facts and finalities.
If there is little that one can do, it must be done early, otherwise accept the inevitable.

275.   *Menang' ilmang'ati oltipilit lemenang' apa ake.*
The enemy does not perish at a place where he was not meant to perish.

Stresses the importance of predestination and the hopelessness of striving to upset an already laid-out pattern. Said when a person wishes another ill.

276.   *Teneng'ueyu olderoni naa enkaji e ng'otonye elo.*
When a rat rots, it is to its own mother's house that it returns.

(When a person gets into trouble, he goes back home.)

277.   *Todua mijo aitayu kailus nintayu kaiting.'*
See that you do not strive to exceed limits; in the process you might waste all prospects.

PROVERBS ON OBVIOUS ASPECTS OF LIFE

278.   *Meeta oltorroboni olng'ejuk.*
There is no new Dorobo (hunter).

(They are all adept in hunting.)

A person easily learns what is practised around him.

279. *Meeta olameyu olonyori.*
There is never a dry season that is green.
(Said of things that are obvious). Dry seasons have dry grass.

280. *Miomon iltorrobo eng'orno.*
Do not beg butter of the Dorobo (hunters).
(They are bound not to have it.)

281. *Mediak empito eneima oltidu.*
The sinew does not miss (the place) where the needle has passed.

282. *Eder olayioni o menye, neder entito o ng'otonye.*
The boy holds counsel with his father and the girl with her mother.
This proverb simply emphasises the practice, and is quoted when one is seen diverging from it or from any other norm.

PROVERBS ON LIFE IN GENERAL

283. *Miar keon tiorrondo oyiara.*
Do not kill yourself from the cooking *orrondo*.
This proverb is based on story no 23. Often quoted when a person aims at something through opportunism. He is warned that he might be making the wrong choice.

284. *Sanag olgoo lolee.*
The chest of a man is an entangled thick bush.
This proverb expresses the fact that what one sees outwardly, when looking at a person, is only the tip of the iceberg, for a man/woman is capable of hiding feelings and problems in order to appear contented and happy.

285. *Eisiash embae nabo oltome.*
One arrow can knock down the elephant.

286. *Etii muuka ilkeek.*
Something hovers about the trees.
Not easy to arrive at a literal translation. Often said when a person insists on doing what he has been warned against. Also made when there are imminent problems that are difficult to solve.

287. *Meji olayioni kaji itopokie.*
A boy (man) is not asked where (how) he recovered.

Once a person has acquired property, he is not asked how he obtained it.

288. *Merumae oishuaa.*
People cannot check on each other's stomachs.

[No one can tell whether one has eaten or not.]

289. *Elatia nainosa nkishu.*
It is the neighbours who feed on each other's stock.

[Stresses the importance of neighbours.]

290. *Toponie sancha ramatare.*
Carry on with a lover as you tend flock.

[Do not neglect any important duty for a less important one.]

291. *Ilosekin intokitin naa ilmairrot.*
Things are tricky and they are cornered.

(Life is not easy, it is a struggle.)

292. *Mejung'oyu enkutuk naata enkaret.*
The mouth with a weapon cannot be inherited.

Once a person is able to defend himself verbally, others cannot appropriate his property.

293. *Emunyak kilikuai negogong'.*
The message was ridden with fortune as well as with evil.

Often said when someone is sent out with an important message, but the person he is sent to may, or may not, be found.

294. *Koko isieku, aa ng'ole kiyae ang'ata naa nena iyie.*
This is a common saying which, when translated literally, becomes nonsensical.

Often said when a person fails to accomplish what he had set out to do. This proverb is quoted on his return.

295. *Menyaanyuk enchikati enkutuk o enolkurum.*
The fart of the mouth and that of the bottom are not the same.

Abusive talk smells more than a fart.

296. *Mme shata omut kima.*

It (he) is not wood that fire burns up. Often said when one person is fed up with another, and wishes them ill.

297. *Etapaashayie anaa enkaji oontoyie.*
It has gone the opposite way, like the houses of girls do.

Girls practise building houses outside the home, following no pattern, such as the one followed in a normal settlement.

Often quoted when something takes an unexpected turn, or when someone does an unexpected thing.

298. *Merotokinoyu enitadaare.*
You cannot defecate at a place where you have fed.

(One does not abuse those he has received hospitality from).

299. *Eiba enkoliai enedupita.*
The widow does not like a burning place.

(Having no male support, she normally tries to avoid trouble.)

300. *Derrat imbaa edede.*
Issues can be discussed when they are truthful.

301. *Tijing'a loonyuni nimijing' iloonyisho.*
Be among those who are awaited, but not among those who wait.

The former is the more comfortable of the two, considering that the latter is riddled with anxiety. This proverb originates from wartime when those at home would be anxiously awaiting the armies and the outcome of the battle.

302. *Siamo turia lewa.*
Delegation, be fearful of gentlemen.

Said to stress the importance of counsel and what it can accomplish.

303. *Eng'ari esajati oloilelee.*
The piece of the shank (of animals) can be shared.

(A small thing can be shared by many people.)

304. *Erruesh olenkaina enaimurruai*
The elephant can trip over a creeping plant.

Despite his size and might, he is still vulnerable, and could easily trip over a little plant.

305. *Meeta iltuli kiririo.*
The buttocks have no comparison.

306. *Emuro nadung'o porori.*
Age-sets are like a broken hind-leg.

307. *Meya esile nkujit.*
A debt cannot be carried away by the grass.

If you borrow during the dry season and then the rains come, you cannot forget to pay your debts. A time of plenty does not wipe away debts.

308. *Meng'or olekutuk kulukuok.*
He that pronounces a curse does not direct it at the soil.

(If it does not aim at a person it would bounce back on the utterer.)

309. *Nchirrakinot noolewa oomurata.*
Gentlemen face each other in the open.

(Discourages underhand behaviour.)

310. *Milo ilgum eranyi.*
Do not go gathering fruit when a dance is taking place.

(Do not perform an irrelevant task at an inappropriate time.)

311. *Mining' inaajo olome.*
Do not believe what a physically hurt person says.

(He could say more than what actually took place.)

312. *Menyaanyuk oturu o onuk.*
He that digs out is not the same as he who buries.

It is better to speak out than to keep problems within yourself. One gets a feeling of relief after discussing issues that are bothersome.

313. *Meikitikitoyu oloota esumash.*
You cannot tickle a hungry person.

(He would not laugh.)

Make sure the other person is satisfied, or is in the same situation as you, before you involve him in anything.

314. *Meipaayu eidurri.*
It is not possible to do a dance when you are moving home.

Both these are opposing tasks, and need concerted effort and attention. Do the right thing at the right time.

315. *Miimie kewan murra o kwenyi.*
Do not let the big things as well as the evil ones pass you.

If you cannot perform great acts, you might end up having to perform evil ones. Take the initiative, do not wait until you have no choice.

316. *Mapal kaotiki eetae maitoki.*
I will not stop daring as long as apology exists.

If you want to block the occurrence of an incident, you must remember to block all possible loopholes.

317. *Enyaanyuk kang'a o kaiusho.*
They are both equally bad.

Often said when a man realises that a person he had always thought was good is just as bad as the rest. Also used when two equally bad situations present themselves.

318. *Menya olkileleng'i emala.*
A gourd does not eat a goat's dropping.

(Similar to the Swahili proverb: *Kidogo kidogo hujaza kibaba*)

CHAPTER SIX

Songs and Poetry

Songs and poetry are an essential part of life in many communities. In societies where traditional customs are strongly adhered to, there are certain rituals that are observed to the accompaniment of songs, dirges and other poetic forms. Apart from these ritual tunes, there are also songs that are composed spontaneously as the occasion demands. These include some lullabies, love songs, war songs and political songs. But whatever function they serve, songs and poetry embody a people's philosophy, beliefs, values and, sometimes, their historical development.

The Maasai, as we have already noted, have various socio-political organizations, including the age-set and age-grade systems. These systems are marked by rites of passage which are composed of rituals, ceremonies and festivities. During these activities there is dancing and singing. Ritual songs include initiation songs, birth and naming songs, prayer, war and other songs. There are also prayers and blessings which, although not sang, constitute an important part of these rituals. Songs sang by children include lullabies, teasing songs, and rhymes.

Songs and poems have been classified according to their function, but this arrangement overlaps with the age and sex of the singers. Thus we have war songs, only sang by warriors, and blessings which, although chanted in every ritual function, are a speciality of the elders. Different types of songs have different names which describe their functional significance and translating their respective titles to, for example, war song or praise song, does not fully illustrate the meaning of the original word. For this reason, the original title has been retained in some cases.

The Maasai, as a predominantly pastoral people, centre their ideas and activities around their livestock and their immediate surroundings. Their imagery is drawn from a pastoral setting. They sing about colours, shapes and behaviour of cattle, as well as the sizes and shapes of their horns. They talk of the buffalo-shaped horns of cattle and their yellow colour is compared with colostrum. Tall people are said to be bamboos.

There are equally unique images that are drawn from cultures whose mode of subsistence is agriculture, hunting or fishing.

In this chapter, an effort has been made to give a broad perspective of the material that exists by giving samples of the various types of songs and poetry. This sample does not provide enough scope to enable the reader to grasp the depth of the poetry, its mode of expression, and other unique nuances. One would need to look at a reasonable selection of each genre, rather than an odd piece here and there, to appreciate these songs fully. It is, however, hoped that the footnotes and the introductory chapter on the historical, social and cultural background of the Maasai will assist the reader in understanding this selection of songs, poems and prayers.

Many Maasai songs consist of phrases which are sang by different people, one reciting a fragment, others chanting melodic refrains. There is also accompanying body movement and rocking in rhythm with the song. Other common gestures that accompany singing include thrusting supportive hands at the singer in approval of what she says (usually women) and, depending on the emotion being expressed, some people get into fits (often associated with men but by no means uncommon to women).

The strophes in these poems are an addition by the author, and are based on the natural break in the translation. In some cases, however, it has not been possible to retain them in single lines. No effort has been made to include phonetic symbols and diacritical marks or music notes for the songs. These are necessary for a complete appreciation of any music.

For review exercises, students are advised to collect songs and poetry from their own communities. The type and function of each piece should be given, with an explanation of its theme and significance within the community. An analysis of the dominant literary features and style should also be done.

1.   A Children's Rhyme and Lullaby

Eetuo nkishu ang' olmong'i arroi
(Eetuo ntariang' olmeregeshi)
Narum te lusie nemaipang'aki
Tigirayu iyie monyit e yieyio
Matara olmoruo otapashipasha
Oota surutia neeta mairina

Inyio olkipapa maishira empuoto
Kainyioo eishiruni metii Ie papa?
Parmuat Ie yieyio lolchoni ronkai
Ong'or Iltatua neing'uari eitashe
Kintederrita ilcholo Ie nanga
Nedo enang'a enye ilmoshomporeta
Pororongos, entalala, mutaangai ai
Enterepenyi ai naijo orupante.
Naijo orupante.

Our cattle have come with the oxen with buffalo-shaped
horns
(Our sheep have come with the rams)
I peep through the window but will not go and meet them
Keep quiet my beloved little one
Let me thrash the spoilt old man
The one dressed in coils and beads
Get up brother and let us call the alarm.
Whom do we alert when my brother is missing?
Parmuat of my mother's with the slender built.
The one whom the *Iltatua* shoot but leave standing
The one fondled by the corners of the gown
His gown as red as the beads.

Explanation

Little girls are often charged with the duty of baby-sitting for their younger siblings while their mothers are milking or doing other domestic duties. It seems that this lullaby was composed at evening time when cattle, goats and sheep were returning home from grazing.

2. Osinkolio looltorrobo

Kiti kiti, hooyie pae

Ntoyie olparakuo le kishu,

Naaminyiaru hooyie pae manang' entawuo tenkaina ehoiyie pae heeho!

Neisulaki hooyie pae inentawuo botor neitu eikau, ehoiyie pae heeho!

Ng'oto kilelu hooyie pae miyagiyagu entarasai, ehoiyie pae heeho

Nkeno kishomi hooyie pae ning'uaa elusie patina, ehoiyie pae heeho

Ena naimu hooyie pae Ole Nkaikoni etarishe, ehoiyie pae heeho

Niar osirua hooyie pae niar entarakuet enuta, ehoiyie pae heeho

Ejo ilparakuo hooyie pae eji mikirisio kirisio, ehoiyie pae heeho

Teneru olkiteng' hooyie pae neru munkarro toldoinyio, ehoiyie pae heeho

Neru' osikiria hooyie pae neru olosira marae, ehoiyie pae heeho

Needo olkiteng' hooyie pae nebaiki enkai, olmeut! Ehoiyie pae heeho

Kumok intare hooyie pae neibor kidong'o, nkoiliin! Ehoiyie pae heeho

Kumok inkerra hooyie pae naa nkumot ejing', bitiro! Ehoiyie paeheeho

Amur esuntai hooyie pae olmairroto liauluo, ehoiyie pae heeho

Pee eikieki hooyie pae enkawuo ang' labuny nikirru! Ehoiyie pae heeho

226

A Dorobo (Teasing) Song[1]

Kiti kiti[2]
The girls of the pastoralists that rear cattle[3]
They that handle the colostrum of the heifer with hands
Especially that of a heifer that is late giving forth[4]

Mother Kilelu, do not come leisurely
Shut the gateway but leave a little opening
Through which Ole Nkaikoni may come after the kill
Having killed an eland and a pregnant antelope
The pastoralists say we are not equal, yet we are
When the ox lows, the buffalo echoes on the hill
The donkey brays, so does the striped-bottomed![5]
Tall is the ox, it touches the sky, giraffe!
The goats are many and have white tails, gazelles!
The sheep are numerous and live in holes, warthogs!

I plaster the wall as well as the outside attic
So that our shapely bow could be hung
The one on which We depend!

1. The song is composed by the Maasai to ridicule the Dorobo and their way of life.
2. A n exclamation of sneering.
3. As opposed to the hunters (or Dorobo) who "rear" wild animals.
4. The later a heifer gives forth the thicker and smoother its milk gets.
5. The zebra.

3.   Esuyiore

Maiseyie osinkolio Ie teipa
Maisisa iltiapukuro Eima entepesi narresho
Naishayie ilkimula

Chorus

Hooe hooyioe hoe hoyioho hooyia
Kainyioo sa naiting'ida koyiombo loolayiok oturia olkokoyoi

Koyiombo mira oltung'ani
Nimira sii enkiteng'
Ira ake enkuyukui napeto
Naishori kule oltiren

Nabo layiok o ilkaseron
Kepiyaya nkidong'o
Nabo olkaisiodi o olayioni
Mang'arie pooki osaroi

Oloolayiok oiguana
Mikiida enkiguana
Neidia enkakenya nanyokie
Naitaeku ilmaai

Nimijo iyie enyorrata kinyori
Ilkimojik loonkejek eing'ori
O ilpuluta loo nkonyek
Peyie elo olmarenke nkadoru
Nchere ekweta olayioni
Koyiombo obolibolo olorrok
Ijo ololchata otoyio
Koyiombo le mbaash enteipa
Erreshore oosirkon ilo

Eilepa enkalem inkokua
Memurata koyiombo
Nikijo kiashu toltarge
Negila lala toltarge

Nikijo kinang'u torinka
Neng'urrorri endukuya
Nikijo kisuaku te kule
Neisuaku Enkai osarge

Esira enkomerei enkong'u
Nesira olodo – kashi
Neyia olkirapash inkipa
Neyia sikitok entawuo
Nemaisho ilkaisiod een

Koyiombo oitadoikio enkeju enkumoto
Nashula lasuria o ntarai
Naning' olorrishet peyie ejo karurum
Nikijo sere meishuro elatimi
Lenkaji e ng'oto koyiombo

Ero tenikweta teneitu
Kira ake iyiook olkinyor
Kiti kiti mikiok osaroi olili
Lenkang' nakwetie olayioni

A Teasing Song to Taunt Uncircumcised Boys

Let us sing the song of the evening
And praise the covered ones[1]
They have passed through the thicket[2]
That has taken all the covered ones

Chorus
What on earth makes Koyiombo[3] arrogant
If he has feared the Kikuyu[4]

Koyiombo you are neither a human being
Nor are you a cow

You are only a dirty puppy
That is given milk off the hearth

The boys are one with the brown birds
They both have rolled-up tails[5]
The flincher is one with a boy
I share osaroi[6] with neither of them

You councillor boy
May your counselling fail
There comes the glowing morning
That brings the hordes

But it is not for the love of you that they come
They come to observe the toes
As well as the eye-lids
And rumour spreads far that
The boy has flinched

Koyiombo whose legs peel
Like a dry tree bark
Koyiombo who leaves at the evening time
And goes hunting for the asses[7]

The knife has risen up to the pleaides
Before Koyiombo is circumcised
When we tried to hook it down
The hooks got broken

When we tried to throw it down with a club
Its head broke off
When we tried to splash it down with milk
God splashed down blood
The pied wagtail has printed eyes

And superb starling is the colour of the birth fluid
As well as that of the heifers milk[8]
None will I let the flinchers wear[9]

Koyiombo has plunged his foot into a hole
Where snakes and cobras reside
We heard his leg being chewed
And we said "May the ritual trees[10] die
Those of the house of Koyiombo's mother"

Boy whether you flinch or not
We like it either way
No, no, we will not drink the smelly osaroi
Of the home where the boy has flinched

1. Uncircumcised boys.
2. Women who have had sexual relations with uncircumcised boys.
3. Refers to the uncircumcised.
4. The Kikuyu and the Dorobo (Hunters) are often employed to do all carry out tasks such as circumcision.
5. Reference is here made to the penis.
6. A mixture of curdled milk and blood that is drunk by initiates. Once a boy flinches during circumcision, the others boycott his osaroi.
7. Uninitiated boys often relieve their sexual desires by dealing with asses.
8. Yellow.
9. There are some especially beautiful birds' feathers that the boys who flinch during circumcision are not permitted to wear.
10. These are ritual branches that are planted beside the house of the initiate's mother.

Explanation

As already stated, circumcision is an essential operation in Maasai society. This song is sang to the candidate on the eve of the operation, and is accompanied by spitting, pinching and exposing the nakedness of the initiate. This is to make him build up courage, so that he can go through the operation without flinching, an act that not only shames him, but also dishonours his parents. Every movement he makes is closely observed, and the slightest movement such as flipping the eyelids is enough to make one be declared a coward. This is what the hordes mentioned in stanza four come to witness, in order to spread the rumour accordingly.

As is evident from this song, uncircumcised boys are said to be dirty, incapable of holding council, and are generally despised. Notice how they are compared with dirty "brown birds" and "puppies", and their skin is said to peel like "the bark of a tree". If they flinch during circumcision, their *osaroi* is not shared by their age-mates and they are not permitted to wear the choice birds' feathers that are worn on the crown. The operation is performed normally by hunters or other agricultural groups such as the Kikuyu (see chorus). The song shows how bravery is worshipped by the Maasai.

4.   Osinkolio Loonkituaak

Emuto kinyamal esupat
Esupat nairi nkukurto
Neiri nosarge o ne kule

Etaekuo enkaji ang' enaleng'
Etaekutuo kule neyeku olker
Enkolong' natumi nosim ai
Netumi neng'ida olmarei lang'
Neng'ida enainosa o enaele
Neng'ida ng'otonye enoto osim
Neng'ida ilpayiani ear intoto

Enkai ai miking'orie olmoruo
Miking'orie olekekuno moitie
Oloshomo rukoro o njing'eta
Nelotu etang'asa eliyio enkaji ai
Etang'asa nchasho oltiren o nerruat

Miking'orie man-enkop loltarin
Olapa oidipie ng'otonye ntaleng'o
Enkiponu lomon neiperno
Nejoki pa-ntare, pa-supen
Pa-supen lai akaji ade ijing'?

Ekalo nanu enkaji enoshi ake
Enkaji emugie nasioki enkong'u
Enkaji e kishirtit olchoni
Nemeeta enkurrukur naitiamie
Enkaji e kilulung'a olepet
Kilulung'a oloyeku oleteipa

Enkai ai nasai aatasayia
Enkai irrugu nkonyek abori
Enkai ai nimintayu ntabo
Aitayu ilmurran lang' Ie polos
Ileme layiok neme selenken
Impurpurri meidimari nchoki

Nchoo ntomonok inkera
Nchoo pooki miiliar
Metii enamakua itejo aisho
Metii enkiberie enkoshoke
Neleku endia nainosa enenye openy

Neisho ina kinguranie nkera
Nedoiki naidaikie enkusaka
Inaatejo erropil iltaikan
Inaatejo emelok intare
Nejo olmuriang' peyie ejo olkuluk

Ndiain naayanyit ilewa
Naajokini tinyiku nejo ayia
Tinyiku mainosie enkiyio enkop
Maitainyie enchonkorro nosim ai
Ntumain nikitejo saing'ang'ie
Naing'ang'ie olkipoket kishomi
Neing'angie ilmosorin ilmoruak
Neingang'ie ilpayiani ilchekuti

Ilili niropil nosim ai
Ilili mikinyim ing'oruo
Ilmurran looltaikan ake onyim
Nimikinyim sii lelo enadede

Patim ai nemeiro nairorie
Tenkae kata mairoro tenkaji ang'
Airo mainosa lomon supati
Sidan lang' lemetii enkurrarre.

Women's Prayer Song

Dusk has found us still preoccupied
Preoccupied with the pleasantry of cleaning gourds
The gourds of milk and of blood

The luscious ones have dawned on us
The milk has arrived and so has the ram[1]

The day the beloved one is received
Delight descends on the entire home
She that has eaten and she that has worn (ochre)[2]
Delight fills the mother for the repose obtained
Delight smothers the elders as they play with pebbles[3]

My God, do not leave me at the mercy of the man
At his habitually moody whims
He that rounds the village
Arriving when loneliness has filled the house
Settling on the walls as well as on the bed
Not at the mercy of a wanderer with unsteady affection
He whose mother had completed all rituals due to him[4]
He to whom guests come saying: "My friend, my dear
Where will you spend tonight?"

I am bound to the usual house
The house of the fair one that catches the eye
The house with slippery hide
With no toddler to mess up
The house with the full gourds
Full in the morning and evening

Oh God who is worshipped I beg thee
Oh God lower thine eyes and look down
My God do not make blunders
By creating those that are half warriors
Those who are neither lads nor maidens
The sluggish ones that cannot tend flock[5]

Give children to the womenfolk
Give them all do not disparage them
For there is none that is unsuited once given
There is none whose womb is timid
Excepting the bitch that has eaten[6] her own

Whilst we play with the children
She that mauled her own was gripped with regret

Those who thought the pigtails were sweet-scented[7]
Those who thought the goats are delicious[8]
It may have been typhoid or foot and mouth disease

The bitches that adore males
Who comply when asked to get closer
Come close and let's destroy the baby
Let's crush him to a pulp

The poor ones we have dubbed 'deluders'
For they delude the gates with wedding gourds[9]
They delude the elders with beer gourds [10]
And they delude them too with shepherds[11]

You smell both bad and good my beloved
You smell but the females do not sneer at you
Only warriors with pigtails sneer
But their sneers do not last[12]

My beloved that does not talk yet I talk to him
Let us chat at our house at a later date
Let us talk of good news
The good news without slander

1. The ram that the women slaughter and eat when a baby is born.
2. During this celebration women dress up, mix ochre with the fat from the ram and put it on their bodies. So, if the meat gets finished the ochre mixture is usually enough for a large number of people.
3. The game known as Enkeshui in Maasai. (bao in Swahili) is played with pebbles.
4. And can, therefore afford to be careless.
5. Barren women are known to grow fat and sluggish.
6. A woman is said to have "eaten" her child if she has sexual intercourse during pregnancy resulting in a miscarriage. Some innocent women have gone through undue suffering because of this belief.
7. The warriors' pigtails, alludes to sexual intercourse.

8. An expectant woman normally avoids eating meat from a dead animal unless it has been investigated and proved harmless to the foetus. A few still defy the advice resulting in miscarriage.

9. A small gourd with beer in it used for blessing the bride when she is being led away in marriage.

10. These are great big gourds used for brewing beer during all festivities including marriage.

11. Young uninitiated boys often tend the flock.

12. For soon they too would long to marry and start the process of procreation which is associated with baby dirt.

Explanation

This women's song was originally sang when a child was born but it is also often heard in other festivities. It is accompanied by slow dancing with the soloist singing the main part and others the rejoinder. Women take turns as soloists.

The song is basically meant to welcome a new baby with great delight. Everyone is kept pleasantly occupied cleaning gourds, eating, making themselves up and making merry. But as it progresses it becomes a prayer for children by those who do not have them and for those who want more. It also expresses displeasure at husbands for providing inadequate and unsteady affection and at their preference for younger and more beautiful company.

5. Osinkolio Loo nkituaak

Parsae tadamu ena sile
Esile nemelak nkishu
Nemelak enkikuei natudung'uo
Nemelak enkare naokoki
Nemelak olumbuani atadoikio
Enkerai oltung'ani nalak

Chorus
Hoyiayio ehoo, hoyiayio
Ayok ayooki Enkai ai

Enkai nasai atasayia
Nasai toonaishi o te kule
Toning'u naanare etuumate
Enare nedung'i olmasi onyil
Osidai odung'i te kule

Patim ai maaru naing'odeu
Nkatampo e Nkai aimariri
Pee aaisho tendorrop nosim ai
Nosim ai natijing'ie enkutu
Natijing'ie oloikarri anaa ilmurran

Nayieng'ie ololtuala osekeno
Oloseken olopeny neimany
Meeta enkirotet nkishu ang'
Aisho nosim indaiki supati

A Women's Prayer Song

O thou who is worshipped remember this debt
The debt that cows do not pay
Tree branches that I cut do not pay it[1]
The water that I fetch for him[2] does not pay it
If I go inside the well[3] it does not pay
It is only the human child that would pay it

Chorus
I come early to my God

O God who is worshipped I pray to thee
Thou who is prayed to with beer and with milk
Listen to what best suits womenfolk
It suits when long greasy hair is shaven[4]
The beautiful one that is shaven with milk

My beloved one whom I pamper is never scolded
I look up at God's clouds
So that he could in short grant me repose[5]
The beloved one of whom I have fed
I have entered the meat-camp like the warriors[6]

The distinguished ox with the bell have I slaughtered
The one the owner swears by
There is none among our cattle that is favourite
I grant my beloved one the best of foods.

1. Thorn bushes for fencing the village enclosure.
2. For the husband. Women in Maasai perform almost all the duties in the home.
3. To water the flock, a tough job that is normally done by men, but from which women are not exempted.
4. Women keep long hair before the child is weaned. This hair is, customarily, not washed with water, but grease is applied to it. When the child is weaned, this hair is shaved off with the use of milk in place of water.
5. Child infant.
6. And eaten big oxen as warriors do in meat camps *olpuli* (ilpuli pl). The pregnant women are normally granted the delicacies that their pregnancies "demand". This includes big oxen.

Explanation

This too is a prayer song, but it is more of a lament, that may have been sang first by childless women. It expresses the sorry state of childless women in the Maasai community, the sorrow and the pains they go through. It goes to prove the truth of the proverb: "Children are the bright moon."

6. Osinkolio loo nkituaak

Aasai aomon Papa lai Ie Nkai
Aasai aomon Iltuati oltareto

Nchooki ntokitin kumok naomon
Nchooki sialibi olcholo lematum

Nikincho oloigari opiyaya lonkulak
Le nkeseni e yieyio naitore sikitok
Nchooki enkukuri naisamis enkerai
Nchooki eleketiet empolos nemalak

Etejo naisho kiyieu entomono
Etejo nkera inono kiyieu entomono

Women's Prayer Song

I plead and pray to thee, my father of the heavens
I pray to thee through the *Iltuati* and *Iltareto*[1]

Grant me the many things that I ask of you
Grant me the cloak with the corners[2]
Grant me the rolled up skirt with urine[3]
Of the beloved one that I suckle
Grant me the smelly gourd of the infant
Grant me the waist belt that I shall not unfasten[4]

The producers of children say we want maternity
Thy children say we want maternity

1. The older members (age-sets) of society. These are retired elders who are assigned the responsibility of offering sacrifices on behalf of the group. But it should be stressed that they are not prayed to.
2. Tartared on the edges by over-use during maternity.
3. The skirts are usually wrinkled from the baby sitting and wetting it.
4. Worn by women with small babies and normally put away when the baby dies.

Explanation

This prayer song, like the two before it, requests God to grant children to the womenfolk. But notice how indirectly this request is put in this song. It talks of all the things associated with babies.

7. Irrepeta Oolkamaniki Loolpurko Errep Noolkidemi Onkulie

Enyor Emusunkui olodua
Neisulaki enenkare – narok
Eirragie Pareron tioriong'

Enoonkurman metudung'i
Siriri naata ilasho mankek
Naigilie olmari ole Nesenke
Laleyio ehoo, hoo iyio laleyio ehoo (Chorus)

Ore eranyisho mampai e sirit ai
Nagira amuk nanu enkutuk
Mme ntoki nalimu maata
Nkatampo Enkai aomon
Meinyiaku Enkai te sipitali
Ololtaika orru Naitiku

Yieyio lai ng'oto Naitiku
Enalepito isiruai olwuampa
Nimioshie enchata nairoishi
Siriri olong'u tenelotu

Maitieu aikilikuana ntae
Enkop naitipat Pukoret
Ootu enosa ilomon peyie aning
Te suntai enkaji ang' tara

Aning'ito eji olchurrai orresho
Eitipatita Reyio nalepo
Enaigilie ilmepunya emunge
Iloolkishau emparinko
Atiiaaka ole Kipuri owuasa
Misuj ilturua mikisul
Tijing'a enailuda maruate
Nainosie oltir ilong'oi

Eshomo olosioki iloipi
Neito ilkeek ilakedok
Neing'uari olopeny enara
Loltuati opi metisiri

Ilmolelian loosikitok
Oishiru ntawua neponu
Nadung'ie ololming'ani Rripo
Nadung'ie ole Ntiako ḳusaka
Elangilang'a ololming'ani
Lenkaisi edung'i suya
Olchani Ii auluo otukurre
Oinosie ntasati enchenche
Milo enchankar ng'oto kisimpol
Ng'otonye olmurrani le sayiet
Olorikito Malancha enkereri
Ntashat naaudo esinko

Eiririunye emutiy enchan
Nang'as arrep nabo sirit
Atang'asa arrep naing'asia osioki
Najulito olorru Kimeriai
Neoiki ole mpoke oloing'ang'e
Le nkitipai oo nkujit

Taoiki enkitipai e kule
Naibung'ie nchilalo ilaimutia

Praises for Ilkamaniki Age-Group sang by Noolkidemi and others

My gall loves the Mzungu
Especially the one from Enkare Narok
For laying bare Pareron[1] of the ranch
To be shared among the warriors
Siriri with the ornamental calves
That ole Nesenke returned for (to the raid)

Chorus

Whilst those of my age are dancing
I sit with my mouth shut
Not for want of what to say
I am praying to God's clouds
For God to return from hospital
The pig-tailed one brother to Naitiku

Oh mother, mother to Naitiku
The one milking the beige ones (from the raid)
Do not hit the spotted siriri[2]
With a heavy stick when she comes

I dare not ask you
The country from which pukoret[3] originates
Come and talk news[4] against the wall of our house
Tonight so that I may hear

I hear that from the narrow *olchurrai*
Comes Reyio[5] with milk aplenty

Compelling warriors with well-fitting legbands[6] to return
playfully to Emparinko (country)

I have told the proud Ole Kipuri
Not to keep embarrassing company of lazy people
Go along with the brave ones
Whose shields are dented

The quick one has run to the shades[7]
The climbers have taken to the trees
Leaving the owner of the fight
Whose father is *oltuati* to be branded[8]

Those of the Ilmolelian clan[9]
That come when the heifers call out
I share out Rripo[10] with Ololming'ani
And Kusaka[11] with Ole Ntiako

The Ololming'ani criss-crosses
As we share Suya[12]
The shade outside has grown bare
As the ladies chat below it
Don't you argue mother of Kisimpol
Mother of the favourite warrior
Led by the striped Malancha[13]
From the nine ridges of sinko

The dusk and the rain have together descended
As I sing praises of one group (of warriors)
I start with the one that is first to wonder
Among whom is he of Kimeriai's mother
Ole mpoke leaked on the atmosphere (air)
At the lush drizzly country

Do leak on the drizzle land where milk is plenty
And where spears have developed gaps.

1, 2, 3, Names of cows.

4. Sing songs in praises of cattle, i.e., Eoko or Enkijuka.

5. Name of cow.

6. The legband looks clumsy on short-legged people. Well-fitting because the warriors are tall.

7. The cowardly one.

8. Same warrior in previous verse. Reference is made here to the marking of the shield with an "olong"u"' mark to signify bravery.

9. Ilmolelian clan are reknowned for their cowardice, but have come here to the rescue.

10, 11, 12 and 13. Names of cows.

Explanation

This is a praise song that was composed by a young woman called Nolkidemi for the Ilkamaniki age-group of Purko (Kajiado). This is the age-group of men who were warriors in the mid-fifties. She sings praises of warriors, cites names of their relations, and recounts their accomplishments during raids, the names of cows that were obtained, and their sources. Notice that she also mentions the warriors who are known for their cowardice.

There are tunes that gain popularity in time and are copied and sang as they are, but often the names and places are substituted for others, depending on the area and time.

8.   Irrepeta Esiankiki

Etukusho olmoruo tiauluo
Neyau enkushoto oltiren
Akiti enkushoto olpayian lai
Mirrar ilmoru le nkima
Amu iyie otiaaka oloo Namerae
Ino irraga enkaji e mampai
Neme enkerai nang'arie kina

Neme enaikau pantawuo
Niyiolo kibirot inkabur
Meiba nkiri tenetumo

Lopayian irragie matata
Mairoto sirkon pee kipuo

Airoto nempirdai ashipa
Naitoki airot Noolmong'i
Ayiolo ajo oloika ade alo
Namanya emarti enkurrarru
Namanya enkurrarru ole Kaigil
Laashomie nkiri bata
Elong'o sampu oo Mosomba
Naikuso Ilkokoyo Ie Nteyia

Chorus

Laleyio ehoo, hee hiyioo laleyio eho

A Woman's Song

A man went into a fit outside the village
Coming to the hearth with it
Calm down my husband
Crush not the firestones
For you are the one who told Namerae's brother
To go and spend at the young woman's house
And he is neither a child with whom I have shared the breast
Nor is he the first born of my co-wife
And you know the flesh of petit-ribbed ones
Do not mind coming together

Lay down your fury old man
Let us load the donkeys and move on
I have loaded Nempirdai[1] with merry
Have done the same with Noolmong'[2]
Knowing that I am going to the high ground
Where he with the fluffy ostrich headdress lives
Where Ole Kaigil's head-dress resides
The place where my flesh felt unsafe[3]
The dapple spear, brother to Mosomba
Who wiped out the Kikuyus of Ndeyia

1, 2, Names of donkeys.

3. Was beaten by her husband.

Explanation

This is a kind of song that is sang in festivities when each woman takes time to express her experiences and thoughts. The composer seems to have had rather dramatic experiences although she takes them with good humour at the expense of her jealous husband.

9. Irrepeta e Saetuan

Nkuapi naamanya iltiyan lang'
Ino nkena mincho kilang'
Oyiayio hoo laleyio ehoyiaayio (Chorus)

Emanya ole kipuri owuasa
Le ng'oto Nakae Ilmotioo

Nemanya ilmeori eiriamari
Lololkatira Embirika

Nelo amanya enkerai oolmurran
Leng'oto kitai oltepesi

Nemanya ole Esho lolgisoi
Le ng'oto Ntitai eneika

Nelo amanya ologeli osur atua
Enting'ida naishuyie Nkunyinyi

Amen isiankikin tena kop
Neisulaki inoonkidong'i

Sasin ilmurran lirorierie
Neima nkiri enkuretisho

Era kulo tualan okuni
Linkodo nkidong'i nikiya

Kinkonyaitie oltuala oikodo nkumok
Lole Sampurri loolpapit

Kiwaita temanyata ole Ping'ua
Isototo nkayiok erashe

Kiwaita ole Rakua lolgisoi
Oishuyie Naingolingola

Enchira naanetu nkidong'i
Ole Ping'ua lempere olkiteng'

Praise song of Saetuan*

Count the locations where our bamboos [1] live
And miss not any

The proud ole Kipuri of Nakae's mother
Lives at Ilmotioo

The identical twins of Ole Olkatira
Live by the waterhole

The warrior's son of Kitai's mother
Lives at Oltepesi

Ole Esho of the ring of Ntitai's mother
Lives at the high ground

The thicket of Ologeli
Holds the proud brother to Nkunyinyi

I despise the young women of this country
Especially those of the Nkidong'i clan

The warriors with whom romance are thin
And their flesh is drenched with cowardice

Three bells[2] have you decorated
But we have taken them

We have repatriated the highly decorated bell
of Ole Sampurri[3] with long hair

At the manyatta we have taken Ole Ping'ua
While you the diviner boys[4] are gathered

We have taken Ole Rakua with the ring
On whom naing'oling'ola depends

You the Nkidong'i may cry bitterly
For Ole Ping'ua with the spear that is worth an ox
Oyiayio hoo laleyio ehoyiaayio

(Repeated after every verse)

*Saetuan is the young woman who composed the praises for the Ilkololik age-group of
  Purko in Kajiado district when they were warriors.

1. The warriors who are as tall as bamboos.

2. Warriors with bells on the legs.

3. His mother is Samburu.

4. All the Iloibonok (Laibons) or diviners came from Nkidong'i section (clan).

Explanation

This song praises the same group of warriors as those in song **7** but this one only refers to their relatives and their home areas. It also teases and provokes the Nkidong'i warriors (these are from another olosho or section) for being too cowardly to defend their group from the adjoining Purko section. Their girls are, therefore, despised for the cowardice of their warriors.

10. Irrepeta e Mopoi

Kaji Kirrepieki Ololtibili
Meishoru enkolong' olpurkel
Mikirrepi te saa sita
Nailiarie oladalu nkishu
Nimikirrepi etadoyie enkolong'
Meya irrepeta oldalati
Enkolong' ake nalotu ene wueji
Nerrepi olodoru ng'amaro

Eitu ashurtaki entilata ina
Olalaa ooki naishi
Atanapa enyorrata olchore lai
Ebaiki apa ara enkiti kerai
Atanapa entilata tolodua
Metubulu anaa nkolong'i

Mapik enyorrata olchore lai
Elukunya natii ilbeli
Etirisha ilkimojik ondapi
Nerish entanun o emoinyua
Nedoyio enyorrata olchore lai

Alo eneirragie ng'aturan
Enenapieki nkera ake apik
Metubulu anaa nkolong'i

Oltung'ani oiba nanyor ilmurran
Ng'oru nabo nagol nias
Tikirrie obaribara iltuli
Meshomo aipang' te Nairobi
Tipika emuatata olng'ojine
Nipik olowuaru ronkai
Ore pee ekenyua eserian intare
Napal Ole ng'oto Talash
Tang'orokoki oloibor kume
Maitashalunyie loolpapit

Love song by Mopoi

When could thy praises be sang, Ololtibili?
For this scorching summer heat prevent it
They cannot be sang at midday
For then, the sun weakens the cattle
They cannot be sang at sunset
For the sun will set with the praises
Oh, when the sun gets to that point
(pointing to the position of the sun about 9 a.m.)
Praises of he with the scarlet one will be sang

I developed admiration for you
Not at the drinking hall
I have stored the love of my love
Since I was just a little girl
I have stored it at the gall bladder
To nurture it day by day

I dare not store this precious love of my love
At the head, for the mind abounds with changes
It has edged between the fingers and the palm
As well as the spleen and the liver
The love of my love has gone down
To where babies lie
I store it where babies are carried
To keep it growing day by day.

He that detests my loving the warriors
Find one tough thing to do
Scrape the road with your buttocks
Until you reach Nairobi
Put a hyena at the sheep pen
As well as the slim beast (cheetah)
If by the morning the sheep are safe
I will give up the brother of Talash
Then you can bleed the white-nosed one (donkey)
To purge me from the long-haired one

Explanation

This romantic love song was composed by a woman from Matapato section in praise of a man called Ololtibili whom she loved. She provokes her husband to do the impossible before she can end her relationship with this man.

11. Enkipolosa (Ilmatapato)

Ajul Ole Siamito olmeing'atie enkop ilonito
Le enaloki e yieyio natii enkutoto
Tonyoku larridaki lai enkaina ematua
Tiatua ilmirisho looltaikan likincho
Abuaaki emutiy o endaruna
Olmurrani lai lenkila enkopiro

Pee mejo Enkai nemejo enkop
Kalo ting'idai ele lemebuak ebuaki
Najoki mara nanu oltingidai Ie toki
Ara ake oibeloyie emurt osina
Loonkishu naitong'or enkonom
Naatemena entito elepito

Nemenu enkayioni nairritita
Nememut entonata olchani etaleng'o osupatei

Atayieua nanu olmurrani le nkila enkopiro
Ine likae mayiapi naashal olopeny naponie
Kurruk kurruk oibor enemuati ng'oroyiok
Neme tenkop ang' eiborrie
Nerok enkila naishopito
Neme tenkop ang' eishopo
Tolikioki ake ilkiushin irruka
Loosiria likituata enkaji oonaapi ronkeni king'oru

Abuaaki emutiy endaruna
Olmurrani lai loonaapi ronkeni
Mejo Enkai nemejo enkop
Kalo ting'idai lido lemebuak ebuaki

Mara olmurrani loonaapi ronkeni
Olting'idai le toki
Ara ake oibeloye emurt osina
Lonkishu naitong'or enkonom
Naamen entito elepito
Nemen eji enkayioni nairritita
Nememut entonata olchani etaleng'o osupatei

Atayieua olmurrani lenkila enkopiro
Naashal olayioni Ie likae mayiapi naponie

253

Enkipolosa War Song (Ilmatapato, 1977)

Ole Siamito's colour is changing[1]
As he fails to lift the tough hides from the ground[2]
The shields of our large manyatta situated between ridges
Do struggle on my beloved
With thine arm strapped against thy side[3]
For thou art with the winning party

I call out loud at twilight as well as in the morn[4]
I the warrior with the black cloak
So that neither the heavens nor the earth can say
I am arrogant, for not calling out loud enough like the others
My answer is that I am not at all arrogant
But a humble being whose neck is weighed down by poverty
Poverty of a herd that barely numbers fifty
A herd that is despised by the girl who milks
As well as by the boy who tends
A herd that does not finish a mere foot of a tree
When it is lush with vegetation

I the warrior of the black cloak
Now require those of the weak owner
From foreign lands to boost my herd

Crow, crow who wears a white band
On the place where women wear coils
You have not just worn this band in our country
You wear a black cloak
But not just in our country
Tell me where those of the Siria are
Whose humps are like anthills
For we of the thin spears are dying for them

I call out at twilight as well as in the morn
I the warrior of the long thin spear
So that neither the heavens nor the earth should say
I am arrogant for not calling out loud enough like the others

I the warrior of the long thin spear
Am not at all arrogant
But a humble being whose neck is weighed down by poverty
Poverty of a herd that falls below fifty
A herd that is despised by the girl who milks
As well as by the boy who tends
A herd that does not finish a mere foot of a tree
when it is lush with vegetation

I the warrior of the black cloak
Now require those of the weak owner
From foreign lands to boost my herd

1. From bleeding.
2. Shields.
3. Hurt from the raid.
4. Song sang at evening and morning.

Explanation

This is a common war song. This particular version was recorded in 1977 during *Eunoto*, a graduation ceremony from warriorhood to elderhood, for the Matapato section in Kajiado district. It is often sang very early in the morning, or at dusk, and it is meant to give the warriors the spirit and courage to enable them to fight and raid other sections. It is sang with a very high pitch by one soloist alone as a prayer. The worriors do this when naked, " black cloak".

12. Eoko (Ole Pere)

Oyie majo duo kalotu ena nabanji
Eitu ajo yieyio Ko res o Makooi
Namishiri ntaua sidain ole Ping'ua
Namishiri ilotot enyori enkop
Neimie oloing'oni kirapash lemaal oltiili

Maroroi naata emua reko nakurito oleng' ileleru
Nkarash olkiteng' lai oishopito buluu
Naitaa elang'ata euapata teneilepaki Ole Polos
Omanya yiook ilmeiseyieki lole Dikir
Otamoo nchoo ogela ilaramatie
Ke enaiding'a ai oolmong'i shiloin ena ana kakua?
Ayiolo ajo enkinyoti ai sidai oolmong'i shiloin
Maikodo lemekenyu eirragita te ndikir
Nanyokie ilpayiani nkutukie etoni aakes enkurma

Aininche nekwa kulie ana kakua?
Ayiolo ajo ninche nekwa olaram odo enkitipet lekiripa.
Nedo ntaua meela neitoki ntaua enkiborra nanare ilorikan
Ilmutende lemeisho enkaripo eisiadu penyo

Aininche nekwa kulie ana kakua?
Ee pae oleng'oti lai oolmong'i lemepono arroi
Lemaikunja eseshata napuku ilkumok aa wuasin
Neyupuyup lolerai lemeidimu irruka are

Aininche nekua kulie ana kakua?
Nayiolo ajo ninche nekua sandikon iloing'ok e Meirurae
Naibung'a ilera enchepati nedar enkorui amanu tentim nasur
Neriku enkashe nashuroi ilepeta sapuki mouarak oo namba e
sogo

Aininche nekua kulie ana kakua?
Nayiolo ajo ninche nekua napiroki nangan olkiu obo
Ijo nangan emusis eilepaki nairobi enkiyang'et
Naijorie olkiteng' lai lenanga nakuyiana ilkurreta

Aininche nekua kulie ana kakua?
Ayiolo ajo ninche nekua olamayio lai oru nkorkorri
Naibayioki emuti iloshon naning'o olumbuani
Lembene eyiogiyiogu enoompisai nememira e Mwangi

Translation

I would never have thought I would come this far
Before telling you that I am Ole Kores
The legs of whose beautiful heifers are branded
As they move on the green landscape

There goes Maroroi [1] with the spotted ochre colour
Then that ox of mine that is dressed in blue
Who takes a quick flight up the high country of Ole Polos
Where we, the brave sons of Ole Dikir live
Whose cattle are used to paddock grazing

Is that it or is it another?
My selected herd whose settlement is crowded
Let us decorate those for whom the morning
Will not find as they lie in high country
Where the elders' gums are red as they harvest flour

Are they the ones over there or are they not?
I know it is they the red heifers with hrown ears
Though they have not been smeared with ochre
Ones that are well suited with patches
And whose hearts are too soft to permit them to delay

Are they the ones there or are they not?
Yes those are my unbranded oxen with buffalo-like horns
Of which the majority are glittering grey
As they march through Olerai unable to carry two humps

Are those others mine or are they others?
Indeed they are the mighty oxen of Meirurae[2]
Whose bells echo through a dense forest
As they are accompanied by the heifer with milk aplenty
And with mighty horns obtained from a country that I dare not say.

Are those others mine or are they not?
I know they are the ones all of the same colour
Looking like the Kanga[3] cloths as they ascend
The country of cool air
And where my patterned ox stretches his legs

Are those over there mine too, or are they not?
I know they are a part of our army with loud bells
From a country where devastation is not permitted
And from where the Lumbua comes carrying a bag
Of money for those of Mwangi's that have not been sold[4]

Explanation

This is a poem that is half sang and half spoken and is known as **Eoko** in Maa. It is spoken (or sang) by men, mainly warriors, ilmurran, to relate their accomplishments in raids. They are normally highly poetic and rhythmic. Note the repetitions and the imagery.

Ole Pere, the composer is from the Purko section of Narok district. This Eoko was recorded at his home in 1976.

1, 2 Names of cows.

3. Printed sheets are often worn during various festivities and are called kangas in Swahili. He is comparing the colour of cattle with the prints on the cloths.

4. The Lumbua seeks to buy what was obtained from raiding Mwangi.

13.   Enkijuka

Ole Pere

Entasupa lomurran – Ipa (Others)
Aikiyiololo toi ninye anaa aimikiyiololo
Mikiyiolo iyie (*Others*)

Mikiyiololo amu nanu oshi eji Ole Kores
Ololong' olgisoi oibung'a ilmoekin intashat
Naiki nkalkures ilasho ilapaitin lemesesh eing'orom Ilasho
nyewaitie

Others Ee pae enenye

Oloota ntaua sapuki ilaron lemebaiki empejoto
Oonum ilang'at likidung'u nkorkorri
Aairritayie ilatampo lolkingi lemeidimu enkiyieu

Others Enenye

Aata olarus lemouo oilomito esidano kimishir
Oriku noo kilapa enkanasa nemeidurrie ilkinyie

Aata olkiteng' omanita olorika aigil ong'uan
Lenkiteng' ai kirotet naing'uaa olerumpe oduaya enkolong'
Oinosita empuk Ilumbua
Aata olarro mugie ololong' emouo
Opiroki ntaua naakweni nkutukie olaram lekeyian
Lenkop namiri iltung'ana etoni anaa nkishu
Naeni ntaua mugiein too mukuntani

Aata olkiteng' oodo omisimis irashat
Lemelita enkorkor eitalam inkejek
Oigilie entureishi nemepono endaata

Aata olkiteng' oimisie erashata lemeeny ebulu
Lenkorkor lemeidimu ilmong'i leitu eing'at olaram

Edooyo ake enkereri olkoroe lemeked ilkeek
Odung'oki ilkurreta ooirinita enkorkor
Olalai oirisha oltikana Ie ngatet oure Ilmaasae.

Praise Song of Ole Pere

Soloist:	Greetings to you comrade warriors!
Others:	Greetings!
Soloist:	Do you know or do you not know me?
Others:	We do not know you.
Soloist:	I know that you know me not for I am he who is known as Ole Pere who wears a loose ring
	And who owns stout steers and a healthy herd that bears during months of plenty
Others:	Yes it is him indeed!
Soloist:	He that owns heifers with large stomachs
	For whom the meadow is insufficient
	But who get stuffed at the valleys
	Where cow bells are removed[1]
	As they are grazed together with those of the King's
	That are overweighed by fat
Others:	It is him!
Soloist:	I have the blue one with the horn
	Whose beauty resists branding
	Who leads the large herd of Kilapa[2]
	Whose numbers pose difficulty when moving homes
	I have an ox that is four times circled with stripes
	Of my favourite cow from Olerumpe[3]

Where the sun is seen as it descends[4]
From a place where the Lumbua eat flour

I have a maroon buffalo with a loose horn
That has fattened among smiling heifers
From a country where people are sold
Whilst they are seated like cattle
And where maroon heifers are tied in shambas

I have a tall ox with dark patches
with wide strides and an obvious bell sound
As it leads young unbranded heifers
To repeated grazing

I have an ox that is camouflaged by patches and who
has not declined to grow
And whose mighty bell overweighs those oxen

A patch stretches over the colobus monkey
That does not climb trees[5]
Among thin oxen whose bells are wound twice
But mine had conquered the *Ng'atet*[6] anthrax
That the Maasai fear.

1. To prevent them from being discovered.

2. Name of cow.

3. Place.

4. High ground.

5. An ox the colour of the Colobus monkey.

6. Ng'atet is another name for Narok or Enkare-Narok.

Explanation

Ole Pere is also the composer of the *eoko* above (**12**). *Enkijuka* is spoken
very fast but with a rhythm like that of *eoko* with brief pauses that allow

equally brief responses of encouragement. He opens by introducing himself to the other warriors who say they do not know him, then verse after verse he sings praises of himself, using his cattle as illustrations. He praises their body sizes, the shapes and size of their horns, their colours, the sounds of their bells, as well as their gait and behaviour. The audience (other warriors) listen intently, and after every verse they say: "It is yours", "It is him", "Yes it is", etc., to urge him on.

14. Emayian

Oo duo kitotoni, naai nchoo yiook kitoni, Naai
Tenikinya endaa, iloinosa oloing'uaitie, metareto yiook, Naai
Metareto ilpayiani enaisho, Naai
Ilootooko o loing'uaitie, Naai
Metareto pooki, Naai
Metareto ntomonok, Naai
Naai ntoisho doi iyiook, Naai
Intoiki ilonito lemeudo, Naai
Naai nchoo yiook kiaku ilpayiani, Naai
Metajara nkishu ilpaashien
Metukurro nkera oltiren
Tiaaki enkima meyupuyupo
Meinosa inaaikuti

Oo duo ena kerai eewuo, tiaki doi miya olojong'a tena kop, Naai
Tiaaki mikiroroki nkera nkung', Naai
Taa oreteti oshe ntona, Naai
Mikiyau sii iyie Enkai, Naai
Taa oipotori, Naai
Oipotoo Maasai, Naai
Oipotoo Ashumba, Naai
Meiruko Enkai oledukuya, Naai
Meiruko emagilani, Naai
Entoikinoto, Naai

Entoiki olari, Naai
Entoiki olameynaai

Blessing

Now that we are seated, O God, let us be seated – Let it be[1]
When we eat food, those who ate and those who smelt, may it nurture us
May beer nurture the elders
Those who drank and those who smelt it
May it nurture them all
May it nurture the ladies
Make us bear on hides without holes[2]
God, make us elders
May the calves fill the pens
May the cattle fill the homesteads
May the children play at the hearth
Tell the fire to stay burning
Let it eat the ritual meats[3]

How about this child[4] who has come, make her not take flies from this land[5]
May the children greet her knees[6]
May she grow to be lucky
Be oreteti[7] tree with the spread out roots
May God bring you back
May you be one that people talk about
One that the Maasai talk of
One that other peoples talk of

May God hear the prayer of him who was the first man
Make us bear for each other
Make us produce in time of plenty
Make us produce in time of famine

1. Said by the audience after each utterance by the person who is conducting the blessing as a way of stressing his request. Could be rendered better as: "O God hear our prayer."
2. Literally, women bear children on the beds that have hides on them. The "holes" are symbolic of infant mortality.
3. The ritual meat is Enaikuti pl. Inaaikuti and it consists of the meat from the right-hand side of the ram, eaten by the women when a child is born.
4. Reference is here made to the Maasai way of greeting where the children bending reach only the knees of older members of society.
5. Symbolic of ailments.
6. Reference is here made to the Maasai way of greeting where the children bending reach only the knees of older members of society.
7. Symbolizes long life, strength and sturdiness. Its root is often used for many rituals.

Explanation

This is a typical blessing in its context. It was recorded live at Ole Polos, see footnote 4, at the close of a session where oral literature forms were relayed and discussed. Although blessings vary in different situations, the diction and presentation is always the same. One person utters the blessing, while others join in with 'let it be' or 'may God hear our prayers'.

Bibliography

Akivaga, K. and Odaga, B. Oral Literature: *A School Certificate Course*. Nairobi: Heinemann Educational Books, 1982.

Finnegan, Ruth. *Oral Literature in Africa*. London: Oxford University Press, 1976.

Hollis, A.C. *The Maasai: Their Language and Folklore*, London: Oxford University Press, 1904.

Lo Liyong, Taban. *Popular Cultures of East Africa*. Nairobi: Longman, 1972.

Mbiti, l.S. *Akamba Stories*. London: Oxford University Press, 1964.

Mwangi, Rose. *Kikuyu Folktales*. Nairobi: East African Literature Bureau, 1974.

Okot p'Bitek. *Hare and Hornbill*. London: Heinemann Educational Books, 1978.

Ole Sankan, S.S. *The Maasai*. Nairobi: Kenya Literature Bureau, 1979.

Tucker and Mpaayei, J.T. A Maasai Grammar with Vocabulary. London: Longmans, Green & Co., 1955

www.ingramcontent.com/pod-product-compliance
Lightning Source LLC
Chambersburg PA
CBHW050633280326
41932CB00015B/2633